"Spectrum women have a voice that needs to be heard. They need people to understand the challenges they face in daily life, and to recognise their talents and many achievements. The coherent explanations and wise adv[...] highly recommended for women w[...]icians."

—*Tony Attwood, PhD, Adjunct* [...] *eensland and author of* The Comp[...] *me and* Asperger's Syndrome: A Guide for Parents and Professionals.

"For too many years, women on the spectrum have been pushed aside in terms of diagnosis, intervention, and support. It took a long time for professionals to finally understand and recognize the complexity and richness of the female profile of ASD. Spectrum Women's book is a breakthrough in many ways. Firsthand accounts and professionals combine their views and experience to provide rich and valuable information. I salute this initiative because this book will become a fundamental resource for the ASD community, families, and professionals."

—*Isabelle Hénault, PhD, psychologist & sexologist and author of* Asperger's Syndrome and Sexuality: From Adolescence through Adulthood

"*Spectrum Women* more than fills a gap, it addresses the huge void and absence of critical information to best understand, support, and develop meaningful relationships with autistic women. Written eloquently by women who have experienced first-hand the misconceptions, misinformation, and lack of recognition of the unique characteristics and abilities of autistic women, *Spectrum Women* will become the voice and the essential work that will help to further advance the inclusion, acceptance, and appreciation of so many individuals who have been marginalized for so many years."

—*Barry M. Prizant, PhD, Adjunct Professor at Brown University and author of* Uniquely Human: A Different Way of Seeing Autism

"*Spectrum Women: Walking to the Beat of Autism* brings us the voice of spectrum women, adding multi-faceted layers of autism knowledge previously unavailable to professionals and laypeople alike. Throughout the chapters, the writers not only share their lives, but often bare the intimate recesses of their souls with the reader. This book marks a pivotal moment in the history of autism as we now have a definitive resource on autistic women available to us."

—Nelle Frances, founder of AspergerChild

"*Spectrum Women* is a beautiful tapestry woven in wisdom, humour, and hope. I found myself laughing out loud and quietly nodding with each resonating reflection of life within its pages. In a world of misinformation around autism, with these spectrum sisters, you are in good and safe hands."

—Rachael Lee Harris, psychotherapist and author of<br>Contemplative Therapy for Clients on the Autism Spectrum

"By far this is the best book I have read about autistic females. As an autistic woman, wife, and mother to a daughter on the spectrum, this book is such a treat. This book gives a sense of belonging, packed full of valuable information, honest insights and great advice, wrapped beautifully together with Dr Michelle Garnett's supporting views. The 15 autistic authors share their personal experiences, covering many aspects of life for fellow Spectrum Women from disclosure, sensory issues, communication, health, anxiety, and self-care to relationships, parenthood, and employment. It's the full package. *Spectrum Women: Walking to the Beat of Autism* will help so many autistic women around the world and will be valuable information for partners, parents, and professionals. Together this tribe of truly amazing women (my autism mentors) have written an absolutely brilliant masterpiece. You are my Dream Team, ladies."

—Anne Skov Jensen, autism advocate, public<br>speaker, and a proud spectrum sister

"Filling a yawning gap in the autism literature with a combination of lived experience and research, recognition of women on the autism spectrum comes of age. In addition to these pioneering authors bringing awareness, acceptance, and appreciation of females on the autism spectrum to new heights, this amazing contribution teaches everyone the beauty of human diversity."

*—Stephen Shore, EdD, internationally known educator, author, and presenter on issues related to the autism spectrum*

"*Spectrum Women: Walking to the Beat of Autism* is so much more than the average book about autism; it is a collection of works that addresses a significant gap in the publishing world. Informative, emotionally charged, and honest, the chapters guide the reader through a variety of experiences. Through multiple autistic voices and clearly defined summations that acknowledge and validate each writer's experiences from a clinician's understanding, *Spectrum Women: Walking to the Beat of Autism* is a necessary read for professionals, families, and any woman who belongs within this amazing tribe."

*—Rebecca Vine Foggo, BA Psych, MA Autism, Doctoral Researcher (Autism)*

"*Spectrum Women* is a powerful resource to own. This book offers the previously unknown and untold experiences of a vast demographic of autistic women allowing other individuals on the spectrum, their parents, educators, and anyone involved in wanting to learn more by understanding and sharing their unique perspectives and challenges. But most of all, this book allows people to realise that a diagnosis doesn't have to be and shouldn't be seen as doom and gloom. Allow these women to transport you into their minds and their hearts to gain a new perspective of knowledge."

*—Nichole Conolly, autistic individual and Graduate Certificate in Autism Studies, University of Wollongong*

"A friend once told me that getting an autism diagnosis in midlife was like finding the Rosetta Stone to herself. This marvellously honest and historically important book will be that Rosetta Stone for many women on the spectrum who will recognize aspects of their own lived experience on every page. I am in awe of the practical wisdom and uplifting encouragement assembled here by these wise elders of their tribe."

—*Steve Silberman, author of* NeuroTribes: The Legacy of Autism and the History of Neurodiversity

# spectrum women

*by the same author*

**Exploring Depression, and Beating the Blues**
A CBT Self-Help Guide to Understanding and Coping with
Depression in Asperger's Syndrome (ASD-Level 1)
*Tony Attwood and Michelle Garnett*
*Illustrated by Colin Thompson*
ISBN 978 1 84905 502 4
eISBN 978 0 85700 907 4

**CBT to Help Young People with Asperger's Syndrome (Autism
Spectrum Disorder) to Understand and Express Affection**
A Manual for Professionals
*Tony Attwood and Michelle Garnett*
ISBN 978 1 84905 412 6
eISBN 978 0 85700 801 5

**From Like to Love for Young People with Asperger's
Syndrome (Autism Spectrum Disorder)**
Learning How to Express and Enjoy Affection with Family and Friends
*Tony Attwood and Michelle Garnett*
ISBN 978 1 84905 436 2
eISBN 978 0 85700 777 3


*of related interest*

**Been There. Done That. Try This!**
An Aspie's Guide to Life on Earth
*Edited by Tony Attwood, Craig R. Evans and Anita Lesko*
ISBN 978 1 84905 964 0
eISBN 978 0 85700 871 8

# spectrum women

## Walking to the Beat of Autism

*Edited by Barb Cook*
*and Dr. Michelle Garnett*
*Foreword by Lisa Morgan*

**The Spectrum Women Mentors:**
ARtemisia, Maura Campbell, Samantha Craft, Jen Elcheson,
Dena Gassner, Liane Holliday Willey, Christine Jenkins,
Renata Jurkévythz, Anita Lesko, Becca Lory, Terri Mayne,
Jeanette Purkis, Kate Ross, Catriona Stewart

Jessica Kingsley *Publishers*
London and Philadelphia

First published in 2018
by Jessica Kingsley Publishers
73 Collier Street
London N1 9BE, UK
and
400 Market Street, Suite 400
Philadelphia, PA 19106, USA

*www.jkp.com*

**Library of Congress Cataloging in Publication Data**
A CIP catalog record for this book is available from the Library of Congress

**British Library Cataloguing in Publication Data**
A CIP catalogue record for this book is available from the British Library

ISBN 978 1 78592 434 7
eISBN 978 1 78450 806 7

Printed and bound in Great Britain

*This book is dedicated to all our spectrum sisters: those who have been misdiagnosed, mistreated, or misunderstood in the past and to those where the future awaits, in finding their voices through their own unique journey.*

## Content Warning

Within the scope of this book, you may find some of the chapters more difficult to read than others due to the subject matter covered within them, especially if they speak to your personal experiences or fears for the future.

We have decided to be very open—for instance, about how being autistic can leave us vulnerable to violence and abuse—since we believe it is important for you to be able to recognize the dangers and to impart knowledge on how to keep yourself safe. We thought it would be wrong not to highlight such risks, but if you are concerned that certain topics might prove upsetting or distressing for you, you may wish to skip particular chapters or sections of this book.

# Contents

# Foreword

Stop! Are you ready to know what it feels like to be an autistic woman? To be immersed in the lives of these women on the spectrum who have shared their personal experiences so vividly it will be as if you are walking in their shoes?

Hello, Reader. In your hands you are holding pages and pages of lived experience, wisdom, and support written by autistic women, to be able to learn from at any time you need help, or when you just want to feel as if you belong. This book can be used as a map to unravel the confusion and soften the hurt that living life as an autistic woman can bring in so many different ways.

Have you ever wanted a direct line to experienced autistic women to ask the hard questions and get help navigating the endless confusion of life on the spectrum? Women you could have access to at any time of the day or night, to help you figure things out? They are within the pages of this book.

Do you want to know how it feels to be understood and to know that someone out there has had the same experiences you have had in life? To finally celebrate your life on the spectrum with others who know how sweet successes can be when they are strived for while in the trenches of a life that doesn't make much sense most of the time?

Maybe there was a conversation you thought went well, only to find out the person you were speaking with is so angry they won't talk to you anymore. Perhaps an unfair situation at work is too difficult to figure out on your own and you need some guidance on how to proceed. Sometimes the isolation and loneliness of being misunderstood feels impenetrable. All of these topics and more are covered in the book by women who have been there and lived those experiences out and learned valuable truths they are now passing on to you.

I, too, am an autistic woman, diagnosed later in life, with plenty of my own lived experiences to share, yet I finally understood more about who I really am within the pages of this book. I remember being left out of activities in school, feeling alone and misunderstood at work, and just not belonging to this world. As I read the book, I started feeling as if I belonged. I felt what it's like to be on the "inside" for once, for knowing what they were talking about, the language they were using, and the world they described.

I felt like I was part of the vibrant, intelligent, creative, empathetic, proactive, wise, and thoughtful group of women who have much to give to any reader who wants to know more about what life as an autistic woman is all about. It was so comforting.

Yes, the people who wrote this book are autistic women, heroines in their own right as they have shared their personal lives for the sake of other women on the spectrum. They are your cheerleaders as you navigate life on the spectrum. Can you hear them? Oh, they are probably using the silent clap knowing all too well that real clapping hurts the ears.

*Lisa Morgan, MEd*

Author of *Living through Suicide Loss with an Autistic Spectrum Disorder (ASD): An Insider Guide for Individuals, Family, Friends, and Professional Responders*

# Preface

Autistic Pride. This is where it all started one fateful evening in June, last year. I (Barb Cook) could be precise on date and time, but will let it slide this time, just to coerce you a little into reading some more. I mean, prefaces aren't usually the most exciting part of the book, but how this book evolved most certainly was for us. Us—the women of this book.

The book had its humble beginnings rooted in a conversation by the writers' team of *Spectrum Women Magazine*. Autistic Pride Day was fast approaching and it was suggested by Jeanette (Purkis)—with prompting from Mr. Kitty's tapping paw—that we should write a collaboration of stories on what Autistic Pride meant to us.

It was halfway through this idea flinging chat that, for some reason, the idea popped into my head that we should all write a book together. Hell, we do have a lot to offer, and we are all on the autism spectrum, plus we have experience—years and decades of experience—sitting within us that needed to be shared.

"You know, it did give me a thought, Renata (Jurkévythz), that we should all write a book together, maybe called *Spectrum Women*, each giving our personal insights. Like a book that is empowerment and mentoring to fellow autistic women?" Those, my exact words, midway through our discussion, had set the wheels in motion—on a train, down a hill, without any brakes...

Within hours a proposal was whisked away to Jessica of Jessica Kingsley Publishers—you might have noticed the imprint on the book (bit of a giveaway)—about how much the women and identifying women of the autism spectrum needed a candid, honest, and open-hearted book written by those who "get" them, live a life like them, and want to share with them that they don't need to navigate this life feeling alone.

We expanded the fold to include autistic women who were not just exclusive to the *Spectrum Women Magazine* writers' team. The number of ideas was immense and topics became tailored into chapters to cover what we felt were an essential start to this mission. Now, keeping you on that word "mission"—reminiscent of a Bond movie—M (Maura Campbell) became my left-hand (I'm left-handed) side-kick, the woman behind the woman, my sanity, my sounding board, my second pair of eyes, my friend with a sense of humor so dark that you needed a torch, the person who helped me make it all the way to the end. Without M, I don't think I could have pulled this all together as brilliantly as we did. (This was not a paid advertisement.)

There are a lot of considerations to be taken into account when pulling a book like this together, and I am sure there will be parts that some of you may not agree with, and that is fine. We all have our insights and personal views which make us different; we embrace that. Keeping this in mind, we tried to encompass a wide diversity of thought, terminology, and writing styles used, while embracing our own personal choices.

As this book caters for a global audience while being mindful of how identification can impact both the individual and the community who views them, we have decided on encompassing some of the following terminology:

- **Identity-first language.** Identity-first language has been mostly used as this is the preferred method for people identifying as being on the autism spectrum.
- **General identification.** Person/woman/girl/those on the spectrum. "With autism" has been used in context academically and historically.
- **Autism spectrum disorder (ASD).** ASD has been used instead of autism spectrum condition (ASC) for academic purposes. This is not a reflection of our personal choice in identification.
- **Asperger syndrome, Asperger's, and the personal identifying term of aspie.** We recognize that Asperger syndrome was removed from the current *Diagnostic and Statistical Manual of Mental Disorders* (DSM-5) and was brought together under the Autism Spectrum Disorder classification. At time of printing of this book, the *International Classification of Diseases* (ICD-10) still formally recognizes Asperger syndrome as a diagnosis. We have included these terms to encompass those who were/are diagnosed with Asperger syndrome and in a historical sense for academia.
- **High and low functioning.** We agreed that the terminology of high and low functioning is an outdated and segregating description of people on the autism spectrum.
- **Neurotypical (NT) and non-autistic** have been used interchangeably to identify persons not on the autism spectrum.

We each have our own unique way in which we identify, write, and view the world. Even though we could have enforced one particular way, a similar style for all, it wouldn't have been a true representation of our voices, our very own and unique voices.

The academic side of this book was something we wanted to embrace alongside our personal accounts. Even though the women of this book are the "experts," we needed to ensure that the health professionals and academic community embraced what we had to offer from our personal experience and insights. Dr. Michelle Garnett complements each chapter throughout this book, giving her own views from clinical experience and research around women and girls on the autism spectrum. Dr. Garnett's unique gift of over 20 years' experience from working in the field of ASDs, alongside Professor Tony Attwood, shines through with each chapter she provides commentary on, with sincere and genuine compassion. Dr. Garnett brings forth to the reader the value and worth that each and every female on the autism spectrum has to offer while providing advice and demonstrated strategies in creating a more fulfilling life.

The information and personal journeys within this book are from our own unique perception and experience of the world around us, each of us living in different circumstances, making no two stories alike. But we share a common theme—to give you the reader a glimpse into each of our lives—and I am sure you will all feel a connection, whether it is with all of us or just one or two. Even the smallest amount of information, wisdom or insight that can set you on a different path of personal happiness certainly makes this project all worthwhile.

> We are Spectrum Women and we are here for each other to mentor, validate, support, and share with you that your life has purpose, has meaning, has value. Within the arms of Spectrum Women, take back your power, the power to be unashamedly and uniquely you. (Barb Cook)

# Prologue

*Barb Cook*

Where does the story begin?

You would think by the time we hit midlife, we would have enough insight and knowledge to understand the world around us or at least have a grasp on what is expected while occupying planet earth... Obviously not. Well, obviously not was my case until I hit my 40s.

My diagnosis of Asperger syndrome didn't eventuate until I was six weeks shy of my 40th birthday. You know that saying "life begins at 40"? Well, that statement couldn't have been more spot on if it tried.

"Congratulations, here is your certificate on surviving life thus far, now this will give you a clue as to what life is really all about. Asperger's, good luck...tallyho."

It was those words that scrolled through my head, like subtitles on a foreign movie. In the background a bugle "tada-ing" ensued: "let the hunt begin"—the hunt for knowledge in my case.

After fudging my way through the past 40 years, I finally had some clarity and a sense of freeing from the internal anguish that I was never, ever going to understand this damn strange world around me. I did actually believe I was losing my mind at one point as I could not fathom, for the life of me, how people existed on, let alone navigated life on terra firma. As far as I could ascertain, I was the problem, and no matter how hard I tried mimicking or masking who I essentially was, I just couldn't perform naturally like my fellow non-autistic beings. And I was tired of it all.

Up until this point, I had literally resigned myself away to never being able to function "appropriately" in society. Until that one fateful day...

The local community center in the small town in which I was residing had brought together a day of speakers centered on women's health and well-being. Venturing in and positioning myself at the back of the room—a spot I readily scan for on arrival for such do's—had me sitting there flicking through brochures while doing my damnedest to filter out the awfully high-pitched chit-chat that irritated like a splinter in an index finger, one that is embedded too deeply to dig out, but will constantly remind you just how annoying it is.

There were interesting presentations to be had, and I smiled when they announced the next speaker was running late for her presentation—"that is so me," I thought—so they would bring forward the following speaker of the morning.

As the speaker warbled away their insights of a life full of wonderment and wellness, it became enormously obvious the "late" presenter was trying her utmost to sneak up to her chair at the back of the stage where she would perform. Obviously, the furniture got annoyed with her lateness and added to her challenges of taking her seat quietly. Those bloody tables and chairs certainly know how to maneuver themselves into position, ready to strike at the most inappropriate moments. With a trip, and thud, she had arrived.

With forgotten notes and wild, windswept hair, the furniture-challenged presenter took stage. A local doctor. With my analytical and judgmental thoughts, I questioned internally: how on earth did she become a doctor if she can't even win a duel with the chair? And she's fat. Really, how can you be fat, uncoordinated, and be a doctor? For some reason I had been conditioned to believe that those who offer help with our health should be a shining example of just that. Perfection, wellness, measure up to the figures we are led to believe we must strive for. There was that rigid conditioned thinking again...

But the rigidness waned as she spoke. The words were not of perfection but about accepting yourself, being kind to yourself, and that we all are valuable and deserve a life that makes us happy. She cared, deeply.

When I reflect on how I charged up like a rampant bull after her presentation, hoping for an opportunity to speak with her—well, more like I just opened my mouth and a tidal wave of words poured forth—I did wonder if she thought I had lost my mind. Well, that was what I was thinking that she might be thinking as we tend to overthink EVERYTHING and more so after an incident like this. STOP THINKING! But in reality she just stood there and smiled, took in everything I was saying and told me to come and see her at her little practice nearby. When I told her I thought I was "crazy," she just looked at me with compassion and said, "No, you're not."

It takes just a moment like this to completely change your world, set you on a path to try to find yourself again. I know so many ladies who are getting a diagnosis later in life and the impact it has, not just on understanding ourselves; it is literally life-changing.

It does take some time to rediscover who you are. After what seems like a lifetime of never understanding the world, let alone yourself, you have to take the time to go back and reflect on your life to move forward. So there I was, a middle-aged woman who was basically starting life over again. I had to untrain all the misconceptions about how I should behave, what was expected, and to let go of what other people thought. That was a hard one.

But my past started to make a lot more sense.

When you don't understand yourself, it is hard to accept not just what is happening but why it is happening. It is virtually impossible to rationalize with yourself when you don't understand why you feel such an outsider, an alien.

But it does change.

So where does the story begin? With you. It doesn't have to start at the beginning and it doesn't have to feel as if it is all over before you got the chance to begin. It is never too late to find happiness, and that is our ultimate goal. To find peace within, to find where we belong and to be valued for who we are. Repeat after me: "We deserve this."

Now heading on to 50, I have finally transitioned into another phase of my life. Nearly ten years later I can actually say I emerged on the other side. Light at the end of the tunnel...well, no, that would be a train, and you don't want to be standing there waiting for it to run you down... But strange humor and metaphors aside—whoever came up with metaphors, silly idea—we have every opportunity to step up and say: "This is how I want my life to be, not that of the expected norm. This is my life and I want to live it my way." Repeat: "This is my life..." I can see you're getting the hang of this.

But how do we go about this, how can we bring happiness into our lives if we're feeling so entrenched in a system that doesn't work for us? We have to reach out, ask for help, find our tribe. Stop trying to fit into everyone else's expectations, take a step back, re-evaluate, and rebuild your way.

It is OK to reflect on what could have been, but don't stay there. As with many women who were identified later in life, experience comes. And it is from this experience that we certainly know what doesn't work for us. Time to find out what does...

Within these pages that follow is a lifetime of experience waiting to be shared with you, by women just like you. The Spectrum Women know your pain, your challenges, your heartache. They have been there, survived, embraced, and evolved.

Imparting their wisdom, the Spectrum Women open up a doorway for you to step through, out into a new way of thinking and loving yourself for who you truly are—a step on a journey for you to explore.

It is this journey, one of self-discovery, reconnecting, and researching, that will be put into gear, shifting each time to a higher level of understanding about ourselves with a kind prompting, not just from "Us" and our words, but also from another. Friend of the Spectrum Women, Dr. Michelle, joins us on our journey, creating unison between our intimate knowledge and her richness of experience in the clinical and academic, which is also reinforced by her sincere compassion and desire to help Spectrum Women, just like us, and just like you, to have fulfilling lives that we most certainly deserve. Within her words you can take comfort that we will be heard and respected, but she too will guide you along a path, still very much your own, with added wisdom and knowledge that she imparts.

But don't think for a minute that this book is designed just for those of us who have been on this path for years or decades; this book is for all ages and for all points of the journey you are on.

Whether you are just at the beginning or have been traveling this path for some time, the Spectrum Women welcome you into their lives. The front door is open, the kettle is on... Come on in, you are welcomed, you are home.

## CHAPTER 1

# Finding Your Tribe

*Maura Campbell*

## Pursuing a diagnosis

I pressed the pause button and asked my husband a question: "What do you think of how he just reacted?" We were watching *Adam* (2009), a romantic movie in which the lead character is autistic. We had been watching a lot of movies and documentaries about autism since our son's diagnosis about six months earlier. We were scared, confused, and hungry for information. Adam had just caught his girlfriend out on a lie and was not taking it at all well. My husband thought it was an extreme overreaction. I thought it was exactly how I would have reacted if I found myself in the same situation.

"What was your eureka moment, the moment you thought for sure you might have Asperger syndrome?" The doctor leaned forward in her chair and gave me an encouraging smile. I told her about the night I pressed the pause button. That was the first moment I really *knew*. I was relieved that she was taking me seriously. The reams of typed-up notes I was nervously clutching, containing meticulously recorded bullet-point lists, were probably her first clue.

When I made some initial enquiries about going for adult autism diagnosis, I was advised that the first step was to talk to my general practitioner. I had been devouring books and scouring the internet to learn as much as I could about autism and kept coming across statements that made me think, *But that sounds like me.* I was intending to pursue a private diagnosis. The doctor suggested we try our local health trust first and I agreed. After languishing for months on a waiting list, I was asked intrusive and irrelevant questions by mental health professionals in the psychiatry department, who frankly seemed to have very little knowledge of autism—"When do you think your Asperger's first started?" was a particular favorite. I was then passed across to the psychology department who eventually deemed me "too high-functioning" to be invited for assessment. I was fine with that—there were probably others who needed the assessment more than me and I understood that services were stretched—but it was frustrating to have wasted so much time when I had a burning urge to know whether Asperger's was the answer to a question I had only recently thought to ask.

And so I boarded a train and was assessed in a private clinic about a hundred miles away. *People have traveled further to find themselves,* I thought. I was excited and nervous. My nervousness was not because I feared a diagnosis of autism; it was because I feared I might not get one. I needn't have worried. I was told there was "no doubt about it." I felt a surge of relief. I finally had an explanation for why I always felt like the rest of the world was judging me and finding me wanting, why I was out of my depth at social events and exhausted afterwards, why I was so anxious all the time, why noises that other people barely noticed were excruciating for me, why day-to-day functioning sometimes seemed so overwhelming. Instead of constantly feeling frustrated with myself for struggling with certain things, I could now take pride in having made it this far on my own. At 44 years of age, I finally knew who I was. I grinned the whole way home.

It is a common enough story. As diagnosis rates for children are increasing, a growing number of mothers are recognizing the reason for their own differences and the challenges they experienced in childhood and young adulthood.

## Why are fewer females diagnosed as autistic?

Women tend to be either diagnosed later in life or missed altogether for a range of reasons. We are more socially adept and less rigid than our male counterparts, and so we tend to fly under the radar. We are better at masking our challenges and blending in, perhaps because we are under more social pressure to do so. We may be perceived as simply shy. Our intense interests in childhood are more typical (albeit more intense) and therefore less noticeable— boy bands or ponies, for instance. We may also move on to new topics of interest more quickly than males. Many professionals will only give a diagnosis if they judge that your ability to "function" is being severely impacted, which seems unfair since it effectively penalizes you for putting in the work to manage your challenges.

Importantly, the diagnostic criteria are skewed towards the male presentation of autism. Indeed, the earliest writing on the specific presentation of autism in females was by pioneering autistic women.[1] The scientific community is starting to play catch-up, which must be welcomed, and I suspect we could see a leveling out of the male/female diagnostic ratio in the future. It remains to be seen whether we will ever get to a point where there are equal numbers across both genders.

Most of the autistic women I know were diagnosed in adulthood and, like me, regard it as a positive experience. Motherhood is not the only catalyst—for some a specific incident has triggered a crisis or they have been led towards diagnosis by a build-up of mental health challenges. Those who were diagnosed at a younger age may

---

1    See the Recommended Resources section at the back of the book.

report a more ambivalent or even hostile reaction to the diagnosis, which is understandable given the stronger desire to fit in; a typical teenager feels self-conscious enough without having to confront the idea of having a "disorder" as well.

I sometimes wonder what would have happened if I had been diagnosed earlier. Would I have made better life choices and been spared unnecessary heartache? Or would it have become an excuse to retreat from the world and avoid living a full life? The simple fact is I have no way of knowing.

Some women decide not to pursue a formal diagnosis, which is a perfectly valid choice. Since diagnosis by the state is usually not that easy to come by, as my own experience has shown, the cost of private diagnosis may be a factor. Or, for some, it is enough to have figured it out for themselves. Some people may be concerned about what others will think of them; if they are a mother, they may be fearful that they will be "blamed" for their child's condition.

There are, of course, online tools available, such as the autism quotient test. While they are not sufficiently robust to provide a definitive assessment, they can give you a decent indication of whether you might be on the spectrum.

Something else to weigh in the balance is that if you have an autism diagnosis in your medical records, there may be certain occupations, such as in the armed forces, where it could count against you. You may also be restricted in terms of emigrating to other countries.

## Running the gauntlet of myths, misconceptions, and stereotypes

If the only information you had was from movies and TV programs, you would be forgiven for thinking there are two distinct types of autistic person—the non-verbal savant or the geeky genius with zero social skills—since those are the most common presentations in the media. I have lost count of the number of times people have asked me, after I mentioned that my son is autistic, what his "special ability" is (I tell them he can eat his own body weight in pizza).

Most women on the spectrum are neither of those things, of course. Autism is a complex condition with many different presentations. No two individuals are the same. It is a non-linear spectrum and each person has their own set of talents and challenges. It is one of the aspects of the condition I find most interesting, though I can see how it creates problems for service providers. Services are usually delivered under the banner of learning disability (even though most autistics do not have an intellectual disability) or mental health (even though autism is not, of itself, a mental health condition). I can understand the desire to categorize us, but the level of support people require varies so enormously that it is impossible to put us all into one box.

You often see statements along the lines of "a person cannot have autism if..." Apparently, to fit others' idea of what autism is—to be "autistic enough"—we must be completely incapable of, for instance, making friends, maintaining eye contact, or understanding idioms and metaphors.

Perhaps the most damaging claim is that autistics do not empathize. Many of us have the opposite problem—we feel too much. I need to avoid listening to the news on the days when the sadness in the world completely overwhelms me. Despite ample evidence to the contrary, the stereotype of the sociopathic loner still persists.

Another myth that particularly bugs me is that we are humorless automatons. Autistics are among the wittiest people I know and our humor is rarely at the expense of someone else. It is usually playful, self-deprecating, and full of wonderful word play.

There is an entire collection of myths dedicated to the causes of autism. Many of these are harmful and, at best, they are a distraction. There is a scientific consensus that genetics play a major role, with estimates of the extent to which autism is attributable to genetic factors ranging from 50% to 95%. The noisy speculation about causes has fueled a mini-industry of unscrupulous people pedaling a "cure" for autism or claiming they can "recover" autistic children, effectively monetizing parental fears. Scaremongers often present autism as a fate worse than death and point to an autism "epidemic," ignoring the fact that the rise in diagnosis rates is a result of improved detection and the reimagining of autism as a spectrum condition as opposed to a rare childhood "disease."

## Disclosing that you are autistic

"Out and proud" is not necessarily right for everyone. I know many people who have chosen not to disclose their diagnosis for entirely valid reasons and I completely respect their decision. It depends very much on personal circumstances.

Disclosure made sense for me at the time. I was at a stage in my life where I didn't feel I had to prove myself, since I was in a stable relationship and well established in my career, and so there was no real downside. The fact that I had a child on the spectrum was also a factor; having decided early on to be open about his diagnosis, it seemed wrong to be coy about mine.

In fact, I pretty much burst out of the aspie closet immediately. I was so euphoric on the day of the diagnosis that I simply couldn't wait to tell the world. Finally, my whole life up to that point made sense! It was a hugely significant moment and I wanted to share it. It didn't occur to me that other people might not see it the same way. I ended up feeling deflated and anxious when I received a muted reaction. I had thought people would be more curious.

Telling people seemed to make them uncomfortable, but they didn't say why. Did no one believe me? Did they think I was making my son's autism all about me, that I was attention-seeking? Did they think I was some sort of imposter? Few things make me as anxious as not knowing what other people are thinking—life would be so much easier if people could just say what they mean and mean what they say.

It is worth taking a bit of time to think about whether to disclose your diagnosis. What is said cannot subsequently be unsaid. You might want some time to get used to the idea yourself before talking to others about it. You may also want to think about the order in which to tell people and how best to do it. You don't need to tell everyone. As a rule of thumb, you could ask yourself whether telling a person or group of people you are autistic is likely to have mainly positive or negative consequences for you. People may not react the way you anticipate. They may be unsure how to respond for fear of saying the wrong thing. Be prepared for awkward silences. Given our ability to mask, a woman's diagnosis may be more of a surprise to her family, friends, and colleagues.

People may have their own expectations, preconceptions or prejudices. I had a friend say to me, "You can't be autistic—people like you." It was meant kindly but it exposed how the general populace equates disclosing you are autistic with admitting to being defective. The underlying problem is how the world still sees autism. The terminology that surrounds it tends to be overly pathologized. Take the word "diagnosis," for example—Jen Elcheson uses the phrase "professionally identified" instead, or you could say your autism has been "confirmed."

Descriptions of autism are usually deficits-based and we are often described as "suffering" from autism or Asperger's. People may see you as having a medical problem. When I "came out," I was asked a couple of times what treatment I was receiving. No matter how hard I tried to tell people that the diagnosis was a positive event, a confirmation of who I already was, they behaved as though I was conveying bad news. What I learned from this was that people do not always receive information in the same way as you present it to them. They often apply their own filters, overlaying what you have said with their own assumptions.

You may well be challenged on why you would want to "label" yourself in this way. Most people struggle with the idea that you would want to identify as anything other than "normal" (whatever that means!) and a few people may even think you have an ulterior motive—that you are trying to claim benefits, for instance. I have often found myself in a position where I have had to explain or even defend my decision to pursue a diagnosis in the first place. I tell people that I just really needed to know and feared that people would not believe me if I self-diagnosed.

I have no regrets about putting it out there. If anyone should think less of me because I am on the autistic spectrum, that's their problem.

## The benefits of a diagnosis

For me, the benefits of obtaining an autism diagnosis greatly outweighed the negatives. It was like taking off a corset I didn't know I had been wearing. I could finally breathe.

Having a name for my differences has allowed me to gain a deeper understanding of myself, why I think or behave in certain ways and how I may come across to other people. I have been able to build upon the coping strategies I had already been developing without knowing why I needed to, such as carving out time to be alone.

Having a formal diagnosis affords you a certain credibility when you give your opinion on issues relating to autism, especially if you can draw on direct experience. A key benefit for me of a formal diagnosis is that it has made me a lot more confident as a parent because I now trust my own instincts much more than I did before. It has also provided me with opportunities to educate and inform other people about autism, and to advocate on behalf of those within our community who may not be in as good a position to do so for themselves. I can challenge head-on the damaging myths and misconceptions in a way that is more impactful than if I were talking solely as a parent of an autistic child.

As well as making me a more confident mother, it has allowed me to articulate my own needs better. I have been able to ask for reasonable accommodations in the workplace to reduce sensory discomfort. I now find it easier to manage my social energy and avoid burnout since I can explain why I may need to leave a social event early, or forgo it entirely, without causing offense. I have learned what will recharge my social battery and what will drain it. I feel less guilty about making time to restore.

You will quickly find out who will accommodate and celebrate your new sense of self with you and who will see it as a weapon with which to beat you. Your respect and appreciation of the former will grow and you will learn not to waste your valuable time on the latter.

But perhaps the biggest benefit has been the opportunity to join a community of people who just "get it," people with whom I can relax. I can take off the mask and unapologetically be me. I am still in the process of figuring out, nearly six years on, who "me" really is, but I have been helped tremendously in that journey by learning about the experiences of others. It feels good to pay it forward.

I have met so many wonderful people since I was diagnosed who would never have been a part of my life otherwise, including several of the contributors to this book. While not every autistic person I have come across has been someone with whom I have wanted a friendship—as with any group, there will be some people you get on with better than others, and being autistic doesn't give you immunity from being an asshole—I have generally found people within the autistic community to be honest, straightforward, and non-judgmental, and to have a well-developed sense of fairness and social justice. These are qualities I hugely admire and to which I aspire.

Other autistic women inspire and encourage me every day and my life is richer for knowing them. There is something incredibly validating about hearing the words "me too." It means I am no longer alone. I have found true acceptance at last. I have found my tribe.

## Dr. Michelle Garnett on diagnosis in women

Like Maura, many women on the autism spectrum deliberated about whether or not they should seek a formal diagnosis, weighing up the potential costs and benefits. Having made that sometimes difficult and painful decision, there is a long and time-consuming road ahead before they find someone with the knowledge to make an accurate diagnosis. Research shows that, at the time of writing, the average age of being diagnosed with ASD Level 1 for boys around the world is 8 years old, while for girls the average age is 13. There are many pathways to diagnosis for girls and women, and we have found that these include:

- The initial diagnosis of a different condition, particularly social anxiety, attention-deficit disorder (ADD) or attention-deficit/hyperactivity disorder (ADHD), selective mutism, depression including bipolar disorder, gender dysphoria, obsessive-compulsive disorder, or anorexia nervosa—this is a common pathway for adolescent girls.

- A common pathway for women is the diagnosis of an autism spectrum disorder in one of their children or another family member.
- Another common pathway for women is the internet— discovering female descriptions of having Asperger syndrome and resonating so well with those descriptions.

It has certainly been the case historically that far fewer females have been diagnosed with autism than males, with the ratio standing at approximately one female for every four males since the early 1990s. However, as Maura astutely describes, we suspect that we will see a leveling out of this diagnostic ratio. Recently, a fascinating research study conducted in Scotland (Rutherford *et al.*, 2016) showed prevalence rates across the genders at 5.5 boys for every 1 girl for very young children, 3.5:1 for children and adolescents overall, 2.3:1 for adolescents only, and 1.8:1 in adulthood. These findings not only indicate that the true prevalence of ASD in women is far higher than once thought, but also underline that females are being diagnosed much later.

In considering whether or not to pursue a diagnosis, I think it is helpful to consider the advantages of a diagnosis, which I see as being these:

- **Relief.** Prior to receiving a diagnosis, many people project into the confusion of who they are with a variety of labels that are self-critical and judgmental, including "weird," "defective," and "psycho," each denoting in loud, clashing tones, "Something is wrong with me!" It can come as an enormous relief to discover that there is nothing "wrong," much that is very right, and a lot that is different.

- **Clarity.** A diagnosis has often been described by women as being "the missing piece of the jigsaw puzzle." The diagnosis can end the seeking and the confusion to the question of "Who am I?" There is suddenly a literature base, research findings, and fascinating facts to answer lifelong questions.
- **Belonging.** Maura has put this so well in her words "Finding your Tribe." Thanks to our burgeoning knowledge of brain function, we are at the dawn of the age of embracing neuro-diversity. Embracing neurodiversity provides acceptance and understanding, especially among those who intimately know the reality of living with neurological difference.
- **Strategies.** Once a person identifies with being on the spectrum, they can learn from others in their tribe about how to cope with other people's ignorance, sensory issues, emotional dysregulation, and alexithymia, among other things.
- **Family.** Being aware of the diagnosis can assist the whole family, so that true understanding, non-judgmental acceptance, accommodations, and empathic attunement can occur.

To conclude, my own advice on whether or not to seek a diagnosis if you are curious is: just do it—and the earlier the better. It answers the question and ends the speculation. It is my experience that our young girls on the autism spectrum need to know about their difference as early as possible in a factual, celebratory, and empathic way to allow them to grow into and appreciate who they are, instead of living by their own and others' ignorant judgments.

CHAPTER 2

# Growing up on the Spectrum

*Jen Elcheson and Barb Cook*

## Early days to maturity—*Jen Elcheson*

### Childhood

I somehow knew from the age of two and a half that there was something profoundly different about me and that it was a result of the workings of my brain. I grew up in the 1980s and 1990s and, until age 17, nobody knew I was autistic with learning disabilities. Navigating the outer world seemed so easy for everyone, but not for me. It was downright nonsensical, chaotic, and muddled. Learning things required patience, extra instruction, and a visual explanation (if available). As others seemingly cruised through life knowing how to do things, mundane or otherwise, their senses effortlessly canceling out external stimuli, I was taking it all in to a higher intensity.

Everything was too fast, loud, difficult, scary, itchy, smelly, and just TOO MUCH! I'm certain I had anxiety from birth. Anything outside my routine comfort zone frightened/overwhelmed me, even 'fun' activities. I was a picky eater. My sensory processing needs ranged from sensory avoidant to sensory seeking. I loved pleasant smells but hated bad ones. I liked shiny, soft textures, bold colors, and stretchy materials. I had a collection of bathing suits because I loved how the spandex material felt with the new clothes smell upon getting a new one. I remember walking around, often talking or singing to myself, with my trusted security blanket, a bottle of something to smell or a bathing suit, as if it was no big deal. Other kids I knew didn't behave in such idiosyncratic ways and I knew I stood out.

I liked adults, but disliked being around other kids. They were always in my space, noisy, irritating, crying over ludicrous things, and making up ridiculous games with constantly changing rules. I often hid in my room with books, ponies, and dolls. Socializing felt prickly and cringy. I now realize I was full of anxiety, exhaustion, and frustration, and could not properly identify my feelings. The kids mom picked to be my friends did not feel like friends. They tolerated me at most. That is, when they weren't calling me a weirdo or ostracizing me.

Upon seeing a psychologist at age three, he told my mom she was raising an eccentric and to love and accept me. That was great advice and all, but no answers to explain my ways of being. I was not alone in this experience. I've met a lot of autistics who were not identified until later and who were considered odd, different, or eccentric as children rather than autistic. There was simply no information at the time. Even now, society is still in the early stages of understanding autism.

## School

School equaled an abundance of social and academic challenges. How I moved, played, processed, stimmed, or talked, I was mocked for it. Adding to the frustration, my neurodivergent younger brother was immediately identified in kindergarten as dyslexic and as having attention-deficit/hyperactivity disorder (ADHD) when I was likely seen as a having "problem behaviors." I wasn't assessed or evaluated for anything—I suspect because I was a girl who *appeared* capable.

Lack of social understanding and other factors resulted in me repeating kindergarten. I was frequently on the "thinking bench" first year. I didn't know why I was put there, let alone know what I was supposed to be thinking about. Eventually, I realized kids lied about me to the teacher to avoid playing with me. Sometimes I got to brush the teacher's hair to prevent any issues. (Mrs A., wherever you are, thanks for meeting my odd sensory needs—really.)

The bullying continued the following year as kids were aware of me repeating a grade. Then the year after my teacher had the audacity to mock me for stimming in class, further encouraging the kids to be nasty.

I also regrettably learned to bully kids back. I thought *everyone* was bullying me and couldn't discern who liked me/who didn't. I couldn't read body language/social cues. If others were nice to me, I didn't believe them. I would sometimes push them away, resulting in no friends until I realized nobody would like me if I continued. I began making some friends in late elementary school. I was tired of being the kid everyone hated and I wanted friends.

I started to teach myself how to pass and blend in with others, using what I was reading or watching as guidelines. For example, there were a few book series I *loved* and collected. Many kids didn't understand why I had such an intense interest in these books, but they encompassed important social themes. They were more than a pastime, rather a crash course in social skills I didn't innately have. One would think I was teaching myself a new language, a hidden curriculum. In many ways I was.

Academically, I struggled with unidentified learning disabilities that teachers saw as lazy/defiant acts of refusal and inattentiveness. I received average marks in some subjects, but continually failed math and science. Processing verbal instructions came slowly or they always sounded garbled. I did best in language arts, but, being a literal thinker, couldn't fully comprehend abstract language until later. I wasn't a gifted autistic who could read classic literature or encyclopedias by any means.

I had/still have gross/fine motor delays. I was unable to hold a pencil or use scissors for years. I felt inferior and couldn't regulate emotions well. The meltdowns in and out of school were combinations of sensory overload, continuous academic failures, exasperation from trying to make/keep friends, and bullying. Although many girls on the spectrum hide their difficulties, saving their meltdowns for home, I could only hold it together to a certain extent. Emotional regulation problems made this challenging. I'm amazed that I made it through school.

**Teen years**

My teens were similarly trying. I habitually strived to hide any quirks that would single me out. There was some bullying in the beginning, but it eventually stopped after switching schools and my ability to pass strengthened. I had always struggled with anxiety, but the new kid on the block was depression. Because I actively worked really hard to fit in, it became very tiresome. I remember skipping school to go home and sleep.

I learned to pass by observing others, watching shows/movies, devouring young adult contemporary fiction, and collecting women's magazines. They were all intense interests, but definitely not a healthy way to acquire realistic social skills. Unfortunately, I became very rigid about being this supposed "normal" version of myself and it really messed with my identity. In hindsight, I felt as if I was playing different roles and acting them out. I was a social chameleon. How I presented depended on who I was around. I also found by imitating the actions of others or through quietly observing I would get into fewer social "SNAFUs" (Situation Normal, All Fucked Up).

With the information out now, I know that passing, although a privilege in itself, is daunting, and can greatly confuse and hamper the development of one's true identity, all to make the neuromajority comfortable. While there are social skills necessary to get us by in life, we should not have to change our entire presentation so people will accept us. Being so focused on fitting in, I had pretty much stopped caring about academics and grades. I wanted to fit in with the kids I hung out with. I also began to obsess awkwardly about looking and acting as much like my peers as I could and about boys.

Meltdowns mainly transpired at home, but I recall having a really intense one at school over a misunderstanding where friends ignored me after I said something wrong. I wanted to know what I had said wrong and fix it, but when no one would talk to me, I ended up extremely distraught. I started attending counseling. I wanted to know why I kept struggling but was not prepared for the answer.

I was identified at 17. I am sure my preoccupations over pop culture, boys, and friends were a dead giveaway to the clinicians, along with information my mom provided. The last thing I would have imagined was an autism diagnosis. I knew I had ADHD and learning disabilities like my brother, and they too were confirmed. However, it was a shock hearing my primary diagnosis was Asperger syndrome. In hindsight, I knew it was true deep down, but oh did I fight it! I didn't want to be the weird girl anymore; I thought I learned to hide that stuff! I felt shame and guilt, which I internalized until I finally learned to accept myself eight years later when something finally changed my perception.

### Young adulthood

My early young adult years consisted of failed relationships and jobs, so I decided to go to vocational school. I eventually found my niche in supporting autistic/neurodivergent kids when I started studying.

I cannot explain my sudden interest in autism; I was just strongly drawn to it and eager to learn. When I met the kids, I was stunned at how much they reminded me of my younger self. Years of denial peeled away and I knew exactly why I had to support them. *The professionals who identified this in me had it right all along: I AM actually autistic!* As many of the courses I took involved a lot of self-reflection, I discovered my true autistic self in the process. This eventually led to my current career in working with neurodivergent learners in schools. Basically, I'm currently doing what I can to be the role model I would have wanted. I also write about autism and volunteer with some autistic-run organizations, all online.

**Leaving the nest**

Leaving home was something I stressed over immensely when younger. That changed at 19. I sought independence and moved out. I have no regrets, but I wish I had gone about doing things differently. It wasn't easy. I worked a variety of jobs and lived in a few different places. Jobs didn't work out or the ones I did well in weren't my idea of a career. Eventually, I moved back to my home town to earn my social service work diploma and school support certification. I was anxious about returning to school, but knew that in order to have a decent job I had to study. I am glad I got the courage to make this choice as I am finally in a suitable career and living situation.

Overall, growing up on the spectrum during a time when attitudes and perceptions greatly differed from today made self-acceptance challenging. I'm glad, despite all of the pitfalls I faced, that I could finally get to where accepting my different neurology opened up many opportunities I wouldn't imagine otherwise. I can finally say that I am becoming more of who I am meant to be as I continue through life. I would encourage others to aim for the same!

## Midlife and beyond—*Barb Cook*

### Menopause and aging

"Growing old disgracefully" has always been a statement that rang true with my perception of aging. Not in the sense of causing chaos (but that could be fun) but in the sense that I don't want to grow old like the rest of society.

The common perception of aging is one of gray hair, aching bones, losing our memory, being put out to pasture where society pretty much forgets your existence. Being autistic and having to battle my way through life to be accepted and respected for my worth, I really don't want to go quietly in my twilight years.

Nearing the age of 50, it does now concern me what does lie ahead for us. For me, I still don't think I have reached full maturity, and in a sense I don't think I ever will or want to. Many of us are renowned for looking and acting much younger than our actual biological age. Maybe we have the secret of never growing up, like Peter Pan, maintaining that childlike wonderment? It really does make me ponder.

Unfortunately, the harsh reality is that we are not getting any younger and we need to start planning a future that will positively support us till the day of our final transition off this earthly plane. Once we start hitting those years of 40, 50, and 60, things begin to change both physically and mentally. The years mark the transition into menopause and ending of our childbearing years. Some of us can't wait for this day to come, but for others it can be one of loss. For me, it is a stark reminder of how many quality years I do have left ahead of me.

Hitting perimenopause certainly makes a statement in that "change of life." It doesn't come quietly—well, not for me—but makes me feel like one crazy woman that really doesn't have a grip of her own life anymore. Plus, there are the physical changes that really add to screwing with your head. Periods, which were once predictable, now come early and then eventually change to being late, even up to months at a time. Our bone density declines, with the future prospect of osteoporosis, and unsightly and fast-growing black facial hairs appear as a result of declining levels of estrogen. Oh, and this unpredictability of hormone levels actually matches the unpredictable moods swings—I think there could be a connection there. I was being sarcastic. On a positive, I think it improved my levels of sarcasm.

So, the onslaught continues—foggy thinking. I literally think these past couple of years that I must be getting the onset of some neurological disease as I cannot for the life of me think straight. The sharp thinking, working with 37 tabs open on the computer, isn't so easy anymore. I still have the 37 tabs open, but for the life of me I don't know why half the time! I constantly forget where I put things when I used to be the one who knew where everything was. That mental spark fades and it is seriously frustrating.

Yes, there is more... Let's throw in the hot flushes, the night sweats, the change in body odor, brittle hair, increased risk of breast cancer, and weight gain that never wants to leave again, and you can see this "change of life" really is not much fun at all. I think you can guess why I can't wait for this to be over.

But we can survive this chaos that is prepping us for our twilight years of no longer being chained to the monthly ickiness and pain. There are good-quality supplements to help with sleep and hormone changes. Your doctor can give you options of taking other paths, but please make sure you do your research as a lot of us are sensitive and they may not be suitable for us.

Also, another practical approach is to take up things like yoga or Pilates to help with strengthening our core as our bones and body change. Exercise is good not just for our body, but also our minds. That is one of the biggest things. If we feel OK mentally, we can usually take on these challenges so much better.

As we continue to age, our bodies change in other ways too—arthritis, the aches and pains, cognitive memory fading. They make you wonder one day, *how did my body change to this?* You question yourself and think, *I used to be able to do so much!* We beat ourselves up at not being what we once were.

The prospects ahead of life-threatening diseases like cancer, diabetes, or coronary heart disease become all too real, and more so if they run in the family. Who will look after us, especially if you are, like me, childless and with no close family? Not that we expect our family to care for us in our old age, but it is good to know someone who understands your needs as you age.

We may be hypersensitive to medications, I know I am, but who is going to remind the doctors and carers as we age? We most likely will all have sensitivities to our surroundings, but who is going to ensure, if the time comes when we are placed in the care of a nursing home, that accommodations will be made for us? How do we protect ourselves and point out that we don't like physical contact by strangers, the noises, the lighting, the foods we are served up?

The only way to try to ensure that people know these concerns is to start planning before it is too late. If you have family or someone you completely trust, work with them to plan out what you want when the time comes and you need care. We may not all need this in our later years, but be prepared; I cannot stress this enough. I personally watched my father in the last 18 months of his life be put into a nursing home as he had a debilitating condition, Lewy body disease. Watching a very intelligent, physically powerful, and larger-than-life man stripped pretty much of dignity, no longer being able to care for or feed himself, was incredibly heartbreaking. Through this experience I watched the dynamics of the nursing home, how carers were constantly in and out of his room, the fluorescent lighting that hurt my eyes, the wanderings of fellow patients who would randomly appear in his room due to their dementia, and it certainly hit home. How could I ever live my final days like this?

This stark reality potentially awaits us. But we don't have to let this consume our thoughts in these later years. If we plan now how we would like to spend our days, and preferably with as much support and accommodations that work for us, I believe we can be prepared and still grow in many ways. We still have time to do things that make us happy—just maybe a tweak here or there, accepting the changes and working with them. Life doesn't necessarily need to have a depressing end.

Now for me, what do *I* want in these years of maturity (yeah, I know, I'm laughing too)? To feel happy, to be surrounded by people who get me, actually to ask for help to make my life easier. Do I want to end up in nursing care? Hell, no! But if it happens, I am prepared. I know what I want. I want to have a pet to share these days with me; I want my art, to still be painting, even if it is just with my fingers or toes; I want to listen to music, listen to books if my eyes are failing. I want to have that crazy multicolored short hairdo to show the outside world I'm still worthwhile. All of my life I have loved living in my head, the creative world within, and drawing on this, I know I can still fill my mind with beautiful thoughts and memories as I drift off to that next adventure, next life, wherever that may be...

## Dr. Michelle Garnett on growing up on the spectrum

### Early days to midlife

For so many women, the diagnosis of autism comes late. This means that there are a lot of "missing" years. Some women experience a lifetime of feeling that there is a lot missing—clarity, understanding, validation, support, sense of self, and friendship—so much so that they feel that they themselves were missing from their own lives.

Essentially, many late-diagnosed spectrum women feel that they missed out on life, and consequently there can be a great sense of grief for those "missing years," as well as relief once a diagnosis is made.

Life without the understanding of a diagnosis in the early years is evocatively and accurately described by Jen. A sense of being different starts early, usually during the onset of the social years in kindergarten. Unfortunately, as Jen describes, it is at this very early stage of life that rejection from peers can start also, confirming the sense for the young girl not only that is she different, but she is different in an unlikeable and defective way. When teachers join in with the mocking and rejection, the negative conclusions are confirmed. It is as if the whole world is against you; there is nowhere to turn, no one who will understand, and the ground is prepared for depression, anxiety, and other long-term mental health conditions.

Fortunately for Jen, like many other spectrum women, she was resourceful and smart. She learned early to use the strategies of keen observation of her peers, research (books with important social themes), and imitation (playing different roles and becoming a social chameleon). In true aspie style, she took on these themes to an expert level, and learned the social curriculum as if she was a native to it. Recent research (Ormond *et al.*, 2018) that we have conducted at the Minds & Hearts Clinic compared the profile of 98 girls aged 5–19 with a diagnosis of ASD with 138 boys similarly diagnosed. Results confirmed that girls do indeed utilize the coping mechanisms of observation and imitation to cope with having ASD significantly more than boys do. Ironically, this social prowess, gained via the intellect and with considerable effort, is a reason in itself for the late diagnosis of females on the spectrum.

There are a number of positive protective factors that Jen's story can teach us, these being mirrored in many stories of my own clients, as well as in current research. The first is the *positive power of the use of observation and imitation to cope with social demands*. I like the analogy of moving to a new country where one must assimilate the language and customs of the country in order to be able to find a job and make friends. The trick is not to lose who we are in the process. The primary goal of psychotherapy at Minds & Hearts is to learn to know, accept, and love one's own self, the true self, the person behind the mask.

This is linked to the second positive protective factor, found in the words of the psychologist who saw Jen at three years old, when his advice to Jen's mother was to love and accept Jen as she was. Research has found the world over that people on the autism spectrum do better when they are the recipients of love and support. It is no surprise really that humans do better with love and support! As a clinician working in this field for more than 20 years now, if I could give any advice to a parent of someone on the autism spectrum it would be this: *Love and accept your child now for who they are, as they are, including their autism. Your child is not someone who needs to be fixed, your child is a unique gift and your job is to find out who they are, how they are, and, most importantly of all, how to show them that you love and accept them.*

The third protective factor in Jen's story is that she found an intense interest (or it found her!) that led to a satisfying and meaningful career. Like many on the autism spectrum, Jen has a huge compassionate heart, and as a result has made of her pain a gift to the world so that others do not have to suffer as she did. This is the true meaning of success. I have found over and over in my clinical work that women on the spectrum do best when they tap into their intense interest and hidden talents—for example, intense empathy, as is the case for Jen—and make a career of it.

**Aging on the spectrum**
One of the huge challenges of life for people on the autism spectrum is transition, and probably one of the least researched areas in autism

44

is aging. So we have a massive challenge ahead of us because we can predict that the transition to old age for people on the spectrum will be difficult, but we have very little knowledge and expertise to guide us. Nevertheless, Barb's story paves the way, highlighting that a number of things really help. These include:

- Advance notice—it really helps to know and understand what will happen, physically, cognitively, and emotionally.
- Preparation, including gaining advice and making plans.
- Seeking social support—not the first thought when one is on the spectrum, but crucially important to assist us not only to survive but to thrive.
- Being proactive about minimizing adverse consequences by looking after our health, including taking up things like yoga or Pilates.

I would like to highlight that, genetically, autism is linked to more negative health consequences such as cardiovascular disease and dementia. While this is not great news, I highly recommend finding out, via a family history search, which areas of physical decline may be on the cards for you. To be forewarned is to be forearmed. There are excellent pathways of prevention for many of the known physical diseases associated with age. Taking positive action early is an excellent way of coping with the stressors of change.

# CHAPTER 3

# Identity

## A Beautiful Work in Progress

### *ARtemisia*

Little girls on the spectrum don't know they are on the spectrum. They just sense that they are different somehow. While certain things may come to us very easily, one thing surely will not. And that is feeling as if we are made of the same materials as the other children and adults around us, feeling native to our supposed species—that is, feeling normal. It seems to us that everyone else has been given some sort of script or at least some crucial plot elements, while we have been given blank notebooks, a few obsessions, and a bunch of seemingly arbitrary rules.

Rules are perhaps the first safety ropes we have to hang on to in this topsy-turvy world. "Don't cross at a green light, wash your hands before dinner, never tell a lie, etc." We can follow those things. Then, of course, we discover that people lie all the time and break so many rules we feel as if we have been hanging on to a rope attached to nothing. This is one of many betrayals that we will feel deeply, starting as young humans, that will make us suspicious and skeptical, while at the same time, perpetually susceptible.

We love the look, feel, and smell of those black-and-white composition books that were (and still are) popular in schools. We may love the challenge that they present: "What will you fill me with?" We look at our lives in that same way—what can I fill this with? Anything and everything, of course. There's just one problem... We don't feel as if we have enough personality to put pen to paper, much less fill so many pages. *We then set out to find our personality and fill our notebooks.* Before we write our story, we have to write ourselves. We start by taking in as many other people's stories as we can. Whether we gravitate towards fiction (often of the sci-fi or fantasy variety) or non-fiction (astronomy, history, etc.), we will want to hear, see, or read until our brains are stuffed and spilling over. Reading the dictionary and the encyclopedia used to be standard procedure. Now I'm sure Google and social media are filling the same role, except perhaps with more emphasis on "self-help." It may be random and arbitrary, but so is reading A–Z reference material just because you want to know *everything*.

Television and videos will be another source manual for "How to be a Neurotypical Human," so we voraciously watch series, films, and documentaries. We may gravitate to quirky yet heroic characters that remind us of ourselves, such as *Sherlock* or *The Girl with the Dragon Tattoo*. Some of us more visual thinkers might not be able to focus on stories and linear tales. Art supplies are an absolute necessity in this case so that video gaming isn't the only outlet we have. Creation as well as recreation is important to learn to express. Music is an important language for some of us. Animals will be another area in which we devote time and energy. They may be our solace, our rational creatures in an irrational world. Animals are almost never cruel; they seem to want what we want—love, security, attention, food, outings...pretty basic but necessary stuff. They won't look at us and say, "What did you mean by *that*?" They communicate without words and allow us to do the same.

Then, of course, we go to school, study other people, copy and assimilate everything we see. In this desperate attempt to become "normal" we will emulate others, both the boys and the girls at school, especially the popular ones with whom we may strike up friendships. But we are impostors in their midst; always we feel we may be exposed for the creatures that we are, no matter how many highlights we put in our hair. If we have a best friend who is not on the spectrum, this friend can become both caretaker and cruise director, and without them we can be totally lost in social situations. When Susie left me alone in a room full of boys, it felt as if I was being left alone in a den of snakes. These were not dangerous people, only normal teenagers.

We may take on the characteristics of our friend—their style, their way of speaking, maybe even their accent—but it's highly unlikely we will take on their interests. More likely they will take on ours or at least possess similar ones already. We think of ourselves as loyal, but they may find us clingy and stifling if we insist on having only them as our friend. Even then, nothing will separate us from our "best" friend faster than finding out they aren't really that into what we are into— another one of life's great betrayals. When we are older, we learn that this was perhaps a bit unfair of us, but young Aspergirls are so passionate and, of course, black and white in our thinking.

We might feel like computers perched upon a set of shoulders with an often hostile territory set out below, for our bodies betray us. Dreadful things. Full of piss and blood and pain, accidents and injuries, illness and infirmities, cravings and cramps. We have no basis for comparison. The stomach ailments that often accompany the autism spectrum will be our norm. The amount of pain we may feel simply walking through a mall will be our own secret private hell. Why share something if you assume others must feel it too, or you sense that they don't and it just makes you delve inward with silent self-examination. *What is wrong with me? Why am I so sensitive?* We may think others feel and experience all the same things we do, but that they are somehow tougher, stronger, and more solid. The funny stiff walk some of us possess, coupled with all the comorbid *-axias* and -*imias* and -*osias* that go along with autism spectrum—well, if we aren't falling upstairs, we are throwing ourselves down a bowling alley after forgetting to let go of the ball. We may try to put our head through a closed window to look outside, or miss our mouth completely and poke ourselves in the cheek with a fork. Or, simply, become suddenly wooden and trip over nothing when a handsome stranger looks our way. Oh, the list does go on. Learning to accept that I will always do hilarious things just at the moment I most want to look cool has made life so much better. Being an Aspergirl may be a slapstick comic's dream, but it can be a teenager's nightmare.

We feel emotions, of course, but we may become afraid of them, for so much of life seems set out to violate and offend them. They overwhelm us. We can't always identify them. We may shut them down or try to. The unfairness of life is a violation of all we hold sacred—mainly, logic. And kindness falls within the sphere of logic. How can we "be ourselves" when so much of allowing is feeling, and feeling hurts so badly?

Even after years of life and a successful career, I would be plagued by the same recurring nightmare. I would be alone in an almost empty shopping mall, in a store with a bald, naked mannequin, usually missing an arm. That, I figured out years later, was me. A mannequin—not human, exposed, alone, undressed, unwanted, mute. Feeling empty within, naked without. Even after taking in so much information, so many influences, I still did not feel fully fleshed out.

I have spoken with many women on the spectrum, especially since founding the International Aspergirl Society. We do have such personalities; we maybe just haven't activated them yet. Or maybe we don't want the standard allowance of personality; we want to be heroic, larger than life. And our dismay when we sit in a crowd and find we just want to crawl under a rock—well, it is disappointing to say the least. We become angry at ourselves. We might experience selective mutism. We might lash out, at others or at ourselves, with words or physical abuse, such as punching ourselves in the head or cutting.

After years of this, we will seek spiritual peace, whether through yoga, meditation, prayer, meds, whatever it takes. We search for and usually find ways to achieve and maintain some equilibrium.

We don't give up, resilient queens that we are. We try on different personalities, accents, religions, cultures, the way that neurotypical girls might try on clothes at a department store—which, traditionally, spectrum women hate. It makes sense, as we are doing this every day in a much more symbolic but significant and sometimes exhausting way. This trying-on can lead to many accusations of "faker," "pretender," "chameleon," especially since many of us do possess a talent for mimicry. This at times frantic, lifelong search can lead others to think we are fickle, flighty, changeable, but of course with that contradictory aspie rigidity throughout. No wonder others are confused. Sometimes we confound ourselves.

In this quest for knowledge, we may travel the world on a motorbike, in a camper van, on a plane, a boat, or just in our heads if finances, circumstances or love of home stand in the way. But regardless of whether we outwardly show it or not, we are seekers.

Yes, it does sound extreme. Welcome to life on the spectrum.

Yet throughout our course will remain roughly the same. Our childhood interests, no matter how many times they have vacillated or seemed extinguished, almost always come back. There are core elements of our personalities that will endure. It is always better to be true to one's intrinsic nature. As Tony Attwood has famously said, "It is better to be a first-rate aspie than a second-rate neurotypical." But we can and do expand our talents, including social ones. The mind can and does learn, grow, and adapt. We want to be social not just because of expectation, but also out of basic human caring, wanting to love and be loved by others. While "book learning" may come easy, the path to a Master's in socializing is long and arduous. Aspergirls do not like slow processes, but this one is extremely important to our survival—in the workplace, in the community we inhabit, and in the relationships we acquire.

What you may discover is a woman who, by a relatively young age, has spent so much time studying human nature—from anthropology to etymology, and a lot of other *ologies* to boot—that she has an incredible amount of knowledge, skills, and talents. Often it is hidden in such a quiet, modest, if not withdrawn person that people are shocked when they find out how much she knows and can do. Still, to this day, people say to me, "I had no idea you could do *that*..."—whether it's writing, singing, or performing. And I'm one of the boisterous ones.

The doorway to realizing one's true self is simply *self-expression*. Once that can happen—whether it takes the form of writing, singing, dancing, doing sports, teaching, lecturing, playing a musical instrument, inventing things, all of these and more—a much more satisfying and mature growth process ensues. A demure, silent creature might be a latent anything. We won't know until she begins to self-express. Once this happens, it is quite addictive. Through self-expression we learn confidence. We might take a few knocks if we make mistakes along the way, which we inevitably will. Then we scurry back into our protective bubbles. But once you have a taste of freedom, it is difficult to retreat permanently.

When we are "diagnosed" with Asperger's or any number of subsidiary traits or co-existing conditions, and then told we should "take a pill for this" or "see a therapist for that," of course confidence will flag at times. How can we be all right just as we are and yet an aberration? I personally don't see Asperger's as a disability. I see it as incredible strengths *balanced* with a few deficits. One cannot be brilliant at all things. I am clearly not talking classic autism, although that too can contain some surprising gifts. Our deficits will only wear us down if we let them ruin our credibility, or if we focus on them like a bad debt, or if we are placing too much importance on things that really don't matter, such as being the most popular person on the block.

We must stay flexible. We must learn to let go of the things that no longer serve us, whether it is habits or hairstyles, vices or career paths, our partners, our country, our names. Recently I changed my name, yet again, from Rudy to ARtemisia. Far from being some clever ploy to garner attention, it is merely a snake shedding its skin so that it may renew for the third or thirteenth time. When people call me by my old name, it feels as if they are talking about someone else. When I have to sign "Rudy" to an email or something, *it*, not ARtemisia, feels insincere. I first spoke about the youthfulness of Asperger's in the "Table of Female AS Traits" on my help4aspergers website in 2008. Besides an eternal childlike quality, perhaps it is this not clinging too tightly that allows us to change. We are always happy to try on a new personality, even if our core will always be roughly the same. I do believe many women on the spectrum are into acting, cosplay, Comic-Con, and burlesque for this very reason. The great Temple Grandin herself told me that Halloween was her favorite holiday. We love masks because of the hiding and the springing forth that they allow at the same time. We get to be someone else for a while.

Identity is fluid and the brain almost eternally capable of making new connections, new pathways of consciousness. I've sometimes heard women on the spectrum compare themselves to others: "I'm more autistic than her" and so on. I feel this is a bit prophecy-fulfilling. While finding out we were on the spectrum was the beginning of a joyous movement, it is not the whole symphony. Thinking about Asperger's and autism can and will take up a percentage of our thinking and our lives, but it shouldn't be the only way we identify ourselves. The more our preconceptions become shattered by our mistakes and experiences, the more different we are when we reassemble our thoughts. As long as we are not too damaged from posttraumatic stress disorder (PTSD) or pain and are willing and able to heal, making mistakes is the world's greatest teacher. A woman can change and grow almost up until the very end.

It's an epic quest, this finding of ourselves. And like all quests, we will have some dark moments as well as great rewards. Unlike the quests we see in films, there is no ending. Self-discovery and forging of identity continue until the moment that we die. We are each a beautiful work in progress...

## Dr. Michelle Garnett on identity

ARtemisia articulates well the progression many spectrum women experience as they merge into their true selves. From the early days of so very correctly following the rules, to intense intellectual curiosity and consequent research about how to get it right, through the trials of imitation, overthinking, strong emotions, and perfectionism, a woman emerges with the freedom to be brave enough to make errors and to self-express. Somewhere along this journey, a diagnosis can provide clarity, but it can also be presented or perceived as yet another deficit.

I find in my clinical work that the earlier I can present the diagnosis of Asperger syndrome to a young girl the better. The best time is as soon as the girl starts to notice that she is different, and this usually occurs around the beginning of primary or elementary school. The diagnosis can be presented by a parent or professional, and there are very clear guidelines about the best way to do this (see, for example, Attwood, 2008). In short, start with her strengths! Clearly describe and write these down, including her powerful commitment to honesty, her loyalty, her forthrightness, her ability to spot error, her compassionate heart, her intellectual curiosity, her logic, her talents, etc., etc. Next describe that we all have areas of challenge, and invite her to name some of hers. These may include difficulties in knowing what to say at times, taking longer to process social and emotional information, finding some sensory experiences extremely challenging, etc. She will be delighted to discover that the list of her strength and capacities is far longer than the list of her challenges. Once she understands these lists, let her know that there are others like her—about 1 in 100. Because this unique profile of abilities has been spotted, there is a name for it, and then use the name that you feel most comfortable with, e.g. autism, ASD, Asperger's, Aspergirl. Share positive literature with her, such as Danuta Bulhak-Paterson's wonderful book, *I Am an Aspie Girl*, for children and teenagers and the inspired *Aspergirls* by Rudy Simone for women.

I find that knowing about Asperger syndrome for a girl on the spectrum is a precious gift, providing a logical scientific explanation for differences that she is excruciatingly aware of, but in the absence of such an explanation she has received pejorative labels that are character assassinations, such as "difficult," "lazy," "naughty," "stupid," or "weird." Without a proper explanation, such labels start to form the basis of a negative self-identity.

And ARtemisia is so right; Asperger syndrome (AS) is only one part of who that girl is. Understanding and integrating all aspects of the girl's being with love and compassion is the pathway to freedom, self-fulfillment, and a meaningful life. For example, many girls walk around feeling as though they are computers perched upon a set of shoulders, with the body underneath being the enemy. For example, anorexia nervosa is overrepresented in girls on the spectrum. Emotional dysregulation, including experiencing crippling anxiety and overwhelming rage, is common for girls and women on the spectrum, and is in part a result of lack of awareness or integration of the sense of the body into the self. The girl or woman on the spectrum is her mind, her body, her heart, and her spirit; through all these mediums she expresses her unique self, her personality.

One of the underlying reasons that women on the spectrum struggle with a sense of identity, or expression of personality, is their problems with innate and unthinking perspective taking, or "theory of mind," that are part of the condition. It follows, and there is research to back this, that if one has difficulty understanding another's mind, that person will also have difficulty understanding their own mind. Self-reflection is difficult for a person on the autism spectrum. Often the person knows themselves, their thoughts, and their feelings only in action (including in being), by expressing themselves through writing, talking, drawing, painting, dancing, theater, playing music, doing yoga, meditating, playing sport, being in nature, etc.

This is one of the reasons that a person on the autism spectrum needs love and support. They need to feel all right just as they are, lovable just as they are, in order to be able to take risks and express their true selves. Love, including self-love, overpowers fear.

CHAPTER 4

# Diversity, Gender, Intersectionality, and Feminism

*Catriona Stewart*

## Diversity

When I first started to research autism in 2001, I was, as many people are, immediately "hooked" by this fascinating subject that includes so many areas of exploration: physiology, neurology, psychology, education, sociology, politics, philosophy. Part of the fascination of this "developmental disorder" is that its study demands we ask ourselves the question "What does it mean to be human?"

In preparation for this chapter, like a good researcher, I went to the Merriam-Webster dictionary to look up "developmental." What I found was a range of meanings more complex and interesting than I had expected, including "to cause to grow and differentiate along lines *natural to its kind*" (my emphasis).

What is natural to the human kind? We have evolved over hundreds of thousands of years; we are arguably in some senses an extremely successful species. What Judith Singer articulated in 1998 with the term "neurodiversity," expanded on later by Steve Silberman, was an idea of humanity not as a narrowly defined homogeneous being but as an ever-evolving, heterogeneous species whose evolutionary survival has been dependent on a widely diverse range of developmental phenotypes. That diversity includes what we call the autism spectrum (Silberman, 2015; Singer, 2016).

Unfortunately, humans (as a whole—and, yes, I know I'm generalizing here) are not good at dealing with what they cannot categorize and contain in conceptual boxes, and they have difficulties accepting what is not "like them." Autistic people are hard to categorize, challenging social preconceptions in so many ways, hard to "pin down," tricky to define. What we do know is that autism is found in consistent numbers throughout the human race and that it is a genetically mediated phenomenon, which means autistic people almost certainly have been around a very, very long time.

We suspect that the autistic genome—possibly in terms of a broader autism phenotype—may be responsible for, or at least contribute to, excellence in our capacities in engineering, science, math, music, IT, maybe more. So that begs the question: why is it defined as "a disorder?"

Another Merriam-Webster definition of development is "leading through a succession of changes each of which is preparatory for the next." That's a pretty good definition of life. And we all, autistic or not, will experience that "succession of changes," although some will be easier to cope with than others.

In the first few months after launching the Scottish Women's Autism Network (SWAN), there was one woman who would make asides to the conversation that was taking place, such as "I don't suppose that's something you've experienced," or "You won't ever have found yourself doing that," or "That probably sounds (feeble/daft/whatever) to you," and so on. Eventually, I asked her to meet me for a coffee and I told her about some of my background, early experiences, challenges, griefs, the mistakes I'd made, situations encountered.

One major difference between her and me, I explained, was

that I had 20 years' further life experience. What she saw when we met and founded SWAN together was an older adult autistic woman who had added to her repertoire of social skills, had gained in confidence, had all those years more of life experience and, I'd like to hope, wisdom. I am still continuing to grow *through a succession of changes, each of which is preparatory for the rest*, but I have a few extra years of autistic human development under my belt. We all need time, and the right conditions, to grow and develop.

I object to the term "disorder" for many reasons, but in this context because it is a way of saying someone is not capable of achieving their full human potential, of actively evolving and, most importantly of all, of *growing along the lines natural to their kind*. The greatest barriers of all to autistic people developing their full potential are surely the narrow, limited ideas of what it is to be human and therefore what is "natural to our kind."

## Gender

I'm not going to write in detail of my childhood but I will just mention some of the signposts: bullying in early primary; finding boys better company on the whole than other girls; spending hours at a neighbor's house absorbed in the piles of comics received from American cousins (the neighbors and I stopped pretending I was going around to play with their daughter, and when I showed up they would just point to the pile and say that, yes, there had been a delivery of new Marvels); the "show and tell" I gave at primary school on early land formation in Scotland and the rise and fall of the dinosaurs and fossils; how I only finally understood why my classmates seemed nonplussed more than 40 years later when an old school friend mentioned it in the context of "never forgotten, it was so *weird*."

I was a "tomboy," I was slight and skinny, went everywhere on my bike, ran along the tops of garden walls, climbed trees. Sometimes mistaken for a boy, my mother would exhort, "Don't stride like a boy!" I was also never without a book. *The Jungle Book* was an early favorite, then Arthur Conan Doyle, Arthur Ransome but, yes, Noel Streatfield and other more 'female' books too— anything and everything. I helped the boy next door with his Airfix kits, I begged for a chemistry set; my friend and I played at being *The Man from UNCLE* and witches. Favorite TV programs were *Doctor Who*, *Star Trek*, *The Champions*.

These days, apparently, being a tomboy is no longer a culturally accepted variance on girlhood, exemplified by literary figures such as Scout (*To Kill a Mockingbird*), Jo (*Little Women*), Anne Shirley (*Anne of Green Gables*). Apparently, autistic girls are more likely, along with hirsutism and polycystic ovary syndrome (PCOS), to "suffer from tomboyism." It bothers me, greatly, having raised two girls to their own young adulthood, that young people seem to be under more pressure to conform to fantastical stereotypes of "femaleness" and "maleness" than even my generation, and that being a "tomboy" is now described as a pathology.

There was the gradual disengagement from everything, including learning, which I had loved. Often criticized and humiliated by teaching staff, I was profoundly bored. Best at English, math, and biology, highly able and mostly interested in the natural sciences, I was at an old-fashioned school with old-fashioned parents where girls "didn't do science." School was preparing us to be well-educated young ladies, fit to run a home for a good professional match. I would have hoped by now that sexism and gender stereotyping had improved, but a recent focus group with autistic schoolgirls revealed they are only too aware of gender stereotyping at work and in their lives. And as so many girls express interests or characteristics that mark them out from their non-autistic female peers, that stereotyping takes on specific meaning.

As a teenager, I became depressed, frightened, and lost. Like many adolescents, without power or real agency, I expressed that fear and sadness, and rebelling against a world in which I could see no role for myself or future took the form of self-destructiveness.

I have never wanted to be a boy or a man. I knew I didn't want to grow up to be the kind of woman with which I was being presented, unless by some chance I was going to be Alexandra Bastedo in *The Champions*, all elegant Chanel suits, skilled in karate and telepathic communication, or a female Spock, intellectually rigorous, self-contained but essentially "human." But despite all the years I pleaded with Scotty to "please, please, come back and beam me up," I never did grow pointy ears or transport to Vulcan.

Ideas of gender identity were not discussed in my world until I was a young adult and had left home. Even then, while I was involved in sexual politics, thus having the opportunity and support to consider my sexual and gender identities, I never really doubted my cis identity as a heterosexual female. But I did, at various times in my early adulthood, truly wonder if I had been born into the wrong physiologically sexed body. I have wondered, if I'd had access to the kinds of conversations taking place now around gender identity, whether I might have made some different life choices.

Now, there is a range of choices we can make about sexual or gender identity, including the choice to reject any. Diversity is reflected in our freedom to identify how we choose in terms of, yes, neurodevelopment, but also sexuality and gender. A talk was presented at Cambridge University, UK, in 2017, by the Cambridge University Disabled Students' Campaign, entitled "Autistic People, Not Gendered Minds" (in reference to Professor Baron-Cohen's "extreme male brain" theory of autism). To quote one of the speakers: "Gender variation is natural, neurotype is natural...start by seeing us as people, not as weirdly gendered minds and we'll go from there" (Camneurodiversity, 2017).

Back in the 1970s, I couldn't picture myself in the female role as it was presented all around me, which left me without anything on which to model my own identity or picture a future. This is one of the reasons I feel so passionately about the importance of peer support and providing positive role models.

## Feminism

Between school and post-art school, young adulthood, I made some truly wonderful discoveries.

First was philosophy. At 16 I made friends with some disaffected bright young people. I read just as voraciously as before, but now I was discovering Jean-Paul Sartre, Michel Foucault, Albert Camus, Hermann Hesse, Simone de Beauvoir. I discovered there were people "out there" asking the same questions as I was and presenting, if not answers, at least intelligent, creative, transformative ideas around those questions. Thomas Szasz, along with Foucault, introduced me to the idea that concepts of "normality" and "madness" are not fixed, but contextual and contingent, historically and culturally situated. As, of course, are concepts of gender and autism (Grinker, 2008).

The second was politics and specifically second wave feminism. A woman from one of my college classes asked if I'd be interested in starting a women's group. I had no idea what she meant, but it sounded interesting and so Glasgow School of Art (GSA) Women's Group was born. We held meetings, went to conferences, met women from all over the country who were smart and rebellious and questioning what it meant to be female. We read Germaine Greer, Kate Millett, Andrea Dworkin. We got angry; we mourned and raged.

The eagle-eyed among you may have noticed that the first of my book lists above included only one woman's name. Virago Press launched in 1972 and the Women's Press in 1978. Many women writers who otherwise would have been hidden from view were made accessible. I kept reading: Jane Lazarre, Judy Chicago, Adrienne Rich, Marge Piercy, Alice Walker, Maya Angelou, Angela Carter, Susan Sontag...I could go on.

Feminism was a place where I felt I belonged, where people were having conversations in which I could take part, engaging, stretching, challenging. There were female role models—strong, intelligent, beautiful, grown-up women doing interesting things as writers, presenters, artists, musicians, political activists and commentators, journalists, philosophers. It was both personal and non-personal. As the saying goes, "the personal is political" and engagement in feminism for me led to politics in the wider sociological context. After graduation I was the full-time waged president of GSA's students' union for two years.

My absorption in politics was, well, it was my "intense interest." I worked hard. I was an "arty, Trotskyite, feminist weirdo" (apparently), elected to the NUS Scotland Executive Committee, visiting Greenham Common and helping to organize a unique Sexual Politics conference in 1983 in Edinburgh. I had to pull away to some extent, tired of being angry all the time, and overloaded. But those times—the years of philosophical disaffection and those of engaged feminism—have informed everything I've done since and provided the underpinning for why I chose, years later, to study the lived experiences of Asperger girls for my PhD (Stewart, 2011, 2012).

More recently, I studied with an applied research program in Gender Studies at Stirling University, which was interesting and useful. It offered a different context for my work and a different language, one that contained terms such as "social models of disability" and "intersectionality."

## Intersectionality

I am vocal, articulate, intelligent. I am white, middle class, have a middle-class education (although that's a complex subject—see above!). I have privilege. But some of my personal childhood circumstances, combined with the sexism of my place and time, the communication difficulties involved in autism, and the fact that autism was not recognized in articulate, apparently able girls meant that I spent years of my adulthood desperately seeking a meaning for my life, a sense of self. I operated in environments and contexts that did not play to my strengths or make the most of my natural abilities.

Autism as a diagnostic category is historically recent. In the early 1960s, Lorna Wing conceptualized autism as a spectrum, brought the work of Hans Asperger to world attention and created the diagnosis of Asperger syndrome for individuals not otherwise learning-disabled or speech-delayed. Even although autistic women (who once were girls) have been "out there" in full public view over the years, autism has long been thought of as a "male condition." Autistic females have been invisible in terms of recognition, research, strategic planning, and service provision.

Their specific needs have not been recognized or addressed, and along with autism stereotyping, gender stereotyping has meant that the ways in which they are marginalized or undermined as individuals are complex and multilayered in specific ways. They have been a marginalized group within an already marginalized population. For the non-speaking and/or learning-disabled autistic female, that marginalization becomes even more complex.

A further underserved population is the black and minority ethnic (BME) community. When I go to conferences or other autism events, I look around and see very few non-white faces. Is this an issue of culture? Or of the self-fulfilling cycle of invisibility—if you don't see yourself represented, then you don't identify with what is represented? Second-wave feminism was characterized on some levels by a split between those who perceived gender inequality to be about sex and gender alone (radical feminism) and those who believed it to be about class. There were also complaints that it was mainly driven by white, articulate, middle-class women who wanted to gain the same privileges as their white, male middle-class counterparts and that the concerns and experiences of BME or working-class women were not being given equal voice.

This is intersectionality, where conditions of inequality and marginalization meet and cross over like the intersections of trunk roads or Venn diagrams. What this meant for me in my lived experience relates to being someone not comfortable in my own skin as a female (or possibly just as a human being), underachievement, poor self-esteem, chronic anxiety and fear, poor choices, and so on. Looking back, I can see I survived primarily by my wits, but I was exhausted often to the point of being at my wits' end.

I am fortunate and lucky, with resources, including my brain, verbal ability, determination (a characteristic inherited from my own mother). I have survived. I've had some great times, fascinating experiences and raised two wonderful young women (the "double whammy" and the joys of being an autistic mother are covered in another chapter of this book, so I won't expand on that here). I have learned a lot and had opportunities to grow and develop. I have reached a place now where I am using my full capabilities and where I am able to pursue my passionate agenda for creating social change.

One of the things on my agenda is gaining not just equality for girls and women but equity and, most especially, equity for autistic girls and women. Not all autistic people define themselves as disabled, but for many the social model of disability, which proposes disability as a social construct and contextual, provides some direction as to how to portray the inequities they confront in their lives. What I mean by creating equity is the smoothing out of a terrain that can be full of additional pitfalls for autistic girls, making adjustments, creating the conditions for genuine inclusivity and equality of opportunity, self-esteem, and self-confidence. These require a whole range of things, including access to education, peer-identification, and role models, none of which can happen without visibility.

## In conclusion

Years of "masking" and "winging it" have made not talking about my personal past experiences habitual. Yet when working for my PhD, reading book after book by autistic women—Clare Sainsbury, Liane Holliday Willey, and the late Genevieve Edmonds—I found myself being confronted with stories of my own childhood, my adolescence, my past. Old griefs surfaced and new ones were born as I realized that much of my potential had been wasted for so long, but also that I was not alone, that who I am resonates with others and has value. So I wanted to share some of my own life here, to explain ways in which strong female role models, writers, activists, leaders helped to save my life; why for me autism is a feminist, sociological issue; and why books like this are crucial. Presented with reflections of ourselves, we are able to regain a sense of identity and self-esteem, our relational selves, as we realize we are part of a wider community of "selves." We can retrieve and build on our natural abilities to flourish and develop as human beings, "to work out the possibilities," to grow along lines natural to our kind.

## Dr. Michelle Garnett on diversity, gender, intersectionality, and feminism

In considering diversity, gender, intersectionality, and feminism in the context of autism, each is deeply rooted in historical context. Catriona beautifully describes the historical context of understanding gender, intersectionality, and feminism. I would like to describe the historical context of autism because I think it bears strongly on all of the issues that Catriona raises.

The definition of autism has broadened enormously in the last 40 years since Lorna Wing's seminal paper in 1981 describing Asperger syndrome in English for the first time. When I started working in this area in 1993, these broader definitions of autism were not in the international diagnostic texts for understanding difference, emerging first in the *Diagnostic and Statistical Manual* Fourth Edition (DSM-IV; American Psychiatric Association, 1994).

For the first 20 years after Lorna Wing's paper, research in autism was predominantly focused on the question: Are Asperger's and autism the same? Throughout this time, due to our limited understanding of the various presentations of autism, boys were thought to outnumber girls on the spectrum by four to one. Unfortunately, this meant that most of the current research on how to understand, define, assess, and assist, as well as research on long-term outcomes and positive prognostic factors, has been conducted with male participants.

Clearly, our understanding of autism is still emerging. The leading researchers and thinkers in the area (e.g. Coleman and Gillberg, 2012) are now considering that people who share the diagnosis of autism are such a heterogeneous group of people that there may be a number of different subtypes (constellations) of autism yet to be described and understood, which we may call "the autisms." Certainly, discussion of an autism spectrum, while helpful to understand some of the heterogeneity in autism, is limited in that it implies that autism differs only in severity from a mild to a severe expression.

If a woman on the spectrum has social communication deficits that she can effectively mask at interview, but which affect her so severely that she has no close friends and is underemployed, or if she has no intense interests or repetitive behaviors, but has sensory issues, a single-track mind, and a strong preference for routine, in most clinics across the world she would not receive a diagnosis of autism. She would likely be described as having mental health or personality issues. Her autism would be viewed to be "so mild" that it does not meet diagnostic criteria.

I meet many such women in my clinic who know that their difficulties and differences have not been encapsulated by their previous diagnoses of depression, social anxiety, generalized anxiety disorder, obsessive-compulsive disorder, borderline personality disorder, schizophrenia, schizotypal disorder...and the list could go on. These diagnoses do not describe who she is. They describe the tragic consequences of living in a world that too often misunderstands, underserves, and vilifies minority groups.

There have been too many debates about what constitutes "normal" in our society. Over the last 150 years, medical doctors have had the most influence in definitions of what is abnormal and hence what constitutes a "disorder" that has recognizable features and signs that can be described in a diagnostic text. Autism, as it was first described by the pediatrician Dr. Leo Kanner was understood to be a pervasive developmental disorder (PDD) because all areas of the child's development were functionally impaired. The presentation of such a child's autism was complicated by additional difficulties such as language impairment, learning impairment, and often motor disorders.

It still seems strange to me that I can run a clinic for autism spectrum disorders where I may, in the morning, see a child of nine years of age who cannot speak and twirls beautifully throughout the interview, and in the afternoon see a pediatrician who is on the verge of nervous collapse due to social, emotional, and sensory exhaustion. Both have autism; which is more severe?

Is autism a disorder? It seems that in our society, in order to receive funding and a unique understanding about how one thinks, senses, perceives, and learns, one must be diagnosed with a disorder. As one little boy with Asperger syndrome once said to me, "But why is it called a disorder? There is nothing 'disordered' about me." I entirely agree with him.

Presently, there are considerations that the current diagnostic manuals are outdated because most of their understandings predate what specialists now know about neurology. In our new understandings of neurodiversity, perhaps what we need are "explanatory texts" about the wild and wonderful ways our brains grow and differentiate along lines natural to our kind, and ways to support, accept, and nourish that growth in ways that honor, respect, and encourage the growth of all beings.

CHAPTER 5

# Personal Relationships

*Jen Elcheson and Anita Lesko*

## Finding what works for you—*Jen Elcheson*

### Friends

I think it is safe to assume most human beings of all neurotypes need some kind of connection in life whether through friendships or relationships. Despite having a difficult time making and keeping friends, most of us on the spectrum want to have friends, and having challenges should not negate this need. I struggled with this greatly until, finally, the right people came into my life. I often found myself friends with the wrong people and wondered why I did not connect with them.

Now I know it was due to being naïve, becoming friends too fast, having different expectations, and having nothing in common. Lots of us will settle for any friend, which is not always the greatest idea. Different friendships came and went, with some completely fizzling out and others becoming more of an acquaintance-based relationship. There were also lengthy times where I had no friends at all prior to meeting the right ones, which was not until I was well into my 20s. Fortunately, I had one very close friend throughout high school, but they moved away to attend university and we lost contact.

One handy tool I found for meeting different people was the internet. The internet is an excellent tool for making friends when you are autistic or otherwise neurodivergent. Practicing my interpersonal skills with a variety of people via the internet helped improve how I connected with others and friendships were formed. Some friends turned out to be autistic too, which may explain why we are still friends. Many autistic people I know agree that we usually get on better with other autistics. Mind you, we can be friends with people of all neurological variances including neurotypicals, because what matters is the quality of friendship. What is crucial is realizing that it's all about finding someone you can get along with, who accepts your difference and appreciates you for who you are. Most of my autistic friends are online, although I have met some in real life as well who are wonderful people that I am honored to know.

Friendships rarely come easily to us, but we still deserve to have friends. The internet and its countless online communities have aided autistic people in connecting more than ever, especially with friends who "get" them. For example, autistic activists/advocates often collaborate to make society more inclusive and have become good friends in the process. For me, it was joining online peer-support groups and meeting others with common interests such as music or animals. Friendships tend to fail when there is no common ground.

First, it is important to be safe and get to know someone over time, whether the friendship is online or in person. Some friendships will form faster than others, but it is important to give things time. In the beginning I learned that it was best to keep things as light as possible (which I know is hard for us) and refrain from oversharing personal information or dominating the conversation. Ask the person questions about themselves and establish what you have in common, giving you something to talk about. It is also important never to give up, even if things don't work out.

As I previously said, it may be challenging for us to make friends, but we have to be proactive at times and to persevere in finding a friend with whom we will connect. This is why starting with online friendships or meeting others through people you know is effective. Online, I have found that you can really get to know someone quite well over time through continued correspondence. Not to mention, when you are typing to someone, there is no need for eye contact or worrying when it is your turn to speak. There are also a lot of resources out there on how to relate to others; even though some are not designed for us, we can take some of the material learned and adapt this to our lives.

**Stranger, acquaintance, friend, close friend**
I wish I had known sooner the different levels of friendships with other people as it would have saved me a lot of disappointments when things didn't work out. I actually did not learn this until I attended college.

What I learned was that when we first meet someone, they are a stranger, which is someone we don't know yet. Upon getting to know them a little, they become an acquaintance. We may see them occasionally or often, but we know them on a very surface level. Think co-workers, classmates, or people you are involved with in some kind of mutual activity.

However, once we get to know them a bit more, and perhaps start going for coffee or doing other activities outside of the usual meeting place, they may then become a friend. The depth of the friendship determines whether they end up becoming a close friend or not. Close friends are individuals who know us best and whom we have gotten to know on a deep level over a lengthy period of time. With my close friends, I engage with some often and others not as much, but they still know me quite well. What is important here is learning to discern between these different levels so we can protect ourselves.

71

### Relationships, romantic and otherwise

Relationships mean different things to different people. Those of us on the autism spectrum have relationships as varied as the neuro-majority do and it is completely passé and out of line to say that we are not capable of having them. Relationships for autistic people can be traditional right through to completely unconventional.

I have all kinds of autistic friends/acquaintances of diverse sexualities who are married/in committed relationships, choose to remain on their own, or have a close friend or companion (or more) with whom they may or may not be intimate but whose company they enjoy. I have also come across autistic people who are polyamorous and have more than one partner and those who like casual arrangements. Autistics can also be kink enthusiasts and swingers. So I have to laugh at the assumption that we're *all* asexual and/or without partners. Although there are autistics who are, this notion could not be further from the actual truth. We are all individuals, after all. We may *experience* relationships differently, but we *have* the same kinds of relationships as non-autistics, contrary to the arbitrary assumptions people hold about us.

As with friendships, some autistic people prefer having an autistic partner and others may have no preference. It can also be a challenge when one partner is more social than the other, so it is important to find someone who understands your needs. I generally get along with others who are autistic or neurodivergent in other ways, either as friends or otherwise. It also helps when they are introverted, as there is less pressure to always be social.

I have to confess, I've never really had a conventional romantic relationship. All of my relationships have been long-distance, because I am very particular about who I associate with and I don't reside in a locale where it is easy to meet people. I am also very introverted and prefer my own space. None of these past relationships worked out, so I have come to terms with being single as it seems to work best for me. I find relationships make me anxious and generally do not bring out the best in my character. Perhaps that may change, but I remain uncertain.

I do enjoy the company of a close friend I used to date, until we realized we made better friends than partners. Not everyone has the personality to be around someone else all the time, and that is totally OK. It's all about finding what works best for you. Please don't let outside opinions deter you from having the kind of relationship (or lack thereof) that suits you best. This also applies to those of us who prefer being single. As a single person, I find that society still puts too much pressure on people without partners to have partners, as if it's some kind of Holy Grail. I find this abhorrent! What if we prefer our own company and having the time to do more of what we enjoy?

Of course, there are some of you who would like to be in relationships. I would recommend seeking out different resources. There are even some by autistic people for autistic people, whether it is a blog, book, video, community, or website. For example, my friend ARtemisia, aka Rudy Simone, has written extensively on the subject and even gives webinars. There are also resources aimed at non-autistics that may help us. Experiment.

In closing, friendships and relationships aren't easy for us, but they are possible. It may take more work and more conscious thinking on our part, but these relationships are worth it, and we are worthy of them as well. Good luck!

## Marriage—*Anita Lesko*

I went the first 50 years of my life not knowing I'm on the autism spectrum. I always felt as if I was on the outside of life looking in, unable to get through the "glass" to join in with others. I had not the slightest clue about how to make friends. When I would be standing in line at the grocery store, I'd look at the magazine rack and a lump would soon form in my throat and my eyes would get misty. There would be multiple magazines for soon-to-be brides and wedding planning. I realized there was "something" about me that made friendships impossible, and seeing that display not only made me sad but tormented me. I tried so hard to figure out what was wrong with me.

One evening at work I discovered what "it" was. A co-worker's son had just been diagnosed with Asperger's. She was crying and handed me some literature about it. As I read, all the pieces of the puzzle of my life suddenly fell into place. It was my "aha" moment. I have Asperger's! That night I stopped at the book store and purchased every book they had on it. Of course, I stayed up all night reading. By dawn there was no doubt I had Asperger's. Three weeks later I went for a formal diagnosis from a neuropsychologist.

That discovery changed the course of my life for ever. I have just celebrated the anniversary of the second year of my marriage. Me, the one who felt so lonely inside when I saw those bride magazines, who couldn't even make one friend. I met Abraham when he attended one of my support group meetings. Right after getting my diagnosis, I started an autism support group that I conducted for several years.

Initially, he became an acquaintance, later a friend, then a close friend, then a soulmate. This all occurred over two years. Due to rather unusual outside circumstances, our courtship didn't evolve as a "typical" romance. The full story is too long for this chapter, but it was a very unconventional process. What we both knew was that we couldn't stand being apart from each other, and when in an embrace, we couldn't tell where one body ended and the other began.

Marriage is a job. It entails many responsibilities. It involves two people who must share in this union. I think marriage is taken too lightly by many people in today's society. I've read and heard people state, "So, if it doesn't work out, we'll just get divorced!" That's a sad way to view it. But here's a big difference: neurotypicals in general have many friendships and relationships. To them, it's easy to find the next one.

For me, as someone on the spectrum who *doesn't* have endless friends or opportunities for that, I treasure my relationship with Abraham as the most precious bond on earth. And he feels the same way. That's why our marriage is so strong. We respect each other. We cherish each other. We take care of each other. We *listen* to each other. Communication is the number-one *most* important aspect to keep us, or any couple, together. You must set aside time each day to sit together with a coffee or cup of tea, relax, and simply talk. Share how your day at work went. Any stressors, if you feel anxious about something, or talk about plans for the future. Simply talk.

For individuals on the autism spectrum to entertain the idea of getting married, you must be realistic and be sure each person has quite a good level of independent functioning. Both should have a job. It's about having dignity and respect for each other; allowing your partner to be themselves, and being able to *accept them as they are*; being able to support each other emotionally and spiritually. We view our marriage as an avenue for encouraging each other to become the best that we can be.

We do things for each other which are expressions of our love. It's all the little things that we do each day that make life together grand. We believe our marriage is better and stronger than other couples', specifically neurotypicals (NTs)! We don't play "mind games," the term NTs use. When there's anything needing discussion, that's just what we do. Discuss it. We wouldn't even know *how* to play those mind games.

Abraham and I both have professional careers and work full-time. That in itself is major stress on us. Not only getting up at 3 a.m. each morning, but planning ahead to make lunches, orchestrating breakfast, coffee, ensuring clothes are clean and ready to go. We try to plan out our weekends to catch up on grocery shopping, cooking food for the coming week and freezing it in ready-to-go containers, cleaning the house, doing laundry, shopping for animal food, etc. All of this takes great communication and planning. We work together as a team. We maintain our individuality yet are bonded together as one.

For me, I know I could never be married to a neurotypical guy. They wouldn't understand me, my need for quiet, and my autistic ways. Both Abraham and I have mitochondrial dysfunction. We both understand the sometimes-sudden extreme exhaustion that surfaces. It's not unusual that by Thursday, we're getting totally wiped out, get home, quickly feed all the animals, drink a lot of water, then go to sleep—and it's only 4.30 p.m.!

There needs to be shared interests so you can do a lot of things together. We love being outside when it's cool out, enjoying bird watching, being with our horses and guinea hens. We'll watch a sunrise with a cup of steaming coffee, sitting side by side on a bale of hay, arms around each other. We always savor the simple things in life that become beautiful moments. It is a basic human need to have a sense of peace, comfort, and security. With the right person, marriage can bring you all of those feelings.

## Dr. Michelle Garnett on personal relationships

It is very true that we all need connections in life with the other humans that inhabit the planet with us. In my work with people on the spectrum, I have found that the crux of the suffering for many is the mismatch between the yearning for connection, intimacy, and friendship, while having a neurology that does not provide an innate understanding of how to achieve this.

Personal relationships are just that: intensely personal. Somehow we have to find a way to achieve connections in a way that suits us personally. After reading Jen's and Anita's accounts of friendship and marriage, you may have completely resonated with Jen about finding friends on the internet, or discovering that the single life suits you. On the other hand, you may echo Anita's descriptions about yearning for a soulmate, or the happiness of finding someone also on the spectrum and discovering a way to be with each other that fulfills that yearning at a very deep level. These are deeply meaningful stories about connection, and I know they will resonate with many. If you do not relate to these descriptions of personal relationships, do not despair: there are as many ways of finding a personal connection as there are people on the planet and the myriad of ways the dynamics work between each of these people.

## Friendship

Jen offers true wisdom from her lived experience when she describes that friendship takes time, that there is a definite shift from each level of relatedness, from stranger to close friend, and that there are important guidelines to follow during each stage of the relationship. Understanding the levels of friendship and the guidelines for each will assist in being able to develop true connection and intimacy. Friendship does not come easily for people on the spectrum. Many are surprised at the work involved in friendship. Reciprocity is important. Keeping the other person in mind, remembering information about them, keeping in contact, whether by internet or face to face, showing interest even when tired or truly disinterested in the topic—all of these are important acts of kindness that keep a friendship going.

Friendship is effortful, and even more so when a person is on the spectrum. Why make the effort? There are at least two good reasons. The first is that you truly enjoy the other person's company, which is often about enjoying the same interests or having the same values or life philosophy. Another reason is for emotional support, so that you do not feel so alone. As one autistic person said, "I would choose to always be alone, but I cannot stand the loneliness." Emotional support does not mean that you need to talk about your emotions or even your life situation and problems all the time, but being able to listen when someone talks about their problems, and being able to open up about what life is really like for you is an important aspect to a sense of safety and connection in a friendship. Like Jen, I encourage you to continue to make the effort toward friendship and within friendship, and not to give up. You do not need 50 friends; most of us only need one or two. It is worth the search. I have recommended some resources at the back of the book which may be useful.

## Marriage

I loved reading about Anita's marriage. To yearn for that level of connection for so long and then to find it is truly happiness-making, a wonder, and wonderful. Even so, her story does not have a fairytale ending. Instead, as Anita says, the relationship is a *job*, it entails work and responsibilities. Like-mindedness seems to help. It is interesting that Anita found her soulmate after her 50th birthday. I am guessing that she knew herself and what she needed in life pretty well by the time she met Abraham. Their like-mindedness in the way that they wish to live, work, communicate, socialize, and replenish each other and themselves is a key part of their sense of fulfillment and harmony with each other.

When the relationship is between aspie and neurotypical, there are many areas of potential disharmony, analogous to a clash of two different cultures. In my work I have found, as Anita describes (assuming a good level of independent functioning in each partner), that it is so important to accept the person as they are with dignity and respect. When each partner makes a true effort to be the best partner that they can be in the relationship, there is a meeting ground for intimacy and deep connection.

## CHAPTER 6

# Socializing, Anxiety, and Addictions

*Barb Cook*

Self-medicating was one of the more undesirable coping mechanisms I implemented into my life from a fairly young age. Being offered that first glass of wine by my father at the age of 15 was his idea of getting me used to drinking alcohol in a sensible manner. Boy, was he wrong.

That first head-spinning moment of emptying the wine glass, feeling the warm flush on my cheeks, reminded me of a similar time when I had started smoking at age 12. That first ciggie I drew upon had me nearly choking to death behind the roller-skating rink I was dropped off at most weekends. Once I got the knack of inhaling like a 1940s silver-screen actress, I could feel the sense of calm as the nicotine took hold of my brain, even if it was short-lived.

Apart from the sense of trying to look cool, I felt more in control of my life, and a sense of calm fell on my ever-firing brain cells. Things didn't seem so disordered in these short nicotine-induced peaceful moments of time. But that is all they were: snippets of what I saw could be a temporary break from the ever-anxious mind I possessed.

Being 12 years old, I couldn't really tell my parents that I had decided smoking needed to be an essential part of my life, so I had to resign myself to the odd few cigarettes at the weekend. Little did I know at the time I was setting myself to up to be hooked on a potentially dangerous habit with possible serious health implications for the future.

The same went for the drinking. That one so-called harmless glass of wine set me on a path of wanting more, wanting the feeling of having control over my anxiety and the feeling of confidence I hadn't experienced, especially in the presence of other people.

The last year of high school saw a significant increase in my smoking. I hated life at this point as I was being bullied by fellow students and discarded by the teachers, who looked at me as a failure even though I was incredibly intelligent. I couldn't function in such awful surroundings in that archaic school to which I was sentenced. So, my coping strategy consisted of hiding alone in a local park among the trees and pigeons, puffing the day away. At least nature accepted me.

Home life was no better. My parents had divorced and my dad was now living with another woman who virtually despised my existence, viewing me as the trouble-maker, and I often felt her ugly glares, her never accepting who I was. I was a stranger in this house that only accommodated my dad, his girlfriend, and her young daughter; there was no place for an undiagnosed, angry, and depressed autistic teenage girl.

One of the advantages (in reality, disadvantages) of not feeling welcome at home was that my father would quite obligingly drop me off anywhere I wanted to go, usually to the local pub that had a live DJ on a Friday and Saturday night. Interestingly, even though I am super sensitive to loud sounds and unexpected noises, loud music always seems to soothe me. The louder the better, and at this pub the music was so loud you would feel your chest thump rhythmically with the bellowing beat.

At 16, I would be dropped off at this pub where I would meet with two male friends who were a couple of years older than me. I had always found an easier connection when hanging out with guys, which I didn't consciously realize until around three years later. At this point I still wanted to fit in with the girl crowd, as that was the expected social norm. Society's preconceptions meant that if you hung out with boys, you were labeled cheap, an easy pick-up, or a flirt, especially in the eyes of the other girls; I certainly didn't want to draw any more unwanted attention to myself. When I hung out with these guys, all I was interested in was when we were going fishing next or talking about what motorbikes we would like to have once we had our open license.

But with each pub visit, the alcohol, that deliciously sumptuous temptress of the senses, increasingly became my friend. My tolerance for alcohol was quite surprising. I am not sure if it is due to how frantically my brain works and that it needs a bucket instead of a glass to harness the thoughts, but either way, I was progressively becoming addicted.

When the opportunities arose for going out with a group of people, the pub was usually my first suggestion in meeting up. There I could quickly consume two drinks to help kick-start the calming of the mind. A sip here and a puff of cigarette there was a perfect recipe for me to cope socially. Mind you, prior to arriving at the venue, I would have smoked half a packet of cigarettes just to calm my nerves.

By the time I hit the legal age for drinking at 18, I had already become addicted. The thought of not drinking never crossed my mind, nor did the thought of just how much alcohol was affecting my life, my decisions, and my behavior. To me, in a way drinking was actually helping with my social skills. I became less self-conscious when I had a few drinks under my belt. I could start to understand the dynamics of what people were saying, and was never sure if it was my brain slowing down enough to be able to allow more information in or the other people around me slowing down due to their excessive alcohol consumption.

Since I was so young and naïve, I never realized just how often I put myself in dangerous situations. Back then I was a tall, blonde, good-looking girl with the insight of a ten-year-old. That is why I called myself a "girl," not a "young woman," as I didn't have the maturity that most women of my age possessed. Being desperate to fit in, I would often take unnecessary risks; the added effects of the alcohol certainly contributed to my poor judgment. Guys who I had thought were great company and full of interesting facts actually weren't interested in just being my friend; they wanted a whole lot more and it wasn't until I had consumed too much alcohol that my mind realized it was too late to get out of the situation.

When I look back, I feel a sense of shame creep in at just how easy I must have appeared, when all I was trying to do was find a sense of calm and confidence in connecting with others. I would be genuinely engaged in what guys had to say, often listening intently to the fascinating subjects they would talk about, whereas the non-autistic women would be hanging off their every word with a hidden mission to seduce them later. If you looked deeper, you could see the differences in how we were communicating. Other women would be choosing their prey for the evening, the good-looking guy who had a sense about them of money and a comfortable future they could potentially offer. I, on the other hand, would be talking to any guy; it didn't matter how they looked because I wanted what was in their heads: information. But these guys thought their luck was in when the pretty girl was talking to them and they kept their hidden agenda for later; I never saw it coming.

Some of the most regrettable moments of these younger years were the result of my being so desperate to be liked. I conceded in my mind to those moments of being seduced with the thoughts of *well, just go through with it, I must be special*, but in reality I was a temporary object of sexual urges. If I had turned someone down, walked away, I felt I would have lost not just what I considered a newfound friend, but the potential of gossip starting behind my back that I was a tease or just frigid. I'd had more than my share of taunts in school and I certainly didn't want this continuing for the rest of my life.

Finding a balance with alcohol and anxiety will always be a recipe for disaster. The days that followed the heavy drinking occurred at the weekends, so I was able to function at work during the week, but as the years went by, with a failed marriage at 26, my friend in a bottle started to take on a much darker role. I was still convinced that alcohol was responsible for my being able to function. I started to give up smoking around this time as I began to realize death from smoking was far more intimidating than death by alcohol. Well, that was my logic, but in reality both were killing me.

Removing an unhealthy addiction from one's life isn't that simple, and especially so for me. I just ended up replacing one addiction with another. Well, it wasn't actually another; it was more drinking. Where my hands were kept busy with the smoking previously, a puff here and a sip there soon turned into a sip, another sip, another gulp... Damn it, my drink is finished already, best to get another.

Telling yourself you are not an alcoholic because you don't drink for breakfast is a serious delusion to oneself. I was an alcoholic and I couldn't control it. I needed this to function and to keep my anxiety levels down. So the drinking expanded to Thursday, Friday, Saturday night and Sunday afternoon, and, in the coming years, to pretty much every evening of the week. But even this never seemed enough, and by my mid-30s I finally had a breakdown from trying to juggle the drinking, the anxiety, the stress, the depression—the vicious cycle in which I was stuck. Something had to give.

I had gained so much weight from the constant years of drinking that I could have been classified as obese. You see, the drinks and the huge amounts of sugar they contain, plus my addiction to certain salty, fatty foods that saw me eating mountains of them in one sitting, all contributed to my downfall. I was desperate for some sort of control of this crippling anxiety. What I didn't realize over these years is that I had slowly, but surely, started to turn inward, become more reclusive. Even though the alcohol initially helped with my social prowess, I was finding I was spending more and more time staying home. The internet had become another of my addictions and I would spend pretty much day and night scouring the net for people to talk to and connect with, researching a multitude of topics that would take hold of my information-hungry mind.

By the time I hit 37 I was diagnosed with severe depression. I felt as if I had given up on trying to navigate the world. I was so controlled by the drinking that I didn't have the will to address it by then, so there I sat for many months dying on the inside. I couldn't function at work and eventually, after an unfortunate accident, I went on sick leave for a year. It was here I had to think about what I wanted to do with my life. I couldn't sustain the excessive drinking if I wanted to have some sort of chance of getting back into a happier reality. At this point, my days were spent staring out the window when I wasn't staring at the computer screen, feeling trapped inside my head and trapped inside the house with my fear of stepping back out into the world. It was far too difficult to navigate.

So I made the concerted effort to stop drinking in the New Year. I was going to turn this around myself, so I thought. I managed to stay dry for four and a half months, until one of my beloved cats died a slow and awful death. The day he died was the day that alcohol retook its place, right back where I had left off. I could cope with the pain and the loss of my furry kid as I drowned my sorrows. He was like my child and I was so lost.

As a year passed by, I had a review with Welfare and was extremely lucky to have a person who understood my internal pain without having to explain much. It was as if he just saw through me, and I will never forget the compassion he had for me. I was signed off on sick leave for another year, unable to work; he knew I needed a lot of time to recover and find out who I was, which eventually led to my diagnosis of Asperger syndrome.

Spending time discovering who I was wasn't an easy task. Initially, it was a huge sense of relief, that I wasn't losing my mind, that it wasn't the case that there was no hope for me. But I went through stages, similar to the ones for grief, that still didn't allow time for me to quit drinking. Alcohol was the crutch to dull the painful memories of the past, the failures, the misunderstandings, and the anger at the years I lost in never understanding myself. I literally tried to drown my inner pain. I wasn't ready to take control, just yet.

As I dug through the layers, I began to find a way to reconnect, and this was through newfound online friends in the autism community. For the first time I finally found people who understood me, accepted me, and lived quite a similar life in many ways to me.

I had found my autistic family and I belonged. I never realized just how important a family is, whether blood or not, that completely supports and accepts you; it changed my whole life. I began to venture out and to take part in society again, but on my terms and in my own way.

A realization of how far I had come on this rollercoaster and dangerous journey came a couple of years after my diagnosis. I was asked to help show some of the Australian reptile wildlife at a significant music festival. This event hosted of tens of thousands of people, a multitude of metal bands, tough-looking guys who were gentle giants at heart. Here I was, among the backstage crowds wandering around with a snake attached to me. Did the anxiety get to me? Yeah a little, but I felt in my element. A lot of these people were talented but different, like me, and I felt safe with them, and not one drop of alcohol was involved.

It was my first real significant sign that I could be me without the aid of drinking. And the best part was seeing all the non-autistic population on the other side of the fence, squashing each other madly for a glimpse of their favorite band on stage. Being on the pit side, there was the space and barrier I needed. It was like that safe protected zone we all need in our lives.

I found that I needed to put myself in situations that helped and supported me as a person, rather than try to mask and pretend all the time to fit into an unmanageable role that wasn't designed for my neurology. I started to make peace with myself, be kinder to myself, and try to take heed of how destructive the path actually was I had chosen. When you finally break, life changes you for good in so many ways; it shakes you up and makes you take a good hard look at yourself. When you finally understand who you are, you can attempt to work towards a more sustainable and positive life.

I still drink, but nowhere near as much as I used to. I used to drink to cope; now I drink to relax. I enjoy what I drink and choose what tastes good, rather than drinking to excess anything that I could afford or get my hands on. I am grateful that I still have an intact liver and do wonder if there was a God watching over me through so many reckless times.

Will I ever completely give up? I really don't know, but for now I have taken back some control, gained some insight into what makes me so anxious, self-conscious, and stressed, and tried to put into place measures, as best I can, to keep stressors to a minimum. I know how long I can cope socially and I keep my circle of friends to ones who understand and support me. When people cause me unnecessary stress, I just let go of them and move on. I can't afford to waste energy on things that don't positively serve me.

I now realize that anxiety, a curse to so many autistics, often plays quite a terrible role in our existence. If I had known who I was when I was so much younger and understood why I was different,

I think my path would have been vastly different to the one that I endured. I would have chosen to meet people in the library or a park surrounded by nature, not meet in a pub to drink in order to fit into a role for which I was never designed. I would have chosen work that complemented my way of thinking and downtime consisting of mindfulness and reflective contemplation.

Even though so many years have passed, during which I lived unwisely, I still feel thankful that I survived and from my experiences I hope to shine a light on where I went wrong, how I could have done things differently, and, I hope, to resonate with some of you about how you too can change your life for a less anxious and more forgiving one.

## Dr. Michelle Garnett on socializing, anxiety, and addictions

I could cry reading the early part of this chapter, for the loneliness and isolation Barb experienced through school and beyond, for innocence lost and the depth of years of personal suffering in a wilderness of need and lack of care. Barb's story is the story of too many people on the spectrum, where neurological difference leads to familial and social isolation, depression, anxiety, and self-medication. Initial Australian data from the Autism CRC longitudinal studies, as reported recently by Richdale (2017), showed that 46% of adults on the spectrum aged 25–80 years old reported a current diagnosis of depression and 54% reported an anxiety diagnosis. Croen et al. (2015) examined 1507 adults with autism in California and found that there were high levels of depression and anxiety for this group and high levels of drug and alcohol abuse. Internet addiction levels for people with ASD are underreported but clinical experience indicates they are high. Beyond substance addiction, there are the added dangers of risk of serious assault or accident when drug-affected.

In the teenage years, alcohol and other drugs can seem to provide the answer to anxiety and socializing problems; they are readily available, and it is culturally normative in much of the Western world to use alcohol to excessive levels. The short-term benefits can seem to outweigh the long-term costs. It can take years for the person to recognize that they no longer have control of their use. By then the addiction is entrenched; secondary issues of major depression and shame are likely to have emerged, and effecting positive change is extremely difficult.

## Prevention

Knowing that young women with AS are at risk for developing addictions, it is important for parents of autistic girls to take steps toward prevention. The clues for how are embedded in Barb's story:

- Delay introducing your daughter to alcohol. The research is clear: the later the child starts drinking, the less likely they are to suffer alcohol addiction.
- Personality factors that are linked to addiction include: hopelessness, anxiety, sensitivity, impulsivity, and sensation seeking. If you note any of these early on in your daughter's life, make adaptations to accommodate these tendencies. For example:
    - **Hopelessness.** Consider a course of cognitive behavioral therapy (CBT) or acceptance and commitment therapy (ACT) to recognize and manage this thinking style, e.g. using our book, *Exploring Depression* (Attwood and Garnett, 2016), which was written to assist with a sense of hopelessness. Discover strategies from the positive psychology movement to increase optimism. A good website is: www.pursuit-of-happiness.org

- **Anxiety sensitivity.** Increase awareness of signs of anxiety in the body, and learn ways to manage anxiety on a daily basis.
- **Impulsivity.** Teach your daughter techniques to recognize and manage her impulsivity, using meditation and mindfulness techniques, for example.
- **Sensation seeking.** Arrange activities for your daughter that incorporate risk in a 'safe' way such as high-board diving, BMX riding, skateboarding.
- **Obsessiveness.** Obsessiveness is a sign of high levels of anxiety. Treatment of anxiety will reduce the obsessiveness. This is a lifelong trait and the approach is to manage rather than cure.

• Always know where your daughter is and who she is with. Monitoring and supervision of teenagers is correlated with less substance-related harm.

• Work on your relationship with your daughter by making time to listen. Validate her experiences. You don't have to agree with her point of view, but say that you can hear, see, or understand what she is saying. She needs to self-express and she needs to feel heard. For girls on the spectrum, conversations may occur more easily while doing something else—for example, driving, walking, drawing, knitting, coloring in, gardening, playing with clay or fidget toys.

• Make active steps to increase your daughter's sense of self, self-esteem, positive self-identity, and sense of self-agency. Talk to her about who she is in positive terms to help her find her sense of self. Identify her personality characteristics, strengths, and talents. Give examples. Orchestrate experiences where she can experience the success of her personality and talents in tangible outcomes. Document her experiences in a scrapbook or on an app.

- Balance activities. Girls on the spectrum can rigidly avoid many experiences, depriving themselves of the learning that they can be active agents of change in their own lives. Ensure that there is a mix of easy and difficult experiences each day. At the end of the day make it a practice, perhaps over dinner, to discuss what went well and what didn't. Incorporate validation of her experiences. Resist the temptation to try to resolve everything.

- Ensure she knows how to relax. Being able to relax on cue is often not available for girls on the spectrum. Often, by the time they realize they need to relax, their anxiety is off the chart and they are resistant to any assistance. It is important to learn to relax at a time when she is not under any stress. There are some good apps to help to calm the body down during moments of extreme anxiety. I recommend Breathe, Calm, Breathing Bubbles, Headspace, and Smiling Mind.

- Assist, where you can, to help your daughter find her group. Being able to connect with like-minded peers will bring understanding and support, ending the loneliness. Connection to others is a powerful protective factor militating against reliance on substances.

## Treatment

If addiction is a current concern for the woman on the spectrum, there are many centers around the world for advice and treatment (see the Recommended Resources section at the end of the book). However, there is less understanding about addiction and ASD than we would hope for. Some considerations are:

- There is a lot of judgment and resultant shame and self-condemnation about addiction in our society. Approach yourself with kindness and compassion. Everyone deserves caring and everyone is worthy. Engage in a metacognitive therapy that will teach you to maintain a non-judgmental, present-focused awareness.

- A focus on recovery rather than abstinence is helpful.
- The most successful treatment approaches to addiction involve inpatient care.
- Considerations for a person on the spectrum to maximize success as an inpatient include asking for one's own room rather than a sharing arrangement and that a focus on individual rather than group therapy may be more effective. However, group therapy where all participants have ASD can work well.
- Outpatient care approaches with the most success include a combination of CBT and motivational intervention (MI). Treatment is typically longer than six months and involves relapses.
- Regardless of whether treatment is inpatient or outpatient, it is important that your therapist is aware of your diagnosis so that treatment can be adapted to suit your individual profile. Considerations will include:
  - management of co-existing conditions, including depression and anxiety (see Attwood and Garnett, 2016)
  - accommodations to therapy (see Attwood and Garnett, 2016)
  - social skills training to minimize incentives for substance use.

## CHAPTER 7

# Personal Safety

*Liane Holliday Willey*

It may seem we live in a world where violence and abuse have peaked beyond measure, but a look back through history would show ill will toward others has always been immeasurable. The good news is humanity seems resolutely focused on facing and resolving the damages laid against gender, race, culture, and age. The bad news is that we with autism too often remain ignored—or, worse, dismissed when we look for help or ask for protection. To be sure, things aren't as bad as they used to be. The days when we were hidden from neighbors, locked in institutions, subjected to inhumane experiments and "treatments" are mostly distant realities. Now we have pioneers like Dennis Debbaudt of Autism Risk Management, countless individual and organized autistics giving voice to education and advocacy, government panels looking for ways to infuse dollars and sense into society and education, and community and caregiver groups devoted to understanding and supporting autistics. Now, autistics across the spectrum have a real chance to lead safe and productive lives, but as we work for that chance, we must remain diligent in discussing the abuse that continues to threaten our personal safety.

When I first began sharing details about my life as a member of the autistic community, I was often told I couldn't possibly have autism. I had employment, a husband and children, a desire for a social life of sorts, interest in popular things, a good sense of humor, empathy, and an outgoing personality. Surely someone with these traits couldn't be autistic... Wrong.

Today's understanding of the spectrum has grown to include a wider and far more accurate recognition of the capability of autistics. I'm obviously pleased the stereotypes of autism as a completely debilitating condition are mostly gone, but I'm rather alarmed that our status as capable individuals may well be eroding some of the supports most us will forever need, no matter how well educated, how intelligent, or how integrated into society we may be. Simply put, the recognition that autistics are capable in many valuable and unique ways should not be morphed into a belief that we are beyond the need for tangible supports meant to protect us from imminent dangers that we aren't wired to recognize.

I'm never happy to share my experiences with the nasty biting bits of my reality. I have worked very hard to figure out how I can fit into the ways of the world, and it makes me very uncomfortable to consider how easily I fall out of sync with society. I worry my words will create uneasy feelings and maybe even fear or regression for you, our readers and friends. I'm offering this proposition to any of you who find this chapter too invasive or hard on your heart: use my words as a catalyst for the discussions our community needs to have...add my stories to yours, so yours aren't so lonely...let my history remind you that, despite damaging despair, you can define your own destiny.

## Do we really know what abuse is?

Despite the fact there are only scattered in-depth studies analyzing the relationship between domestic violence and abuse among those on the autism spectrum, there is a strong correlation between the two in anecdotal reports. I wonder if the scientific evidence is still small, because too many people in our community have a naïve and untrained understanding of what constitutes violence or abuse. For example, if I grew up in a household where it was commonplace to receive gentle swats from my mom on the bum for misbehaving, I might not be able to recognize that a co-worker has initiated sexual assault if they patted my bottom when I walked by, and I might not be able to identify a heavy-handed smack on the backside as domestic assault. Literal-thinking autistics might think every swat means they did something out of line, thinking they are the perpetrators and/or in need of the swat, no matter how uncomfortable it felt or how loud our gut yells that something is wrong. In fact, and make no mistake about this, abuse is a multifaceted state that can take many forms including (but not clearly limited to) any word or behavior pushed upon another person in a way that sparks physical, emotional, financial, sexual, negligent shocks, or after-effects.

I realize that's a pretty vague definition. It's hard to give autistics a fully encompassing definition of abuse, because our literal thinking, our need to repress our inner fears of rejection by accepting most anything just to have a friend or a job, and our general trusting nature work against us when we try to figure out if we have been, or are being, abused. In truth, almost everyone has their own definitions of abuse; lawsuits and too often too coarse individualized cultural norms are proof of that.

I had no idea I was a regular victim of abuse until my counselor made it abundantly clear some of my so-called friends, mentors, and trusted bosses were nothing more than abusers who must have picked up on the fact I was an easy mark because of the very things that make me autistic.

With the continued help of my counselor, I've slowly learned to coherently and objectively analyze so many things that have left burn marks and dents on my self-confidence and my psyche, things I may have winced at or been confused by, but things I never knew I could stop or even file charges against. I remember never being able to say no to civic group leaders who asked me to do way more work than others were doing, because I wanted so badly for people to know that, despite my idiosyncrasies, I was smart and capable and a giver. It took years and years to realize in many cases I was the only one doing any work for the cause to which we were all supposedly committed. I took the teaching assignments all my co-workers rejected just so I could show them I was a team player who deserved a tenure position even though I openly complained about meetings and department agendas. When I'd wear a tight sweater, needing the feel of compression for the day, I'd frivolously react to the stares leveled at my chest with something like, "My boobs always look bigger when I have on my winter weight," because even my horrible non-verbal illiteracy could tell their stare was sinister. I tried drugs for roommates who asked me to "go first" so they could tell how strong the strain was, because, heck, I never said no to a dare—a dare was an act of comradery, ya know? No. No, it wasn't. And neither was it an act of comradery when a few dates easily convinced me that dates ended with things I never suspected, liked, or wanted.

As neurotypical as I'm told I appear, I was indeed the kid, the teen, the young adult, the mom, the neighbor, the relative, the co-worker, who was knocked down sticky mud slides by cruel people who walk this earth as if they are at least as good as every kind soul ever was. Even after I was identified as having autism, and it became known I could be easily taken advantage of or misunderstood, I was still the first person cut from the group. I was the first person laughed at. The first person dismissed. The first person ignored. I might be able to forgive the people who took advantage of me when they thought I was fully socially aware of my spot in space, but it's impossible for me now to forgive anyone who took advantage of me if they knew I was a gentle-natured autistic.

I'm told it's important to forgive people for a vast variety of reasons, none of which really resonate with me. Maybe someday I will be able to, down in my bones, identify the concept of forgiveness in a way that makes me feel compelled to explore it, but for now I'm simply trying to rebuild the parts of me that were marred by the cruel nature of others. I'm trying to recognize abuse earlier and more accurately. I think if I can avoid abuse in the first place, I will be in a safer and kinder place from which forgiveness and contented growth can happen.

Any situation driven by any human can quickly turn into an abusive state. There are no rules that make it OK for anyone to treat you in any manner that makes you feel uneasy, queasy, violated, cheated, mistreated, stupid, ignorant, used, or hurt in any way. Consider the examples below and use them to spur journal writings or discussions you can ponder on your own or with a trusted advisor. Try to analyze the concept of abuse according to your beliefs and feelings, not by others' definitions or others' norms. Stretch yourself beyond literal or rigid thinking modes, because abuse is a concept that is malleable when a ne'er-do-well is pulling the strings. Find help as soon as you need it. There are sources available online that do a great job of connecting you with advice or support. The editor of our book, Barb Cook, runs this website and it is fabulous: www.spectrumwomen.com. The days of being alone are over.

## Sexual abuse

There will never be any reason for an intimate partner, a roommate, a spouse, any family member, or any other person(s) you cohabit with, ever to do anything to you in which you aren't truly interested.

While it is often natural for a person to be intrigued by new experiences, especially those that are sexual or romantic, temper your intrigue within the realm of your personal standards of dignity, respect, pain, nurture, freedom, and, above all, personal safety. What may seem like a good idea to spice up sex, for example, may quickly turn into either subtle abuse or downright dangerous happenings. While being careful not to judge any expression of love or lust—I need to be clear on this—predators will typically disguise many behaviors as nothing more than frivolous sadomasochism or playful roughhousing, when in fact they may be setting a ruse with insidious ramifications.

If you feel pressure to engage in intimate acts because of your religion, your culture, because you feel guilty for not doing what your partner might want, or because you think you "owe" someone sex for whatever reason, reach out for counseling until you realize those thoughts have no safe or healthy basis. There is absolutely no set of circumstances under which you are obligated to move beyond your comfort zone. Set this rule and keep it etched in stone: "no means no." Safety words are great, but, above all, NO means stop, quit, get off me, get away from me, let me go, etc., etc., etc.

## Economic abuse

The person who controls the purse strings tends to control the relationship. Control is an integral and often insidious part of abuse. Economic control can happen at work, through the internet, within any personal relationship, at shopping malls, at the bank, or at a social gathering.

Truthfully, it can happen anywhere currency or goods are exchanged. If you face any of these circumstances, resist the will to accept them as the norm or to give in and do as you're being asked, until you can make very sure you aren't part of a predator's con.

- You feel so harassed at work, you want to quit. Beware of this scenario, as it is a common ploy by employers who would have to pay unemployment benefits if they fire you, but none if you quit.
- You'd like to work, but the people you interact with convince you not to, or they refuse to help you get to work, or they convince you that you're needed at home to do chores or watch the kid or animals, or they simply tell you they won't allow it (for any reason, even those that sound nurturing). It's much easier to control someone if they don't have money or outside influences such as co-workers. Keeping you home and alone keeps you an economic prisoner.
- You find you are never included in financial decisions that affect anything to do with you, or the household, or your future security. When someone wants to keep you reliant on them, one of the first things they do is keep you financially ignorant. You can't be independent on any level if you don't have the money to support your independence.
- Co-workers, fellow students, peers, charity groups, religious organizations consistently pressure you or demand you give them money. They might say they will just borrow it or that they should have it for whatever reason (good or bad), but there is never a reason why you are obligated to give your money to anyone.

There are community events, online courses, and classes that can help you learn about personal finance. Even if you have math dyslexia (dyscalculia), you can still try to learn all you can about the rights and wrongs of safe money management, and you can ask for help from social service agencies if your financial situation is just too complicated for you to manage. Bottom line: the list of people who will take advantage of your finances is endless. Be aware and protect your assets.

## Physical abuse

At first glance, this seems like an obvious abuse to detect. But the shrewd predator will know how to hurt you without leaving a visible mark and they will know how to convince you either that they aren't abusing you or that you deserve the abuse they are giving, or that they are sorry and are so thankful they have you to understand they aren't bad people even though they beat you to pieces. So many of us on the spectrum will fall into these traps for all sorts of fine and not so fine reasons. Maybe we have an admirably strong sense of loyalty or a deep sense of empathy and concern. Or maybe we have no self-worth, or a desperate need to keep a friend no matter how horrible the friend is.

I know this kind of abuse far too well. I get sick thinking of the danger into which I put myself. I feel stupid for not seeing I was being abused. I feel guilty, ugly, ashamed, and vengeful. The memories and literal scars from my physical abuse simmer like coals that will always char. I've put together a list of abuses that are totally unacceptable. I've personally experienced 80% of these. I'm admitting to my painful past only to promote discussion that all of us are susceptible to the dark side of bad people and to encourage our community to make some real change in abuse support services.

Here's my list of unacceptable abuses. I hope it isn't your list, but if even one of these things is happening to you, reach out for advice on how to find safety:

- slapping
- shoving
- biting
- choking
- hitting (or threatening) you with anything that can hurt
- keeping you against your will

- holding you down
- stalking
- keeping any medications or dietary needs from you
- keeping you from sleep or necessary rest
- forcing you into unsafe pathways on bikes, in cars, or while you are walking
- breaking windows or doors to find you
- throwing things
- abandoning you
- stopping you from getting, or refusing to help you to get, medical or psychological care
- shutting you out of your home or safe place
- forcing you to be around a dangerous human, pet, or animal.

Counseling has helped me learn not to reopen the wounds these memories left, but it hasn't been easy and I doubt I will ever be able to put everything into a neat little box I can compartmentalize in my brain. Counseling empowered me so that I can guarantee I will find a way to access the authorities if any of these things ever happens to me again. And if that day happens, I will be smart enough to bring along materials, or, better still, a person, to help explain the relationship between autism and physical abuse. I've been a consultant in far too many cases of rape, domestic abuse, and child custody battles to think courts will be able to really understand the seriousness of our abuse largely because our communication styles tend to be too placid, our pain tolerance oddly high or very low, our eye contact vague, and our body language not intense enough to convince a judge we were significantly damaged.

In other words, we don't often look the part of a person who has really been abused, but that's a superficial judgment call and one that can be rectified. If you are involved in (or witness to) any wrongdoing or crime, I strongly suggest you reach out to legal aid representatives and first responders who understand autism, before you make an official report. They can then assume the role of translator and help you share your story in ways that neurotypicals can comprehend, while simultaneously helping you deal with the ramifications of the situation.

## Emotional abuse

It is common for people on the autism spectrum to miss the concept or ramifications of emotional abuse for it can be served up ever so slightly and rationalized ever so cleverly. Although we may be highly empathic, we may not be able to tap into the words or feelings we need to identify emotional abuse. This is a particularly difficult kind of abuse for me. I'm an intensely verbal person who is easily overwhelmed by other people's sadness or pain. I think these two characteristics fight with my reasoning, leaving me in a state of "paralysis by analysis." I have this overwhelming need to pull apart, twist, and rephrase words and subtle nuances all the time, but especially when my thinking gets crumbly by rushes of concern or compassion. My intuition gets squeezed into a dusty corner, making it incredibly difficult for me to decide if I've been insulted or slighted or attacked. Add in a rather weak "theory of mind," and all at once I'm a perfect target for emotional abusers, especially those who like to make paper cuts instead of chainsaw-sized wounds.

From the subtle to the brazen, emotional abuse can come at you through a myriad of ways including (but sadly not limited to):

- broken promises, vows, or agreements
- unequal workloads that leave you bearing most chores or responsibilities, or that force you to handle work you can't do or truly dislike doing

- isolation that keeps you from other friends, co-workers, peers, neighbors—anyone or anything that would give you happiness or independence
- mind games such as convincing you that your feelings are delusional or your instincts are outlandish (gaslighting)
- humiliation of any kind
- disrespect or contempt for your values or lifestyle
- threats and extortions
- condemnation of your looks or clothing, or criticism of your skill sets or intelligence.

The marrow of personal safety needs to be self-defined because it's certain we all have our own threshold of what's acceptable and tolerable. Everyone has different markers for things and situations that cause them angst, sadness, worry, pain, or twinges of suffering. Some things, however, go beyond the pale and straight into the land of cruel and just plain wrong. Please, if you find yourself in any of the scenarios I describe, reach out to your own safety source or to one of the resources recommended in this book. Keep in mind that there is no shame in asking for help, no shame in being a victim, no shame in making your destiny safe.

## Dr. Michelle Garnett on personal safety

Tragically, from both research and clinical experience, it is clear that people on the autism spectrum are among the most vulnerable in our society for verbal, emotional, physical, and sexual abuse, including verbal and physical bullying within both school and workplace environments. It may be tempting to think that it is only the autistic individuals who are non-verbal or who have a co-existing intellectual or learning impairment that are vulnerable. However, as a society, we need far more awareness of the vulnerability of those members of our community who have what is referred to as autism spectrum (level 1 or 2) or Asperger syndrome, particularly girls and women.

Liane very clearly describes the reasons for this vulnerability:

- Individuals on the autism spectrum are not neurologically "wired" to read the intentions of others.
- They may not recognize abuse because of their tendency for literal thinking and self-blame.
- Their inner fears of rejection and/or low self-esteem can lead to an acceptance of certain levels of abuse.
- Their innate social confusion and intricate analysis of social situations can lead to poor judgment and decision-making.
- Their natural tendency to believe in the honesty and innocence of other people can lead to naiveté and vulnerability.
- Perpetrators recognize that the person is unlikely to tell others about the abuse because of their high levels of anxiety and lack of assertiveness skills.

In addition, we know that being the victim of one abusive act is predictive of further abusive acts. Bear and his colleagues (2015) compared rates of bullying among a large sample of students with disability (1027), including ASD, and without disabilities (11,500), and found that having ASD increased the rate of bullying by 50% compared with neurotypical children. Many adults with Asperger syndrome report that bullying from peers started as early as kindergarten. Unfortunately, this means that being bullied at school is another risk factor for later abuse for people with ASD.

To stop this largely hidden problem, we need action at individual, family, school, and community levels.

### Individual

Early recognition for females on the autism spectrum will assist in equipping girls earlier to recognize their vulnerability to potential predators throughout life. Early prevention programs can include: learning how to read non-verbal communication (facial expression, body language) to increase awareness of intention in others, how to recognize and avoid unsafe situations, how to tune in to and be guided by their intuition and gut instinct, development of assertiveness skills, counseling for early bullying and teasing at school, how to ask for help in choosing safe friends and partners, how to love and accept yourself for who you are, to recognize all forms of abuse, to have the self-esteem and self-empowerment to say no, and to report if needed.

It is important to acknowledge here that sociopaths are among our most charming and socially skilled community members; sometimes it can be impossible, with or without autism, to read a person's true intention.

### Family

At the time of diagnosis, it is very important for clinicians to describe to parents and/or carers the risks ahead for the girl on the spectrum and to create a plan for managing these risks, which may include some or all of the above strategies. Adolescent girls are safer from potential harm if their parents always monitor where they are and who they are with. I encourage parents to schedule times to have frank and open discussions with their adolescent girl about the very real risks of sexual and other forms of abuse, and to create plans to militate against risk. These conversations are often needed well into adulthood for our girls on the spectrum. Two excellent books to assist are *Safety Skills for Asperger Women* by Liane Holliday Willey (2011) and *The Aspie Girl's Guide to Being Safe with Men* by Debi Brown (2013).

## School

Educational staff need to be trained both in the female presentation of ASD and in the importance of having consultants available to the school who specialize in autism, even when this means allocating resources to purchase the expertise. Identification and awareness of a girl on the spectrum within school should represent a red flag to members of staff that there are risk factors for bullying and abuse for this girl. Guidance officers need to be trained in how autism can present, and to be open to an understanding of when abuse has occurred for a girl on the spectrum.

## Community

As Liane describes, we cannot afford to shy away from the conversations about abuse, however confronting, painful, or uneasy these conversations are. Only with awareness of the prevalence of the problem and the reasons behind it can we begin to create change. An understanding of the ways in which people on the autism spectrum are vulnerable to predators needs to be incorporated into the education of our medical, health, forensic, justice, and educational professionals to inform the way that they interview, support, educate, and advocate. We need more government funding to support adults on the autism spectrum to be safe in our community, regardless of their level of education or intelligence. For example, in Australia, an excellent organization to educate professionals and organizations in recognizing child sexual abuse is Bravehearts (https://bravehearts.org.au).

## CHAPTER 8

# A Real Parent

*Samantha Craft*

## No universal rulebook

As a schoolteacher, I knew the facts—that effective parenting would lead to a child's psychological well-being, deter from drug and alcohol use and delinquent behavior, and foster a fulfilling life as a responsible member of society. In my mid-20s, I'd thought I had all the parenting resources I needed. Problem is, parenting is largely based on an individual's human traits: personality, intelligence, temperament, character, and moral compass, to name a few. In reality, there is no *universal rulebook* for being a successful human, and, to boot, children and circumstances aren't all the same.

I've always yearned to fit in and abide by the rules, to know what works and what doesn't, to satisfy my fight-or-flight mode with the best route to avoid life's pitfalls. When I was a young mother with three small children, living in a suburban town in Northern California, I desperately wanted to be the "perfect" parent. In efforts to do my best, I convinced myself to create another identity: a woman who could enter the demands of parenting with a persona that didn't stand out from the norm; a tight-lipped, light-hearted, capable superstar who could soar through the sky of parent groups, sports and activities, birthday parties, scrapbooking, and numerous other outings and obligations, with ease. For almost a decade, I abided by this lifestyle, and, as a result, lived as a fraction of myself. Until, one day, I literally imploded and had a nervous breakdown. Overnight, I had transformed from the party queen who hosted a multitude of successful social functions, to a recluse neighbor who was practically friendless. It would be another three years before I was diagnosed with Asperger's.

## The terrifying early years

My early parenting years were nothing like I'd expected or imagined. With the coming of pregnancy, I suffered with miscarriages, severe health complications, weight gain, and postpartum depression. By the time my third son was born, I'd had five pregnancies in less than five years. With my firstborn, despite the numerous pregnancy books I'd rampaged through, I didn't readily recognize my own postpartum baby blues and exhaustion. Nor did I know how to seek out support. Simple motherly things, like how to warm up a baby bottle, were challenging and time consuming. Thoughts of what diapers to use, what size, how to dispose of them, would distract me for days. In the midst of being a new parent, I became obsessed with hobbies—my way of distracting myself from the challenges of the unknown.

The years leading up to my oldest son's seventh birthday were by far the hardest. My first two sons were a mere 18 months apart, with both babies suffering from ongoing insomnia and inconsolable colic. They weren't typical children—at least not like any children I'd read about. Throughout six long months, after my second son was born, my eldest baby was up about every 90 minutes, while my second was up every 30 minutes. Friends thought I was exaggerating, until two volunteered to relieve me for the night.

I remember my fellow schoolteachers advising me to sleep when my children napped, and them not believing that my babies didn't nap. Being an autistic parent increased the genetic chances of my offspring having some type of challenge—sensory integration issues, sleep disturbances, irritable bowel syndrome, generalized anxiety, chronic infections—I just didn't know that yet.

The inability to console my own children and lack of sleep came at a cost. I began hyper-focusing on my own health issues, displacing the fear of not being able to control my environment with an intense fear of my own death. As much as I tried my best to be a good parent, I thought I was failing. As the years passed, I was unable to leave my children with sitters. No helpers lasted more than a couple of visits. It wasn't an unusual occurrence for a sitter to up and leave in the middle of a shift. One night I came home to witness my third-born screeching naked through the house, with a broken bowl atop his head, dressing the furniture with streams of toilet paper, while the adult assigned to provide careful watch stood there helplessly.

## Enter Asperger's

My middle son was diagnosed with Asperger's syndrome at the age of five. I'd searched high and low for answers for his behavior—spinning fits, lining up toys, screaming at the sound of the doorbell, erratic sleep cycles, dangerous aggression, and self-harm. For a couple of years, my middle son was up until midnight with insomnia, my firstborn awake at two in the morning with asthma attacks, and my youngest awakened sporadically by earaches. By then I was physically disabled and unable to work from chronic pain: a condition that would take over a decade to diagnose as a connective tissue disorder.

Some days, I was certain my life could not go on, especially the afternoons when my middle son screamed from his bedroom, tearing everything down off his shelves, while I sheltered the other children in my arms. Finding poop on the table, toothpaste smeared across the bathroom, following my sons from room to room to ensure their safety—these were all normal parts of my parenting days. I'd never sobbed so hard and never felt so lost. Every place I turned for assistance proved futile. Doctors blamed parenting, family said "spank," friends offered book titles.

It was only the passing of time and an outlying faith (that I pulled up from somewhere) that got me through. It's fair to say that mothering, with the coming of autism and other challenges, was nothing like anyone had ever explained.

## Arresting desire and anxiety

My first significant glimpse into the type of parent I wanted to be was found among the tall redwood trees in Northern California during a family therapy demonstration. I was eight years old. In the 1970s, my mother worked as an assistant for a world-renowned family therapist, Virginia Satir. I remember my slender mother and her boyfriend as two volunteers, sitting in adjacent chairs, under the tall evergreen trees. I had entered the half-circle of mostly empty seats and made a pronounced leap into my mother's lap, turning my back purposely away from her boyfriend to display my feelings of unease toward him. My action resulted in a huge sigh from the audience, and an internal compulsion, some four decades later, to cultivate an environment of safety for my children. This keen-edged need to protect my kin is complicated moreover as a result of the way my mind works—in how my brain latches on to a specific ideal and dictates how I should live.

Today, my three sons can detect my penchant for protection, as well as some of my rigid ways of being. They'll shake their head in jest or chuckle lightly at my fretting mannerisms—the fire extinguisher in the bedroom, triple checking of pick-up times, sitting by the phone awaiting updates, repeated reminders of taking precaution.

I am no stranger to extremes. In my early parenting days, I militantly followed the American Food Pyramid Guide. I could not prepare any meal unless each of the food groups was represented. I would sit up late at night fretting over the missing food group— the fruit, the veggie, the protein. Meal planning was notoriously anxiety triggering.

I know that my anxiety plays a key part in parenting. I am likened to other maternal caretakers around the globe, fretting over their beloved ones, with an everlasting desire for them to be happy, healthy, and fulfilled. In other ways, I take my worry to the extreme.

I now view my parental anxiety as an integral part of the way I am. I've learned anxiety is not something I can push away. To deal with my emotional distress, I think back to the character John Forbes Nash, represented in the critically acclaimed film *A Beautiful Mind*. I recall how Nash had imaginary friends who presented as extremely lifelike—distracting images that he could not banish from his mind despite his tedious efforts. Nash eventually learned to stop trying to push the imaginary people away, and, instead, he adapted to living with their presence, without giving the images any further power. As much as I can, I do the same with my anxiety.

## Adaptation and order

One might call me "obsessive" about the concept of time and order, including planning and prepping. Out of all my personality traits, these attributes likely affect my family the most. If things aren't going as scheduled, it is difficult to suppress my panic. It's not uncommon for me to rush someone out the door, even if we are on time. Nor is it uncommon for me to prepare family members, 24 hours in advance, for an upcoming appointment. Catch me off guard about an unexpected change in plans, and my voice speeds up, I pace, and my tone turns from calm to irritated.

I have a tendency to prep to the extreme—a default of my need for predictability. When the boys were small, I recall prepping for a vacation to Disneyland weeks in advance. In total, I packed 15 brown paper bags, one bag for each of the three boys, for each of the five days of the trip. Each individual bag had a pressed change of clothes, nightwear, an activity (e.g. coloring book), and a snack. The act of organizing served to ease my traveling anxiety. The visual image of those 15 brown bags still makes me feel good. Another example: I used to have all the family's Christmas presents bought and wrapped before October.

I learned to stop over-planning during a family trip to Maui. I'd spent months scheduling out everything. I had booked the excursions and even narrowed down what food I would order at what establishment each mealtime! Not long after our plane set down in Hawaii, the island of Maui experienced a freak storm. Most of our plans were canceled. Even the beaches were closed. As I watched multiple palm tree branches break off from the force of the wind, I promised myself never to overthink a vacation itinerary again.

My knack for organizing did come in handy when my middle son was a toddler and struggling to stay out of trouble. I set up a vast play space in our home and would guide my son from one activity to the next, every five minutes, from puzzles, to books, to water coloring, to Play-Doh®, to wooden blocks, to toy cars. I discovered that as long as my son had direction, and was intellectually and physically stimulated, he could focus long enough to stay out of harm's way.

## The importance of humor and logic

When I was a teacher, I had an automobile license plate holder that read, "You can't scare me. I teach middle school." Although I struggle in some areas, such as my need to plan and ever-present anxiety, I am often able to view my own life experiences through the lens of humor and logic to improve my outlook.

Something often missing in parenting tips is the benefit of having a sense of humor. I learned the power of humor when I was transferred from an elementary school to a middle school teaching position. I was so terrified of facing a room full of hormonally charged teenagers that I spent the better half of a weekend writing a letter to the school district pleading my case to remain a fifth grade teacher. Faced with the unavoidable task of interacting with one teen after another, I quickly discovered that being able to laugh at my situation and myself went a long way. This attitude would later enable me to take my own children less seriously, particularly in the middle of spontaneous-toddler-combustion and the like.

My gift for logic has come in handy during my decades of parenting. I am often able to pull away from a heated situation, view an occurrence from a neutral position, and not take things personally. My sons' volcanic emotional outbursts, no matter their ages, didn't shake my security as a parent. Nor did their erratic behaviors lead to my own counteractions. In the teen years, I interpreted my sons' uncouth behaviors as a normal part of transitioning toward adulthood. Each son had his own emotional spell he stumbled through, and I did my best to stand by without spewing ridicule or shame. My belief is, if a parent allows space for a child to express themselves fully, while providing boundaries with unconditional love, that child will grow into an adult with a sense of security and a calm nature.

## Uniquely you

My care for my children extends into upholding their ability to make their own choices and to find their own way. I recognize my sons' unique interests, passions, and opinions. I respect their choices and support their pursuits. I don't have expectations of what vocation they ought to select. I honor my children in their uniqueness and recognize their individual strengths and challenges. I have been cautious to expose them to circumstances that accentuate their abilities, and to avoid situations that constrict their personality and sense of security. For example, when my middle son's behavior was challenging, I made certain to weigh the pros and cons of attending public gatherings, particularly when he couldn't help himself from shouting obscenities. Through childrearing, I learned to see the benefits of each of my child's attributes. Parenting a child with challenges that are atypical has taught me to put the needs of my child above the fear of what other people might assume or think.

In their early years, I immersed my children in a variety of activities, from art school to martial arts. Even though it was difficult for me to leave the house, because of sensory and social challenges, I didn't want my personal struggles to stifle my children's opportunity for growth and experience. Most days, it took all my strength to leave the house. In moments of extreme fatigue, shut down, or spells of chronic pain, I was fortunate to have my then-husband to pick up where I had left off.

## Free thinkers and authority

Because of my tendency to think outside the box, not blindly follow social trends, and lean toward social justice, I have helped to raise free thinkers. My sons question the norm, recognize corruption, and do not commonly accept things at face value. I am not one to push fashion trends. I am frugal. I budget. My boys have had no television programming for most of their youth and they weren't exposed to reality TV and commercials.

While my lived example has led to beneficial outcomes in my sons' upbringing, I recognize I am not a perfect parent. I have areas of imbalance, extreme rigidity, and lack of follow-through. I am prone to indulge my children in some ways and be very restrictive in other ways. I might spoil them with certain gifts, yet obstinately refuse to take them to an unhealthy fast-food establishment.

I am excellent at stating clear expectations and coming up with creative ways to list household chores. On the other hand, I am lousy at following through with disciplinary action. This is largely due to the fact that I don't easily anger, don't hold grudges, and find it impossible to pretend to be upset and to don an authoritarian mask. While I am consistent in certain behaviors, such as being dependable and offering support, I am less consistent in upholding rules. I don't feel like the boss and I don't feel like a friend. Because I can easily see the gray area between right and wrong, I am susceptible to a flexible outlook and influenced by differing opinions. Compromise, collaboration, joint problem-solving are familiar and instinctual. Firmness and the concept of "my way or the highway" are foreign ideals.

## Mama bear and moving forward

I've never held back from providing for my own sons' needs and never will. I am such a mama bear when it comes to doing right by my children. I did not hesitate to hold my eldest back a year in school, when I recognized he was emotionally immature in comparison with his first-grade classmates. Nor did I abide by the stern warnings not to home-school my middle son and keep him in junior high school. Instead, I was quick to pull him into safety—a decision that led to a reduction in my son's school anxiety from 100% to almost nil, and thankfully eliminated all thoughts of taking his own life.

Present day, my sons understand that my brain works a bit differently than other people's and appreciate my ability to put their well-being first. Because of my uniqueness (and self-acceptance), my children more easily accept others' unique quirks. Knowing my struggles, they sometimes assist me with directions, rules and procedures, grocery shopping, instructions, forms, and writing tasks. They understand that I might panic with last-minute changes, that I am notoriously lousy at small talk, and I am apt to place the proverbial foot in my mouth, such as walking into a room full of their friends and announcing, "It sure stinks in here!"

Overall, my sons appreciate my honesty, transparency, willingness to take responsibility for my actions, and ability to validate their own struggles and feelings. When they feel lonely or scared, they know I understand, and, more importantly, they know I believe them and validate their experience. They appreciate my consistency, my thorough explanations—the way I work to expose the unknowns. I have inspired in them the ideals of deep introspection and self-awareness.

My firstborn son, who is studying for a four-year degree at university, has reported that my actions have taught him to have diligence and conviction, to nurture self and others, and to practice tolerance and respect. I have had the pleasure of watching my two oldest sons grow into mature, responsible, caring adults, both of whom are consistently encouraging individuals with solid characters. My youngest remains beautifully childlike in spirit and open-minded in thought. Although I might struggle with physical actions of endearment, such as knowing how to hug or how to provide a supportive pat on the shoulder, I have no barriers when it comes to letting my children know they are loved and cherished.

Moving forward, I am focusing on ways to better myself as a person. For instance, I try to pull away when I am fully immersed in a project, if only for a brief moment, to make fleeting eye contact and reassure an onlooker that I will return my full attention shortly. I practice ways to convey that I have genuine interest in what another is saying and try to remember to ask how someone is feeling, before jumping into a list of information and facts. In times of personal interactions, I sometimes absorb my surroundings, and press pause, as if taking a photo snapshot, in order to feel truly present in that place and time. More recently, I am discovering new ways to incorporate fun into my life, by incorporating activities that don't have an attached intellectual or monetary goal, such as video games.

## Miraculous seeds

My parenting, like my personhood, is a result of numerous factors. Like many others, I am perfect in my imperfections. I am accomplished through my frailties. I am brave in my fear. Ultimately, what makes me an effective parent is my capacity, my openness to love, to try my best, to serve, and to admit I don't have all the answers. In the end, what defines ideal parenting remains an interwoven labyrinth—a journey that is highly dependent on the adventurer herself. It is said that a primary objective of effective parenting is to foster within a child intellectual curiosity and the motivation to learn and grow and accomplish. Perchance it is the parent, who, through the process of the mothering journey, plants those miraculous seeds within herself.

## Dr. Michelle Garnett on parenting

Working with many mothers who are themselves on the autism spectrum, parenting both neurotypical and autistic children, I have discovered that having autism brings gifts as well as challenges to the parenting experience, as Samantha beautifully articulates. One of the overriding gifts of being autistic is when that person chooses a project or a passion, their capacity for success is *phenomenal*. For many autistic mothers, their children become their passion. Often, having grown up undiagnosed, mothers on the spectrum have an intense desire to protect their children from the adversity they themselves experienced. They wish their children to experience the safety, self-acceptance, and happiness that they themselves did not experience. Often they are all too aware of how cruel the world—meaning people—can be.

As a woman on the spectrum embraces motherhood, she often becomes an avid reader or internet researcher, aiming to discover as much as she can about the development of children and how to parent effectively. She stretches herself to confront and master sensory and social challenges for the sake of her children, where her natural reaction would be to shy away. She is commonly idealistic and perfectionistic. These qualities can each be a double-edged sword: at the same time, a source of aspirational energy and goodwill, as well as a whip with which to castigate herself.

I have found in my clinical practice that the qualities and strengths that a woman on the spectrum will commonly bring to parenthood include:

- a thirst for knowledge about children and parenting
- extraordinary tenacity and persistence when the going gets tough
- attention to detail and capacity for intricate problem analysis

- capacity for absorption in mothering tasks and problems
- aspiration to excellence, being the "perfect" mother
- creativity and capacity to think outside of conventional lines to discover original and insightful solutions to parenting problems
- open-mindedness and non-judgmental acceptance of their children without societal expectations or norms
- capacity for calm during emergencies
- a logical approach
- having a sense of humor, however quirky
- capacity to make tough decisions and follow through, despite what others may think or advise
- an honest, authentic, and transparent approach that children recognize and respond to
- a trust that their children will be honest
- an innate understanding of autism and how their autistic child may think, feel, react to, and perceive certain situations
- a well-earned, deep understanding of coping strategies and problem-solving methods that have helped them, which they can then pass on to their children
- a capacity to see life as an exciting adventure and a mystery to absorb and unravel, rather than as a problem to be solved.

Some of the challenges mothers on the spectrum will commonly discuss include:

- Managing the sensory issues of parenting, including the loudness of the screaming and shouting at times, the smells (e.g. children's breath in the morning), and some of the tactile experiences of physical affection (e.g. too much cuddling expected).

- Regulation of their own strong emotions including anxiety, anger, and stress, when she has not been able to develop coping mechanisms for these prior to motherhood, or if there is an onset of postpartum depression (baby blues).
- Assisting their child to understand and manage their strong emotions.
- Organizational difficulties when there is no help available—for example, managing the schedule of a busy household plus all the commitments and appointments, preparing meals three times a day that must have nutritional value.
- Dealing with the small talk at the school gate and other "incidental" social occasions.
- Needing to have regular communication with the teacher and other school staff, especially if their child has special needs such as autism or learning difficulties, and being able to be assertive or make oneself understood.

There is no doubt that women on the spectrum can make awesome mothers. Key factors for success are self-awareness, a good sense of humor, and being able to access support when needed. It can help to have a willingness to prioritize learning, even when that means making mistakes or feeling a sense of failure. I encourage you to find your own tribe, even if that is on the internet, to be able to share the agonies and the ecstasies of motherhood, and to try to resist feeling that you must do it perfectly or on your own!

## CHAPTER 9

# Independence

*Barb Cook*

Living independently is a rite of passage that many people take for granted. Leaving school, getting a job, obtaining your driver's license, buying your first car or motorcycle, moving into your first apartment or home, finding that perfect partner to settle down with, having children...it all seems so very simple, doesn't it?

This idealistic view of how life will be doesn't take into account the fact that each of our lives is different and we need to fathom what will work for us.

So how do we go about this? Take what inspires you and turn it into something that could set you on your path to satisfying employment. Employment is one of the most crucial parts of working towards living independently, and there are so many things tied to having an income.

This moment of inspiration can come at any time in your life. Ascertaining from an early age that I had a love for stationery, art, and patterns, I knew I had some direction toward what I wanted to do with my life later on.

Primary school: "What do you want to be when you grow up?" An artist!! "Hmmm...artists don't make much money."

High school: "What do you want to do as a job when you leave?"

Fashion designer!! "Do you know how hard it is to get into that industry?"

Midway through high school, a move halfway around the world to another country, parents' divorce, everyone hated me, bullying, loneliness…

High School from hell: "What do you want to do when you finish school?" I don't care; get me out of here.

Dropping out of high school in the UK in the 1980s while living in a dying fishing village really doesn't leave you with many prospects. So there I was, no qualifications I could rely on, living in a tiny Housing Association house with my dad who was hardly home. I was virtually living on my own at 15 with the social skills of a five-year-old and with no real idea where my life was headed.

I became rebellious. Now stood an angry hormone-fueled nightmare wanting to strangle the world for not equipping me with the tools I needed. Expressing how I felt was never easy; defiant and rebellious behaviors were the only way I could release the pain and confusion inside.

One random sunny day, the two girls living up the street from me ignited a change in my perspective of the world: they both had motorbikes… I wanted to be like them and it was my first big step in gaining independence through transport. I dreamed how I would ride gracefully around the streets, wearing black leathers…well, black *everything*!

Mind you, I didn't have any issues using public transport. This never really concerned me. I found this as a way to escape and to venture out into the world on my own. Public transport was cheap and fairly reliable. We had a small bus that would come and do the loop around town every hour so I could pretty much predict when and where to go. Pay bus driver, get ticket, find seat…preferably away from everyone else as I could not stand anyone being near me. The same also worked for the train: buy ticket, show ticket, get on train and go. It was fairly safe and you always knew your destination, but I was limited as to where I could go and wanted to explore more.

When I finally got my first motorbike, it was such an incredible feeling of freedom. I was now master of my life; I could do what I wanted, go anywhere I felt like...except...the second day I had my bike, I crashed into the back of a car. Nothing too serious, but it shook me up and I gained a very fast lesson in "respect thy machine." There was a huge amount to learn if I was to manage to stay alive for another year.

Having no friends, I joined a local motorbike club that soon became my new family. This group of people boosted my self-worth and gave me a feeling of belonging, which was something I never thought I would find. I had found a tribe of sorts.

I tried to further my studies by going to a small college, where I was still being ostracized and could never understand why no one would talk to me. I quit after three months; sobbing at the head of the college, I asked why nobody liked or talked to me, but I got no answers.

Failing yet again at trying to further my education, I needed to gain some sort of stable employment. I had a couple of short-term cleaning jobs and eventually, after spending nearly every single day down at the employment center, I scored a job in a local supermarket stacking shelves. It was a very long way from what I had envisioned for myself, but it was stable, predictable work; most importantly, I got paid.

Through work and motorcycling friends I began to learn how the dynamics of social skills worked. I was set up by some co-workers for a party that never existed and was left abandoned miles away from home. They thought this was hilarious; I thought, *Why are people are so mean?* I believed everything they said as truth. I was learning that what people say may not be in your best interests. I soon questioned everything thoroughly to prevent putting myself in future unsafe situations. Being naïve is something I have realized that non-autistics easily detect and they are quick to expose you. I had to learn to toughen up (emotionally and physically), which I did when I switched to a job in the weight-training equipment industry. The factory itself consisted mostly of men, except for two other women and me.

As a woman among a whole factory of men, you would think it would be intimidating. For me, it wasn't. I finally found my feet there; I flourished and began to understand the world in a very different light. Men were much easier to connect with than any woman I had encountered. I was 19 when I joined this company. These guys taught me dynamics of communication far better than so-called "girlfriends." There was no gossip; it was straightforward, say it how it is. I even gained a sense of humor. Guys somehow have got it right and I watched and absorbed everything I could from them. They didn't shun me either; rather, they took me on as an equal, which I never expected, but I also worked hard to show my worth.

In the years leading up to acquiring this job, I was also desperately trying to find a way to live independently. I was living with my dad and his girlfriend then, and things at home were not going well. No one understood me; the way I thought, my sensitivities, my aversions. They put this all down to my rebellious attitude and, in a lot of respects, that added to it. The more stressed I became, the more obnoxious my attitude became.

After moving out and living with a friend, I soon realized I couldn't live with anyone. Everyone had their ways of doing things and they all irritated me enormously. I had nowhere to go when my friend told me I had to leave. I couldn't go back home, as I wasn't wanted there either. Fear of being homeless certainly strikes the fear of God into you. Desperate, I begged my dad to help and he convinced my aunt and uncle to take me in. As much as I loved them, I had to abide by their house rules. I was extremely poor and desperate for money and food. Being family, I assumed it would be OK to eat some of their food, but I soon realized when they put a lock on the kitchen door that it wasn't OK; I wished they had spoken to me directly rather than just lock me out one day. It really hurt me and I couldn't understand.

A couple of months after bouncing to another aunt and uncle, I lived with a boyfriend who was incredibly dangerous. When I was escorted out by police officers who had arrived in six patrol cars for my safety, my dad finally found me a tiny place of my own. Almost 19, I still had no skills in how to go about finding my own place. Dad had done it all for me. To be honest, I was grateful. I finally had my own little room with a single bed, tiny kitchen, and separate bathroom; it was small but safe, and it was my very first space. I had a huge window that looked out on to the street. This big old window became my friend; I could fit on the sill with my cigarette in hand, watching the world drift by. Most importantly, I could keep watch on my motorbike below. This life was far from any of my childhood dreams.

Managing money when you have had no instruction or concept of its value can come as a rude shock as you watch your pay packet vanish within an hour. Rent, power bills, phone bills, fuel for the bike and then food...if you can afford it. Back then, buying food was a hard choice for me, as smoking was one of the things that actually kept my anxiety under some sort of control, even if the prospect of an early death awaited me. Going to the supermarket, which was a sensory nightmare, I would buy the cheapest food I could find: canned tomatoes, bread, rice, potatoes, butter, and cheap budget minced beef were basically my main diet for years. I had no option but to buy only cheap food to help me exist.

Trying to juggle the strain of paying bills without a budget, I eventually had to leave my little unit and go back again to sharing with a friend. Sharing was a much-needed break from the mental torture of being so poverty-stricken. I truly thought I would never make it on my own. Sharing the costs made life much easier.

Still having no clue about budgeting and now having extra money, I subsequently spent it on things like a wardrobe full of black clothing, takeout food, a pricier brand of cigarettes, and too much alcohol. No balance whatsoever. Thursday nights were spent waiting at the ATM for our pay to be deposited. When midnight arrived, our money was in. Off we would race to the local pub to drink until 2 a.m. I felt so independent, but, in reality, I was being damn reckless. Alcohol was another self-medicating tool to help dampen my fierce anxiety and combat self-consciousness. Still, it was a dangerous path, as I ended up talking to all sorts of guys and got myself into some situations that, upon looking back, I wonder how I got out of. Being a pretty young woman at 21, with no sense of danger or social skills, I was extremely lucky to have my friend look out for me. I never saw the hidden agendas that awaited me.

At 22 I finally got together with a guy who had adored me for years. Unfortunately, our perceptions of a relationship were quite different. I was confused while living alongside this person with whom I was supposedly meant to spend the rest of my life. I felt I had lost my independence and felt trapped. A failed marriage on my account by age 25 really does not follow the expectations of this "grand plan" that society holds for us.

I still had no idea of how to fend for myself. Finally, at the age of 26, I rented a house by myself for the first time. Until this point, I really didn't do a lot of housework due to all the tiny places I had lived in, sharing with friends. Furthermore, when I lived in the unit on my own, there was an onsite cleaner who came by weekly. Now I had a huge house to clean, lawns to mow, gardens to maintain, and more bills. Plus, I trusted people; I thought the estate agents were nice honest people... Wrong. "Make sure you do not make any marks in the house…" "Make sure everything is maintained as per original…" "Oh, and there will be regular house inspections to see if you can look after this place," they said with their smug looks. This was the start of many horrifying instances of renting. If the property happens to be OK, it could be the neighbor from hell next door driving you insane by loudly partying every weekend. The screaming arguments, the moldy smell of damp from an aging house, repairs that never get fixed, owners selling the house and giving you a week's notice to leave, the panic of "How do I find another place to rent in a week?" The anxiety, stress, sensory overloads, and sense of despair literally drown you at times.

So, is this what independence is? No, it doesn't have to be if you are armed with the right tools. These days, it is far easier to research where you want to live, as you can filter through properties online to save you on viewing trips. Most applications can be made online. If you see something that appeals to you, try to take the time to visit that street to gauge the particular neighborhood. Are there noisy neighbors, barking dogs, and construction work nearby? If so, look for a place that won't send your sensory perception into chaos. Write out a list of what you ideally want in order of preference. If you can get a good majority of your list of requirements, then you are heading in the right direction. It is pretty much impossible to get everything you want, but there are ways to work with any problems. To screen out noises, have a fan blowing to create a white-noise effect, or get good-quality ear buds to dampen the sounds; if rooms are too bright, use blackout curtains, or buy low-wattage light bulbs for lamps instead of turning on flickering fluorescent lights.

Another thing you will need to consider when setting up in your own space is the cost of furniture. When times were extremely tight, I would create makeshift tables out of the boxes I had used for packing and cover them with cheap second-hand sarongs. You'd be surprised at how easily you can disguise something to give it a feel of hominess. If you are in desperate need of help, you can also turn to certain charities that can help you out with donations of free or inexpensive furniture.

There are many great budgeting tools available online or as apps you can download to your phone to help you manage weekly costs. This gives you an insight into how much you need as an income to survive each week. Ideally, this is something you should plan out first before acquiring your own space. Having an idea of what you can comfortably afford goes a long way in ensuring you will not fall short on rent or essential bills. These things take priority and must be paid on time. Being behind on rent payments can set you up for a future of difficulties in obtaining a place to live or, worse, homelessness.

Keeping receipts for major payments such as rent and bills is essential. I am meticulous at keeping receipts for just about everything, in yearly folders with sections for each month. This proved its worth when I applied for a rental property and was told that I still owed money on a rental from many years before and that I had been placed on a bad tenants' list; estate agents will not consider your application if you are listed there. Luckily for me, I had every single receipt from that property and could produce these to them. It took months to have my name removed from this list, but I was fortunate to have an estate agent who understood what had happened, could visually see all my payments, and ultimately rented me the property.

So, did I end up getting that dream job, that dream life we are all led to believe awaits us? In a sense, yes, but it took many, many obstacles, ups and downs, and heartaches to finally get to a point of contentment. Years of finding which living circumstances worked for me, plus having a mental breakdown at the age of 37 due to work pressures, finally made me wake up one day and ask myself, "What do I want? What will make me happy?" I had gone from working in factories to working for myself as a graphic designer (thanks to my brother for funding me to get this qualification at the age of 24—but I did have to pay him back in work!). I had found a way to use my love for creativity by designing through artwork for businesses, being an editor, then crashing and walking away when it all got too much.

Years later, I'm now back in the realm of design and editing in a field that I personally love and know so well. Combining my love for design, writing, reading, and precision, I have finally found a point in my life where I am happy. Do I make much money? No, not at all, but that doesn't worry me. Do I have the pressures of life put upon me and the pressure I used to put on myself anymore? No.

As my life heads into 50 years of living on this planet, I think I have finally learned what fulfillment and independence are. An independent life is one that makes you happy, however you achieve it. Whether you want that big house or just to live frugally in the bush, the choice is yours and yours alone. Don't let others tell you that you can't do this or that, you need to get married, you need to have children, and you need to have a good education. What you need is a life that makes you feel whole as a person, one that you embrace and makes you smile when you enter each day. Our lives are not long in the grand scheme of things, and we need to change the world's perspective on seeing our qualities, to give us a chance to show who we are. If we are happy in our own independent lives, just think how much more we can give back to the world we live in.

## Dr. Michelle Garnett on independence

While finding a place in the world has its own set of challenges for all of us, being female and on the spectrum brings unique challenges. As Barb eloquently describes, the launch to independence requires certain skills—for example, knowing who you are, what environment or job will suit you, what you can stand, what you can't stand, problem-solving skills, adaptive life skills such as budgeting and knowing how to care for one's body, being able to read people, and learning to be alert to human predators. We also need peer support because family cannot always be there, and it is dangerous to be completely alone in the world. These specific skills and supports may be lacking for a female on the spectrum.

Many girls and women on the spectrum are by nature mimics. In the vacuum of not knowing who they are, they intuitively look to how other women are living to decide how to live their life. The shopping list of job, partner, children may dutifully be checked off, and the woman is left puzzled; she did the "right things" but why does she feel so lost, so desperately unhappy? Others may decide early on that the typical pathway is not for them, and meet varying levels of success trying to attain fulfillment in their own unique way.

There is no easy way in finding one's own place in the world, and Barb's story is one of a tribal elder imparting wisdom to those who are beginning their journey.

- Take what inspires you and turn it into something that could set you on your path to satisfying employment. This superb advice is at the heart of the success of most, if not all, people on the autism spectrum. Fascinating new research conducted in the UK indicates that over 50% of people on the autism spectrum have a passion within the creative arts, more than those who had a passion for IT. Whatever your passion, follow it. Use your creativity and intellect to discover ways around the obstacles, even when you doubt yourself. Do what inspires you, even if you cannot see how it can become your career. It may very well be the reason you get up in the morning, even though you must have a "day job" to pay the bills.

- Find your tribe. For many on the spectrum, finding like-minded people doesn't happen at school or within the workplace; it happens when they are following their passion or their interests. Not everyone will get who you are, but find the people who do. While we all need our solitude at times, we do not thrive in solitude. Research indicates that one of the key factors for success for people on the spectrum is that they had support from other people.
- Avoid black-and-white thinking about people. Not everyone will be on your side, but not everyone is against you either.
- Look out for your safety. A woman on the spectrum needs to build in safeguards for staying safe from physically or sexually abusive predators. The basics include asking friends and family to check out whomever you may choose for a friend or partner: don't drink in bars alone, or drink alcohol or take other drugs in groups of mainly other men, unless there is someone there who can stay sober and look out for you. Learn how to take protective action should you find yourself in an unsafe situation—for example, by attending a martial arts class or a specific Stay Safe or E.S.C.A.P.E. F.A.S.T. class for women.
- Learn how to budget. It is never too late. If you're young, start now. Use an online budgeting or financial planning tool.
- Understand the sensory environment that suits you. Design your living environment around your own needs, also considering the geographical location—for example, central to the city, near a park, or in the country.
- If you are house sharing, ask to negotiate the rules upfront for purchase and sharing of food, sharing of expenses, sharing of household chores including cleaning, expectations about noise levels and times of the day, as well as expectations of visitors and how long they stay. Make the guidelines clear. While rules are broken from time to time, fewer problems

and less hurt are the result of upfront discussions and clear guidelines. Keep a copy of them to refer to as needed during the time you are staying in the house.

- Alcohol and other drugs are commonly used by people to overcome overwhelming social anxiety. Effectively, many of these drugs block the frontal lobes, which is the part of the brain that allows for good planning, interpersonal functioning, and sound judgment. While we may feel that we are better socially when we drink, in reality the reverse is true. Safe, enjoyable, and fulfilling social time is compromised when we take excessive alcohol or illicit drugs. Make a rule for yourself not to cross this boundary, and to find other ways to manage fierce anxiety and combat self-consciousness.

- Recognize problems when they come up and don't personalize them. When there is a problem, it doesn't mean that there's something wrong with you; it just means that there is a problem. Learn how to problem-solve:
  - Define the problem.
  - Brainstorm all possible solutions, including seemingly ridiculous or impossible ones.
  - Make a list of the pros and cons for each solution.
  - Choose a solution based on your analysis.
  - Do it.

Be prepared to try and fail, try again and fail, all the time learning more about who you are, what you need, and what you want. Be compassionate and kind to yourself—you deserve it.

## CHAPTER 10

# Promoting Positive Employment

*Jeanette Purkis*

## My work journey

My experiences of employment as an autistic woman have been varied. There have been big challenges but I have found my way to a job I enjoy.

I left home at age 17 during a recession. It was almost impossible to find a job but I got one working in a fast-food restaurant. After two years I left due to sexual harassment from a manager. I didn't work again for almost ten years following some poor life choices, serious mental illness, and homelessness. When I was 27, I decided to get myself a full-time professional job in order to escape poverty. My journey was pretty stop-start, but I studied and made incremental steps to build my confidence around employment.

I think a lot of people, if they had been in a similar position, would have stayed in the dishwashing job I had at age 27 for the foreseeable future, happy to be employed and in a more positive space than they were before. But for me, I had this huge level of drive and ambition. Basically I thought, *I want a professional job and I won't stop until I get there*. In 2006, feeling ready for full-time work, I successfully applied for a job in the Australian Public Service.

The Public Service has been incredible. The work suits me well and I feel quite at home. I have been in my role for over ten years and have been promoted twice. Despite some challenges and setbacks, my world of work is now enjoyable and rewarding.

## Overview—autism and employment

Employment is important. It can provide financial independence and a sense of inclusion and being part of something bigger. Autistic people can face challenges in gaining suitable employment, but it does not need to be unattainable. Currently we face some of the lowest labor force participation rates of any disability group and some of the highest levels of unemployment (Australian Bureau of Statistics, 2017). However, there are a number of effective strategies which we can put in place to address this disparity. In recent years things have started to change.

### Positives of employing autistic women

Autistic women often have some very useful "soft skills." The term "soft skills" refers to intangible skills such as enthusiasm or loyalty— both things that autistic staff often excel at.

Some workforce skills autistic women may be particularly proficient at include the following:

- This one may sound like a cliché but it is very common that autistic employees are great at noticing the things that others miss, be that in proofreading reports, coding, or testing software. Autistic people can often notice things neurotypical people do not. In a work context this is a significant advantage.
- An employee who has struggled to find and keep a job is likely to be more loyal to their employer than someone who

PROMOTING POSITIVE EMPLOYMENT

has never been unemployed. Autistic people often have that experience. Loyalty impacts positively on employees' productivity and quality of work.

- It took me 41 years to work out that it was possible to do a half-hearted job on something. In the two years since that realization I have never actually done anything half-heartedly, despite realizing it is possible. In my work life, diligence and care in all I do are a huge asset and I am definitely not alone in this.
- Autistic women are often very thoughtful and empathetic. They may provide support and friendship to their colleagues and have a "listening ear." Autistic women are often excellent in caring-type roles such as medicine, psychology, nursing, teaching, or veterinary science.
- Autistic women are often fascinated by a topic which can turn into a career. There are a lot of autistic women working in academia and science, building the knowledge of humanity by pursuing their passionate interest.
- Autistic women may be strongly aware of and invested in diversity and respect for people facing disadvantage. This can mean they are excellent at working in areas such as advocacy and some parts of human resources.
- Autistic employees are often innovative, creative thinkers. This is relevant to a range of different careers. In knowledge-type work there is an obvious benefit from this, but it can translate across to a number of different jobs.
- There is evidence that staff with a disability, including autistic staff members, take less sick leave and fewer unplanned absences than non-disabled staff (Australian Public Service, 2017). If we are in a workplace with a good "fit," then we are likely to be enthusiastic and dedicated. We are often "engaged" staff members—which is exactly what an employer wants.
- An autistic staff member's communication style and

personality often complement the styles and skills of existing team members. In a workplace it is essential to have a variety of people with a range of approaches to the work. The different approach an autistic employee might bring to their role can assist in the performance of their team.

When applying for jobs, you can include your soft skills and positive characteristics in the application and mention them at interview.

When thinking about your own career, it is helpful to view your working life as a journey with no set destination. When setting vague goals as "dream jobs," they rarely eventuate or live up to expectations.

## Barriers to employment for autistic women

There are some barriers to gaining suitable employment which autistic women may experience.

These barriers can often be addressed through building an understanding of autism with managers and colleagues, explaining how things such as sensory issues can impact on work and putting into place measures addressing these barriers.

Difficulties autistic women face can include:

- disruptions from moving through the transition points of completing high school, undertaking further education, and joining the workforce, for a number of reasons
- anxiety
- discrimination and/or bullying
- exclusion or isolation from colleagues
- difficulties understanding work hierarchies
- sensory issues
- difficulties understanding "unwritten rules" and expecta-tions which neurotypical employees seem to know intuitively.

## Gender differences in employment

Some considerations around employment are similar for autistic men and women. However, there are some experiences—positive and negative—which women are more likely to have than their male autistic peers. One lens through which this can be viewed is that of intersectionality. Intersectionality is essentially the idea that people can face disadvantage as a result of belonging to a number of diversity groups. These intersectional lenses can inform a person's experience of life. An autistic woman in the workplace may experience gender bias and discrimination to do with her autism. An autistic man in a similar position may experience discrimination based on his autism but not his gender. Autistic women face all the gender disparities that other women do. However, many gender differences affecting employment do not involve discrimination or bias but do require understanding.

Some gender-based considerations for autistic women employees include:

- The impact of pregnancy and parenthood in the workplace. Governments and/or workplaces in some countries and regions provide a period of paid or unpaid leave for new parents. This may include access to leave or part-time hours when the parent returns to work. If you are a parent or thinking of becoming a parent, check out what is available at your workplace and in your country/region. Find out whether there are laws or policies protecting the rights of expectant mothers and new parents.
- While most managers and employers adhere to the relevant workplace relations laws and company policies, in some cases employees can be subjected to bullying and harassment. This can be focused on their gender. While sexual harassment happens to men as well, the majority

of this behavior is directed at women. Autistic women may struggle to speak up or know what they can do when they experience harassment or bullying. As such it is important to know your rights and responsibilities as an employee. Useful things to be aware of are:

- the relevant information in the workplace/industrial relations laws for your country/region
- what constitutes unlawful or bullying behavior at your workplace
- what your options are if you experience bullying and harassment
- where to go to help address any unwanted behavior.

It is worth doing this research even when you aren't being subjected to bullying or harassment so that you are more able to spot problem behavior if it occurs. In addition, when employees are going through these kinds of issues, it can be emotionally draining and stressful. Having to look for information and what to do "in the heat of the moment" can be very upsetting, so being prepared is a good idea.

- Confidence at work can be a challenge for all women, but autistic women even more so. Some strategies to address this include reminding yourself that many of your colleagues are also not confident and they are putting on a "mask" or "cloak" of confidence so their managers and colleagues think they are. Viewing yourself in a positive light—your skills at work, positive feedback you receive from your managers, and focusing on your strengths—can help with this. Confidence can be a challenge for many of us, so don't feel bad if you do not acquire it quickly as it can take some time. One of the best drivers of confidence is competence in what you do. Building your skills and experience at work—or in activities you do outside of work—can help increase your confidence levels.

- Social, non-work-related elements of your job—for example, your colleagues wanting you to join them for lunch or the work Christmas party—can be a struggle. Women can find it hard to decline offers to attend these events, even if they really do not want to participate. It can help to have a few words prepared to tell your colleagues or manager why you don't want to do these activities. In these situations it is OK to tell a "white lie" if you need to (i.e. an excuse so as to avoid hurting colleagues' feelings).

- Assertiveness is hard for many of us and dealing with interpersonal issues and irritations at work can be overwhelming. In these instances it can be really useful to have a "venting buddy"—someone you can talk to about issues you are having with colleagues or managers. Your venting buddy should not be a colleague or manager or anyone at your workplace as they might pass on your venting to the person you were venting about, which will make things worse! Venting is a really useful thing to do as it diffuses your frustration and anger, but not with the person who is causing the issue.

## Applications and interviews

When applying for jobs and having job interviews, preparation is the key. For many autistic women, a job interview is one of the most challenging things they can do, particularly if they are introverted and lack confidence (which, let's face it, is quite a few of us). Preparation can give you confidence and knowledge, helping you to perform better at the interview. Prior to the interview, find out as much as you can about the job you applied for and research the company at which you applied to work. Look at their vision statement and mission statement if they have one, as these can state what they do, how they plan to do it, and their philosophy as an organization. You can insert this knowledge into your response to interview questions. Practice interviews either with a friend or family member or in the mirror. You won't know the questions you will be asked at the actual interview, but that doesn't matter too much. This is more about preparation and building your confidence.

## Autism-specific jobs

If these are available, you could consider disability/autism employment programs and affirmative measures. This refers to where companies target jobs specifically to autistic talent. These are often in the software and IT industries, but they are in other businesses too. Some large employers offer affirmative measures for applicants with disability (including autism). They are not subsidized jobs but open employment with the same wages and conditions as non-autistic employees in similar roles. These kinds of jobs often have alternative recruitment methods such as no interviews. For some autistic women, these types of jobs open the door to permanent employment.

## "Disclosure"—talking about your autism at work

Knowing what to say about your autism, how much to say, and when to say it is often termed "disclosure." Knowing whether to tell an employer or prospective employer about your autism is frequently a big issue when you join the workforce or change jobs. There is the potential for stigma and discrimination around autism in the minds of employers. Some employers have very little understanding of autism, which can mean they lack confidence in employing an autistic staff member simply because they don't know what it might entail. They might fear expensive workplace adjustments or the autistic staff member taking lots of sick leave.

Disclosure does not need to be a passive or apologetic thing. It is your story to share. You can tailor the information you disclose to different workplaces, and use it as a positive, proactive part of your application. Try not to see it as a negative or something to feel shame or embarrassment about. It is a good idea to elaborate further than "I am autistic" and also talk about how your autism can be an asset in the workplace. For example, if you are applying for a role in software testing, disclosing your autism could involve you promoting yourself through mentioning your great attention to detail and knowledge of different systems. You can also use your disclosure conversation to detail what reasonable workplace adjustments you might need. You can explain to the employer that you need a particular small, low-cost adjustment for sensory issues, which can head off any concerns the employer has about costly workplace modifications.

There are pros and cons for talking about your autism to employers. Some of the positives include that you can access workplace adjustments and supports if you need them, you don't have to keep a "secret," you can feel more comfortable in yourself, and, if any issues arise at work related to your autism (such as having a meltdown at work), it is likely to be much easier to address if key people know you are autistic. The main negatives surrounding disclosure center around potential discrimination in the recruitment processes by your colleagues and managers, underestimating your abilities, or treating you poorly if they know you are autistic.

There are a few key "points" at which you can decide whether and what to tell your employer about your autism. These are:

- when you apply for the job
- at interview
- when you are offered the job
- as soon as you start work
- some time after you start work.

There are also considerations about what to say and who to say it to.

It can help to consider a "strategy" for disclosure and it is usually best to tailor this to each workplace or job for which you apply. You do not need to adhere strictly to your strategy, but it allows you to think about the considerations and what you plan to say well in advance, which can also help you to address anxiety around disclosure.

### Accessing workplace adjustments

Many autistic employees are great at their job but may require adjustments to the workplace in order to manage and do their job well. Adjustments can be to either the physical environment or attitudes of colleagues and managers.

One of the issues that employers may balk at when employing staff on the autism spectrum is the apparently prohibitive cost of providing reasonable workplace adjustments. Many autistic employees do require adjustments to enable them to do their job. However, in many cases the adjustments required do not involve significant cost or effort. When necessary adjustments are put in place, it can mean the difference between autistic employees being underproductive, stressed, and unhappy to being proficient, productive, and engaged in their job. Employers and managers see employee engagement as the key to productivity, so adjustments that result in this are definitely a plus for employers.

Some adjustments commonly sought by autistic employees include:

- Measures to address sensory overload. This can involve changing lights from LED or fluorescent to incandescent. Removing lighting and putting a lamp in the workstation can help and costs very little.
- Providing a quiet space to work.
- Giving clear instructions for a task the employee finds challenging and writing these down.
- Giving reassurance (e.g. saying 'thank you' and showing appreciation for work).
- Providing a mentor or buddy.
- Having an autistic speaker visit the workplace and talk about their experiences. This can assist managers and colleagues to understand autism better.

It can be hard to ask for workplace adjustments, but it is actually in the employer's interest for autistic employees to be able to access measures that enable them to do their job better. In some countries there are government services to support employees with disability to access reasonable adjustments in the workplace.[1]

Autistic women can be valued and productive employees and with the right supports at work, can find their work fulfilling and rewarding. I know I have.

---

1   For example, in Australia there is the Job Access website which has information and guidance on workplace adjustments for employees and managers (www.jobaccess.gov.au).

# Dr. Michelle Garnett on employment

Jeanette is one of the leading stars in understanding what works in employment when you are on the autism spectrum. The chapter is a succinctly stated, clear, positive, and helpful overview. It is factual, matches the research evidence, and has extra credibility because of Jeanette's extraordinary journey from serious mental illness and homelessness to not only being successfully full-time employed within the Australian Public Service, but also being such an excellent contributor, sharing her positive attitude and expertise on autism via public speaking engagements and her successful radio show. Jeanette, like all contributors to this book, is truly an inspiration.

### Strengths and qualities

There is a growing awareness around the world about the qualities, values, and abilities of the person on the autism spectrum, where more and more there is a recognition of the positive attributes in autism leading to an increased bottom line for the company. The value of an autistic person is due not only to their hard work, but also to the skill and knowledge they have acquired about a potential intense interest to practice and study. In addition, an autistic person generally brings values that lead to success. They tend to have a very strong work ethic; they come to work to work, not to socialize. They are often extremely honest, hard-working, committed, and persistent. All of these qualities are highly valued by employers.

Each of your qualities can represent a double-edged sword, and some balance is needed. I suggest making a list of all your strengths, talents, qualities, and values. Next write down how each of these would contribute to your success at work. Write down how each may have a disadvantage. Lastly, write down some strategies and ideas for mitigating the disadvantages.

Success in employing an autistic person is not only fiscal. CEOs have described that the process of enculturation of a company to neurodiversity has had a positive effect on all employees in that company, leading to higher value being placed on acceptance, looking out for other people more, and greater tendency to offer support. With increased understanding and compassion, employee happiness increases across the company. Happy employees are more productive.

## Challenges to acquiring a job

The transition from high school to college or work for people on the autism spectrum is now known to be one of the major challenges of their life, and, as a result, has become the focus of much research and clinical work around the world currently.

One of the major problems in getting work for the woman on the spectrum is other people and ignorance about how autism presents in some. Other people misinterpret her non-verbal communication as being disinterest or somewhat unusual at the job interview, so she may not be successful in gaining the position even if she had the confidence in the first place to apply.

While the problem can be caused by other people, the effects on the girl become her problem. Being ill-treated at school very often leads to significant problems with social anxiety, generalized anxiety disorder, and depressive episodes, among other psychological conditions. Experiencing rejection or needing to mask oneself on a daily basis leads to a negative self-identity and a low sense of self-agency (i.e. a sense that you can be the master of change in your own life).

## Overcoming challenges to getting work

For a girl facing the end of high school, staring at the void in the future, I can recommend the following strategies:

- Accept help from people who have your welfare in mind. Doing it alone may seem safer, but in actual fact it is more dangerous. People have hurt you in the past but that does not mean that everybody in the world will hurt you in the future. There may be one person in the list of people you know and have known who you can confide in and ask for support. The list may include your parents, past teachers, other members of extended family, old friends, counselors, psychologists, or your GP.

- Commence the journey of discovering who you are. You are not defined by other people's thoughts about who you are, or by mood states such as depression and anxiety. Become very aware of your own strengths, personality characteristics, values, and abilities. Find a good counselor or psychologist to assist you to do this. Clues can be found every day in all situations, but especially in what you enjoy and how you find pleasure and satisfaction. As Dumbledore said, "It is our choices...that show what we truly are, far more than our abilities."[2]

- Seek psychological assistance for any depression and anxiety. There are good strategies for dealing with both.

- Find your own tribe. No one is an island; we need support from others. Many women I know have found friendship and strength in blog spots such as Autism Women's Network (AWN), Neurodivergent Rebel, Live Positively Autistic, Musings of an Aspie.

- Start small. You may have a blazing ambition and enormous talent, but it is unreasonable to expect yourself to realize this fully within a short time period. Start with tasks that represent

2    From Rowling, J.K. (1998) *Harry Potter and the Chamber of Secrets*. London: Bloomsbury.

two to three out of ten in terms of anxiety; once these are accomplished, tackle the next ones. For work experience, start with voluntary work if necessary. Do not rate yourself for taking on work that is below your training or not in line with your ambition. Having a "day job" will not only help pay the bills to give you independence, but will give you valuable work experiences that will help inform how to be successful in the work experience of your "dream job."

## A word on disclosure

It is important that Jeanette has listed that there are specific time points within a working life when disclosure may be the best option. Generally, the job application period is not the time to disclose. Many women on the spectrum choose not to disclose. We find that it can instead be useful to use a "spoken social story." This means describing yourself in a succinct sentence to help others understand you, without needing to go into extra detail about your whole profile. For example, to explain difficulties looking at the other person's eyes when talking with someone, one may say: "*I am the sort of person who* needs to look away while you are talking to me to be able to think about what you are saying." To explain a dislike of small talk, one could say: "*I am the sort of person who* loves to talk to other people, but I'm not very good at small talk. I prefer sharing about interesting topics. What are your favorite topics? I like philosophy."

## CHAPTER 11

# Our Sensory Worlds

*Kate Ross, Jen Elcheson, and Barb Cook*

## Sensory seeking, avoiding, and feedback—*Kate Ross*

When I discovered I was aspie at the age of 30, it put my sensory issues into a context that finally made sense; previously, others gave me the impression that I was being "dramatic," when in actuality I was experiencing sensory overload. Conversely, if I stopped when I saw something particularly shiny or colorful that others would otherwise walk past, then I was viewed as "a bit weird." Autistic people can crave and seek sensory input as much as we will reject and avoid it, either outright or by diverting to a different stimulus we can better tolerate. We can exhibit hyper- and hyposensitivity to various stimuli, sometimes going between the two over the same stimulus, depending on the situation. For example, some can be hypersensitive to temperature and touch, significantly reacting to being too hot or cold or to any physical contact, while others can be hyposensitive, sometimes demonstrated by wearing clothing inappropriate for the weather (e.g. shorts and a T-shirt when it's snowing outside) or being unaware of bumping into furniture. Becoming overloaded by sensory input and being unable to process it all can lead to emotional distress and meltdowns, so regulating one's sensory system is essential.

If I'm having a sensitive day at work, feeling quite agitated due to the cacophonous open-plan office, instead of putting in earplugs, I will put on my sound-isolating headphones and listen to music, which creates a "sonic barrier" between me and the noise in the office. So while I'm sensitive to one type of noise, I can tolerate something else in its place because I am in control. Some autistic people (adults and children) need to wear ear defenders most of the time because they are unable to filter out all auditory input as neurotypical people tend to be able to do. At times, if I'm hyper-focused on something (e.g. reading, washing dishes, a crochet project, even walking in the town center getting from one point to another), I can completely zone out and won't notice if someone is talking to me or trying to get my attention—they will have to make themselves quite noticeable if they expect me to notice them!

When it comes to visual stimuli, bright light and glare affect me greatly—I wear sunglasses on completely overcast days, and have taken to wearing subtly tinted glasses which work to minimize eye strain from the blue light of electronic devices. The worst is driving at night-time with LED headlights coming towards me or reflecting in my side mirrors, which hurt my eyes and disrupt my ability to see; I try to avoid driving at night, but sometimes it's not always feasible, so I have been using the subtly tinted glasses, as they are not as dark as typical sunglasses.

This kind of sensitivity can be referred to as scotopic sensitivity syndrome or Meares-Irlen syndrome. On the other side of visual input, there are some visual sensory experiences that I will seek out, particularly anything with bright colors or moving water features—I even find the crackling flames of a bonfire absolutely mesmerizing to watch, as long as it's not too bright. As a child, I loved going to Niagara Falls and watching the water flowing down the river into the waterfall. I could sit quite happily for what felt like ages just watching the water. I also love anything rainbow-colored...and get really weirded out when colors are not in color spectrum order, especially if it is attempting to be rainbow-like!

My sense of smell is quite acute; the difficulty with an overpowering olfactory system is there's no equivalent to earplugs or sunglasses, as holding your nose in public is considered rude! It's easier to manage in one's own environment, by emptying the bin, cleaning regularly, or using candles or odor-neutralizing sprays as needed (only if these don't exacerbate your sensitivities); however, when out in public, the plethora of fragrances and odors can be an assault on one's nose. My simplest and most portable coping strategy is mint chewing gum and lip balm. The gum's strong flavor releases a nice smell too (while freshening your breath!); however, if chewing gum is too strong, wearing lip balm places it naturally and conveniently underneath your nose, acting like an inadvertent filter. If there is a particular fragrance you find pleasing (e.g. citrus, lavender), applying a few drops of essential oil to a small square of fabric which you can take with you would be helpful, especially if the fabric in question is one that you like the feel of for tactile feedback.

When it comes to taste, we all vary widely in what we love and hate. Personally, I like having some spice for flavor where appropriate, but not too much spice for heat. Some on the spectrum experience taste quite strongly, preferring only quite bland foods, or vice versa, preferring strong flavors, spice, and heat. With taste comes texture as well, and again some don't like saucy or juicy foods, preferring dry foods only, or vice versa; the same applies for soft and crunchy foods too. For me, at lunch, I always alternate bites of a sandwich (soft) with a crisp (crunchy), and I don't like having a sandwich without a packet of potato crisps. This will sometimes extend to other meals, but not every meal every time. There are also periods of time where I will only like having certain meals, even if it means alternating between two or three things for a few days!

This is often seen in autistic children (e.g. only wanting sausages and chips day after day), so it's no wonder that this happens with autistic adults as well—we were autistic children at one point! Ever since I was a child, I prefer keeping food separated on a plate; it's a combination of taste, texture, and visual stimuli. When I was a kid and we were having a roast dinner, my dad would mash all his food together on the plate and I could never express why this made me so uncomfortable, so I just made extra sure that nothing on my plate touched.

I could devote a whole chapter to touch and pressure! However, for this overview, it's fair to say that our tolerances vary as much as we do as individuals. I love using a coarse face scrub, as my face doesn't feel clean without it. Also, ever since I was young, I always loved having my hair brushed and my back scratched, as well as firm hugs, especially from my dad and grandpa; I find these experiences very calming, although some would find tight hugs too much to cope with and instead will prefer gentle hugs, if any contact at all. However, certain tickly sensations irritate me, particularly wispy strands of hair flying in my face or scratchy clothing tags; light sensations like this are considered "alerting." We also have certain textures that we like to touch, as well as ones that give us heebie-jeebies—one for me is rusty metal gates!

Proprioception was a term I only came to learn about when I discovered more about autism, especially in relation to how sensory integration affects our daily lives and what sensory stimulation (or stimming) I have been doing since childhood without realizing why. The proprioceptive system is defined as being located in our muscles and joints, providing us with a sense of body awareness and detecting/controlling force and pressure; the proprioceptive system also has an important regulatory role in sensory processing, as proprioceptive input can assist in controlling responses to sensory stimuli (Middletown Centre for Autism, 2017). We seek proprioceptive input through various activities which can be innocuous or self-injurious, such as biting/chewing fingers or non-chewable objects, hitting one's head, or throwing oneself on to the floor, among other things. The Middletown Centre for Autism Sensory Processing Resource recommends a variety of activities to engage the muscles and joints in order to provide proprioceptive feedback, including (but not limited to):

- weight-bearing activities (e.g. crawling, push-ups)
- resistance activities (e.g. pushing/pulling)
- heavy lifting (e.g. carrying books, lifting weights)
- cardiovascular activities (e.g. running, jumping on a trampoline)
- oral activities (e.g. chewing gum, blowing bubbles)
- deep pressure (e.g. tight hugs, weighted blanket/jacket/ lap pad).

I hope this overview has helped you to understand how important our sensory system is, and to think about what your own sensory preferences and aversions are. Awareness of how autistic individuals can be affected by sensory input will enable you to help yourself, a friend, or a family member when they are feeling overloaded and in need of assistance.

## Dyspraxia—*Jen Elcheson*

Many of us on the autism spectrum tend to be clumsy in a variety of ways. I am constantly trying to be aware of my surroundings in relation to where my body is, due to the concern I could be a real danger to myself or others around me. At different times I have struggled to varying degrees with both fine and gross motor movements which still impact my daily life as an adult. Seemingly easy tasks such as food preparation or knowing my left from right are just some of the challenges I face. Dyspraxia, or developmental coordination disorder (DCD), is something that has always been a challenging facet of my life. Even though some motor skills have improved, others remain difficult to grasp.

As a child, I had a very odd presenting gait that often had others rudely remarking on how I walked or ran in a peculiar manner. I found myself getting dizzy easily when on the swings or merry-go-round. I could not throw, kick, hit, catch, or bounce a ball. I was absolutely hopeless and looked ridiculous when trying to follow dance routines in my short-lived tap dance and jazz ballet classes. It seemed that, no matter the activity, I always required that extra help and stood out, which just added to the embarrassment of knowing my body always seemed so out of sync with my brain.

I did not know how to cut with scissors or properly hold a pen or pencil until I was around the age of 14, only realizing the latter after classmates pointed this out. Even though I could not hold a writing apparatus in a conventional way, I still managed to have legible handwriting due to being taught how to print letters by a very talented learning assistance teacher in first grade. I am forever thankful for that woman's help, as someone who always appreciated writing and eventually became a writer. One year in school, I had a teacher who did mostly art projects with the class, which resulted in me melting down and refusing to do said projects because I was so embarrassed by my difficulties. To make matters worse, the teacher just assumed I wasn't trying hard enough, but my brain and hands simply did not work well together. It wasn't that I didn't want to create anything; I honestly couldn't do it at the time.

However, I did learn certain things—for instance, how to tie my shoes (though my bows never look all that nice), ride a bike, skate, and downhill ski. All these activities took extensive practice and care, plus I did not become perfect at them either. In my teens I took martial arts and tennis lessons because I found both fun, even though I still had a difficult time with them. Being able to learn these things to an extent helped improve my coordination in certain ways, but I wasn't "cured."

DCD is something that will be with me for the remainder of my life and will always present challenges for me to tackle. Being autistic, combined with other conditions, does not make life a very easy one at all. Motor planning and executive function will always be a daily challenge and there will be times when I move very slowly as I try and simultaneously process. I still have to be very mindful when moving around places because I will walk into other people or objects (such as tables). Often I have bruises on my body and I honestly have no recall of how I got them. I use public transport as I do not feel comfortable driving.

Lots of things that people do unconsciously and with ease are often difficult for me. The enormous energy I put into getting through my day can literally be quite exhausting. However, over the years I have learned to accept it and try to ask for help and learn ways to work around it. Like anything else in life, sometimes that is the only option.

## Misophonia—*Barb Cook*

**Trigger warning:** This section may cause you to have destructive and raging tendencies. Please ensure no one is present in the room when reading, especially if they have happened to have recently opened a packet of potato chips... Things could get ugly.

Road rage for your ears pretty much sums up how I feel when I hear certain annoying sounds. Annoying is actually quite an understatement when specific sounds flick that switch in your brain that throws you into instant, blindly hot rage.

I discovered my hatred (yes, it is that bad) of certain sounds when I was in my early teens, babysitting a friend's young child. This happy little kid came bounding from the kitchen holding a bag of chips in hand and promptly jumped up on the sofa behind me as I was sitting on the floor. Eagerly opening that packet of potato chips directly behind my head, taking a handful and gleefully stuffing their mouth with them, chomping obliviously away with their mouth open, instantly changed my contented mood into one of a serial killer. This poor little kid could not for the life of them figure out what had happened when I angrily turned around and figuratively burned holes into them. I could have quite nicely asked the kiddie to eat those chips with their mouth shut, but when this feeling strikes you have no control over the response that is so instantly forthcoming. I was, in my mind, thinking of many awful ways I could dispose of the child, bag of chips and all.

It wasn't just chips that sent me into an insane frame of mind; pretty much anyone who ate loudly, slurped, or sucked while they ate; even dogs licking themselves would bring on this rage. I did realize that some sounds would also ignite a vomit reflex reaction, especially the dogs' licking sound. This reaction would also be instant, like the rage, but would also induce another response different from the murderous inclinations. When I heard these sounds, I instantly wanted to run away as far as I could. I could hardly control the feeling that I was going to vomit like a demon over the poor animal before me. Being an animal lover, it certainly has been a challenge to avoid those moments.

So how do we work with these sounds that literally make us mad? With the dogs, I have learned as soon as I hear or see them going for one of those good old cleaning licks (even worse when it is in those nether regions—I can hear you gagging now), I go and give them a pat to distract them for a moment and take them outside if they are an indoor doggie for a short while, or until I can see they have settled. If you're not able to take them outside, maybe take them into another room or take yourself away to another room if you can.

Now back to people. Ideally, we would like to do the same with the humans. Pop them outside until they have finished chomping away. Unfortunately, this is frowned upon. Being prepared for when you know people are going to be eating is one of the best ways to stave off those psychopathic inclinations (insert *American Psycho* music). Having some of those discrete little ear buds can really dampen down the intensity of the mastication. If you are caught in a situation where this is not possible and you can't get away from the situation either, I have found striking up an in-depth conversation actually distracts my brain from the irritating sounds.

There are many other sounds that can send us into these rages, but one thing that is common is that misophonia can be quite debilitating and there is still very little research on this condition. Studies have shown that these sounds trigger in the brain, not in our ears as we would think, initiating our fight-or-flight response (Kumar *et al.*, 2017). When you look at how I feel about eating noises, compared with hearing licking sounds, it really does make sense that this is coming from a neurological reaction: one I feel like beating everyone up, the other I want to run away far as possible.

As with our other sensitivities, we need to find what will work best for us to lessen the impact and to reduce the stress and anxiety these situations can cause, including the anxious lead-up to a situation that we may not be able to avoid. If you know the person well, you may be able to ask them to stop what they are doing or change the way they are doing it, but usually this is not the case and at times can cause unintended offense. Plan your situations as best you can and always carry with you ear buds to give you at least some relief. As with many of our sensitivities, preparation is extremely important to reduce both the possibility of being irritated and the unintended mental flashes of torturing our unaware victim before us...

## Dr. Michelle Garnett on sensory worlds

Temple Grandin is known for saying that she would not change her autism in any way or any form, except to change her sensory processing system. This statement comes as a surprise to neurotypicals who immediately assume that someone on the autism spectrum would prefer to have innately intact social communication neural systems. However, Kate and Barb know differently, as they describe. A differently functioning sensory system is now known to be part and parcel of having ASD, to the extent that it is in the diagnostic criteria (American Psychiatric Association, 2013). Most people on the spectrum experience sensory overload, but there can be hyposensitivity, as Kate describes, where certain sensory experiences are under-registered.

While sensory information is initially detected by our sensory organs, it is actually processed by areas within the frontal lobes. The way the brain processes the sensory information determines our experience of that sensory information. Research to date has shown that sensory processing differences in the brain cannot be eliminated or cured, but it is possible to develop coping strategies over time that assist in eliminating the distress associated with sensory processing difference. At my clinic we find that it is important to use a combination of environmental accommodations and psychological strategies, as both Kate and Barb describe.

### Assessment
Knowing exactly which senses are processing the information differently, and in what ways, is important knowledge to inform

both accommodations and strategies. A clinical psychologist or occupational therapist can provide this assessment; alternatively, you can utilize resources available in the community—for example, the wonderful book, *Sensory Perceptual Issues in Autism and Asperger Syndrome* by Olga Bogdashina (2016).

**Being sensory-ready**
Our sensory system works best when our brain is well rested, well nourished, and oxygenated. When we are stressed, any sensory processing issues will be aggravated. Having a daily routine that supports self-care will go a long way in supporting you to manage your sensory challenges. There are also particular activities you can engage in to assist your body in being ready for the sensory challenges of the day. These are individual to the person, and are usually prescribed by an occupational therapist who understands sensory processing issues. These preparations may include bouncing on a trampoline, using a weighted blanket, starting the day with physical exercise, using body brushing, or listening to certain types of music.

**Environmental accommodations**
It can be very helpful to develop a sensory toolkit to carry around when you are out and about in the world. The toolkit would be customized by you for you, based on your sensory processing system. For example:

- auditory aversion: sound-canceling headphones or earplugs
- olfactory aversion: a favorite essential oil (e.g. lavender)
- tactile aversion: sections of fabric with a corrective tactile experience (e.g. velvet)
- visual aversion: sunglasses, Irlen lenses, or a visor
- taste aversion: peppermints.

## Psychological strategies

Increasing a positive mood and decreasing stress can greatly assist with managing the difficulty of overwhelm in the sensory world. I once met a woman who loved windsocks. She carried photographs of her favorite windsocks in her wallet to assist her to get through the difficulty of the smell of sweaty bodies on the trains in summer, as well as other aversive experiences. In the clinic we have found that treatments for the management of chronic pain, including CBT, mindfulness techniques, and hypnosis, have all been useful in managing the stress of sensory processing differences.

## Dyspraxia

Dyspraxia commonly co-occurs with ASD. Dyspraxia is a lifelong condition that affects a person's capacity to plan and coordinate movement. As Jen describes, it affects fine and gross motor skills and leads to motor clumsiness. However, it can also affect speech and socializing. It can take extra time for a person to plan what to say, and to make the mouth movements needed to express those thoughts. There can be problems with pitch, volume, and tone of voice. They can have difficulty remembering a sequence of instructions, and can take extra time to learn adaptive skills such as cooking and driving. A person can be very aware of their difficulties, and feel social anxiety as a result.

It can be very helpful to know if you have dyspraxia. Having a neurological explanation can remove character assassinations such as thinking of oneself as being slow or lazy. Understanding the neurology behind dyspraxia can lead to greater self-compassion and self-care. This caring approach leads to acceptance of adjustments, such as using typing instead of handwriting, allowing yourself more time, using lists and visual schedules to assist with planning, and taking up sports that are best suited to your body and brain (e.g. swimming, yoga, martial arts, walking, running).

### Misophonia

Misophonia, as Barb describes, is an incredibly stressful condition that typically starts around age 10–13 years and is more common in girls. Other names for misophonia are selective sound sensitivity syndrome and hyperacusis. The reaction is usually to sound, sometimes to certain repetitive movements, and can range from mild to severe. The condition is not fully understood yet, but it is believed to be partly neurological and partly psychological (i.e. exacerbated by tiredness, hunger, anxiety, and stress). It is best managed with a healthy lifestyle and self-care, as well as specific strategies when the triggers occur, which usually include moving away, tuning into a different noise, using distraction, etc. Sometimes antidepressants are prescribed.

## CHAPTER 12

# Communication

*Becca Lory*

One of my favorite ways to tackle any subject is to begin with a dictionary. As a hyperlexic, hyperverbal spectrumite, words are my playground. I love getting to know words and their meanings with autistic intensity. It is only natural that when I am looking to understand a topic or idea, the place to begin is the dictionary.

## Pardon me: Communication stripped down

The handy-dandy online version of the Merriam-Webster Dictionary states that communication is "a process by which information is exchanged between individuals through a common system of symbols, signs, or behavior; the function of pheromones in insect communication; also: exchange of information" (Merriam-Webster, 2017). Insect pheromones aside, this definition looks pretty solid. I was actually fairly surprised to see the word "behavior" included as I often wonder why autistic behavior isn't seen as a form of communication. I think it communicates a lot of information.

But I digress. The definition of communication gives us a great starting point. Of particular interest is the requirement that "information is exchanged" using a "common system." Right away, a red flag goes up for me. Common system? What common system? Who picks this common system? Where do I get one? Immediately, I have questions. This is cause for concern, especially for us spectrumites. We often miss out on group decisions because we don't understand the hidden curriculum agenda. Moreover, if the decision is about commonality, the spectrum is the last place you're going to find it. If there is a common system, it's most definitely not an autistic communication system. Which raises the main issue: if we aren't using the same system, can we communicate? The answer is no. Without a common system, there can be no exchange of information. If we cannot exchange information, we are not communicating. Neurotypical translator, anyone?

## Don't call me, I'll call you: The shapes and sizes of communication

Communication can be broken down into three main categories: verbal communication, non-verbal communication, and written communication. The use of words and sounds to express yourself is referred to as verbal communication. By contrast, non-verbal communication utilizes gestures, facial expressions, and body language as the means for information exchange. Lastly, written communication is any type of interaction using the written word, including signs and symbols. Three vastly different modes to employ when looking to express your needs, wants, and criticisms. How to choose?

For many of us, making that decision is fairly easy. As a words person, I am an author and speaker by nature. For comfort, skill level, and speed, I usually choose some good old-fashioned verbal communication. My mom used to say I could win any argument by simply out-talking the other person. But when I am really looking to communicate, especially regarding my needs and feelings, I much prefer writing. It allows me to take the time to process what I want to say, think of the correct words, and put them all in the right order. Writing is permanent. The spoken word just floats away.

This is not necessarily true for all spectrumites, however. Many of us draw, use sign language, text to talk, and use any number of other assistive communication tools. Yet, somehow, no matter what we are using as a tool to assist in communication, when we communicate with each other, it is always noticeably easier. Why? What is it about spectrumites that allows us to communicate with relative ease with each other but not so easily with those of standard neurology?

I'd say it comes down to two major things: our communication style and the language we use. Because we are most often direct, honest, and do not waste words, our style of communication challenges the societal norms of politeness. With each other, it is a relief that information is being exchanged without flowery words or gray areas. No implied statements. No wasted energy. With those of non-autistic neurology, there is small talk and compliments, hugs and handshakes, all of which still baffles my brain. We cut to the chase. That is not the common system.

Additionally, we use terms and descriptors that are unfamiliar to neurotypicals—words like "stim," "meltdown," "fidget," "sensory overload," and the list goes on. Our literal language is different from most. If you use those words in mixed company, they always require explanation and justification. With each other, that is a layer we do not have to peel away.

Thankfully, especially with the technology in our lives, many people are leaning away from strictly spoken communication and relying much more on non-verbal communication and written communication. In today's world, we often opt to text and email over calling or meeting. Emoticons and group texts have replaced quick chats and dinner meetings. It's not a good or a bad thing; it's just a different thing. Slowly, our system of communication has shifted its priorities, changed methodologies, and morphed into a text-and-symbols world. This shift has been a breath of fresh air for communication on the spectrum.

The fact that it is now socially acceptable to text or email rather than calling has dramatically changed life on the autism spectrum. It evens the playing field. It allows us to contribute. It gives us choices, and choice gives you courage. It's no wonder our changing world is suddenly flooded with such strong advocates. We now have the means with which we can effectively communicate using our strengths, not our challenges.

## "You look tired, angry, sad, bored": Communication challenges on the spectrum

If I had a book for every time somebody told me I looked tired, angry, sad, or bored, my library would be where *Good Reads* looks for its next list. I can be fully engaged in a conversation, listening intently, and inevitably someone will interrupt to ask if I am OK. My standard reply is: "Yes. You can't tell from my face?" Seriously, communication is a lot of work for me. It's not all about the words. The words are secondary to remembering eye contact, monitoring all body language, and maintaining appropriate facial expressions. That's a lot to do on top of remembering your train of thought, choosing the right words, and conveying the correct tone.

As an autistic and an introvert, nothing about any of this

sounds appealing. Not the social. Not the eye contact. Not the body language, nor the facial expressions. Unfortunately, the modern human is a social animal which does not have much success outside of our interdependent, industrialized world. As a result, we end up having to do a lot of communicating and a fair amount of socializing. In fact, social communication is essential unless you manage somehow to live simultaneously all alone and off the grid. Then you only have to communicate with yourself. Easier? Not necessarily. But let's not jump ahead.

The communication challenges of the spectrum don't end there. Have you ever looked up how to be an effective communicator? Granted, the information differs depending on whether you read *Business Week* or *Buzzfeed* but, regardless, there are some common themes. An emphasis on body language, articulation, tone of voice, emotional intelligence, and small talk runs through most of the articles. Some of our favorites, right? And when you look up "barriers to communication," it doesn't get much better. Among the barriers are an overuse of technical language, giving the impression that you aren't listening, providing unsolicited solutions, opinions, and advice, to name a few.

Feeling as if you have a giant arrow pointing at your head blinking "Communication Barrier"? You are not alone. Frankly, there are some social communication skills that are just harder for autistics because they do not come naturally to us. Those skills take extra energy and, most of the time, for any number of reasons, it's energy we don't have to spare. As a result, communication suffers and we isolate. Not exactly a successful endeavor. The good news is that with this shift toward non-verbal and written communication, courtesy of technology, the social rules are changing. The more we move to email and text, the less often affect, tone, body language, and eye contact will matter. Take advantage, spectrumites; the communication field is being leveled.

## Honest to the point of blunt: Attributes of spectrum communication

Over the years I have had my fair share of communication glitches. Some were simple miscommunications and others became meltdowns and burnt bridges. Many of those glitches came from some very particular issues common to spectrum communication that I now refer to as the "usual suspects." These suspects are a group of attributes, particular to spectrum communication, that are the cause of most of our miscommunications, big and small. From our directness to our mutism, the usual suspects just hang around waiting to sabotage every great conversation.

We all have the very basic human distinction of being an introvert, extrovert, or the ever-elusive ambivert. Contrary to popular belief, this distinction has little to do with how we socialize and communicate. Rather, it has everything to do with how we recharge. If you are exhausted from a long day out in the world, how do you choose to spend your evening? Alone, with others, or either? Your answer to that question is the very thing about you that lets you know which category you fit in. It is simply a preference for energy expenditure.

So, is introversion particular to the spectrum? No. Is it common on the spectrum? Yes. In general, socializing is challenging for spectrumites, as is communication. It uses up a lot of energy. Many of us find that when we are depleted we need low-sensory, limited social time, and plenty of freedom to be ourselves. The very nature of those needs means time alone. However, spectrumites come in all flavors. We absolutely have our extroverts and our ambiverts. As with everything spectrum, we are all different.

Another one of my favorite instigators of spectrum communication blunders is our unrestrained directness. Spectrumites have an uncanny ability to tell it EXACTLY like it is, period. We aren't big on flowery language and almost always lack an edit button. That can get you in a ton of social hot water, trust me. I have left many a job after an episode of direct communication. However, I wouldn't trade it if you paid me. Maybe because I consider it a strength most of the time. One of the perks of being direct is that other people tend to respond in kind. Most of the time, directness begets directness. I prefer direct communication. It is clear. It does its job. It doesn't waste time. When vague politeness enters a conversation, I am lost. Floating in the hidden curriculum, being dragged under into the gray abyss of sugar-coated language, over and over. Give me directness over that mess anytime.

Directness, of course, doesn't come alone. It goes hand in hand with another fun one: honesty. We spectrumites love honesty. Again, we tell it EXACTLY like it is. Moreover, we would like it very much if it were returned. Spectrumites are known for our honest nature as we do not understand the function of lying. As such, we rarely do it and we rarely recognize it. In fact, our honest nature can be the very thing that makes us susceptible to communication backfires.

Here is a tiny example. Have you ever answered a rhetorical question? Me too! In fact, I answer them all the time. I often say, "Don't ask any question in front of me, because you will get an answer." The idea of asking a question but not wanting an answer is absurd to me. It seems like a giant waste of time to my spectrum brain. Quite simply, if you don't want an answer, don't ask a question...but that leads me to our next suspect: literalism.

Spectrumites are notorious for taking things literally. We almost always take things at face value. I have become more practiced at not falling victim to these blunders through the years. Though, to this day, I have fallen for every "made ya look" joke ever made at my expense. Joking aside, our struggles with "theory of mind" and literal thinking color our communication skill set. Filtering for sarcasm, irony, metaphors, and figures of speech is another layer added to our communication struggles. It colors how we receive communication, how we process it, and how we return it. Oh, to think of all the jokes that have fallen flat on my spectrum ear, not to mention the attempts of mine that have missed their targets—so many of them the result of my literal mind.

The next of our suspects falls more in the category of processing, but it also greatly affects communication. There is a little thing that happens for spectrumites when we hear a bit of information. It comes into our ears as words but automatically gets translated into the language of our brains—pictures. That translation takes time. We then have to put our picture response together and translate in back out into words to communicate it to others. It is very much like being bilingual. It is time-consuming and exhausting. Over time, I feel we get faster at it, even though the number of pictures continues to increase every day. Nonetheless, there is what I call a small lag in our conversations. It represents not only that translation time but all the other processes our different brains go through to become effective neurotypical translators. That lag, however small, can be long enough to be misinterpreted as rudeness, boredom, and not listening. It is the quiet communication killer.

I have saved the most complicated suspect for last. Maybe because it plagues me when I am most vulnerable and exhausted. Maybe because it is still the greatest mystery to me. Mutism—or, more accurately, selective mutism—is a common symptom of anxiety and overwhelm. And trust me, nothing halts communication faster than a good old episode of mutism. I'm not sure where the words go exactly. It usual feels like huge, foggy fatigue. On heavy social or sensory days it happens the most. First, I struggle to find the words and then I can no longer form them. It is incredibly frustrating and can often exacerbate an already messy situation. It is hard for others to understand that all of a sudden words are not an option. I'm sure many of you have experienced your own version of mutism. I wonder if it differs from mine? I have only just begun to explore this topic for myself and have only gotten as far as to understand the "when" of it. I have yet to understand the "why."

## Talk like a man, look like a lady: Women and communication

The added bonus of being a woman and a spectrumite usually makes communication even more difficult. In general, the female gender is known to rely more heavily on forms of non-verbal communication, such as nodding, eye contact, and facial expressions. Apparently, there is also a preference for communicating sitting down or standing around with others, particularly face-to-face. Well, not this female. My spectrumness has often been the issue in many of my social experiences with neurotypical women. People comment on my lack of emotion, my directness, my strong opinions, and, apparently, my desire to be moving while I talk. All of these things seem to come together in social communication situations somehow to negate my femaleness.

Bossy, stubborn, manipulative, and cold are only a few of the number of negative attributes I hear simply because of my communication style. Spectrum women hear about our "male brains" all the time, and I have had enough. Being direct does not make you masculine. Having an opinion doesn't make you less ladylike, and walking while talking doesn't remove my caring female nature. A distinctive style of communication does not make us less feminine. Spectrum women are strong, direct, assertive, and clear in our ideas. We do not have to be soft. We do not have to wear heels and lipstick. We do not have to sit in intimate, face-to-face, gentle conversations to maintain our femininity. I may talk like a man, but I do so with the pride, courage, and strength that only a spectrumite can possess.

## All by myself: The internal communication system

Since receiving my autism diagnosis, I have been on a journey of self-discovery. I had to learn all about myself, all over again, through the lens of autism. Through regular therapy, I revisited my painful childhood memories, my struggles in work and school, my never-ending poor choices in relationships, and even my rifts with family members. Many times, I would remember with great sadness how hard and long every day had seemed. I was heartbroken for my past self, living so blindly vulnerable in such a bright, loud world.

Sometimes the memories would set me back, sometimes they pushed me further. But no matter the memory, one thing was becoming clear: I had spent the greater part of my life ignoring my own voice and replacing it with the collective voice of others. I had stopped listening to me. I didn't trust myself. So I began to tackle my own inner workings. When exactly had I stopped listening to my own needs? Had I always ignored my body signals so blatantly? How exactly did my inner mantra become "No, don't say that"? It was all very upsetting and I knew it had to change.

I began a path to mindfulness. Mindfulness is usually described as the ability to be fully present, meaning you are truly aware and attentive to where you are and what you are doing. The goal is that you are more effectively dealing with the mistakes of the past and the worries of the future by being entirely consumed with the present. This includes all aspects of your physical, emotional, and mental sensations. This was something I could get behind. But for some reason I was having trouble. Yoga and meditation were encouraged as supplemental exercises, but I simply could not quiet my brain enough.

What was I getting stuck on? It took me a bit to decipher it all as I struggled with many of my internal communications system until I finally realized that those struggles were exactly my problem. No matter how hard I tried to be present, the conversations in my head were only getting louder. It almost sounded like a busy subway platform. Lots of thoughts at all different volumes, at all various times. I needed a conductor or something. Ding, ding, ding! That is exactly what I needed. My brain and body were trying to communicate, but there was no system. I needed to get control of my thoughts, but that meant first I had to listen.

Listening to yourself should not be an issue. That is, of course, unless you can't hear anything. Many of us on the spectrum struggle with our little-known eighth sensory system, interoception. Interoception is most commonly known as the sense that is responsible for detecting your internal regulation responses. Kelly Mahler, in her book *Interoception: The Eighth Sensory System*, describes interoception as a system that "helps us feel many important sensations, such as pain, body temperature, itch, sexual arousal, hunger, thirst, heart rate, breathing rates, muscle tension, pleasant touch, sleepiness and when we need to use the bathroom" (Mahler, 2015, p.1).

This was a revelation to me. For years, I would come home from a long day at work or school only to realize that I hadn't used the bathroom all day or I had forgotten to eat. When asked why, my usual response was that I had forgotten. How could I forget to do such essential activities? Quite simple—my body and brain are poor communicators. I don't get those hunger pangs. On my best days, I hear the audible grumble as a warning that it's time to eat. On my worst days, I don't remember to eat until my blood sugar is so low that I have the dropsies, or I have become so impatient and cranky that I am on the verge of a meltdown. It's not very much fun at all. My interoception meter is broken.

Fortunately, you can improve your interoceptive skills. I began to work on my internal communication system. The more mindful I became, the more I listened to myself in the present, the better my interoception got, and slowly the volume in my brain began to quiet. I began with scheduling a self-care routine, adding in my meals and bathroom breaks. I created sleep hygiene routines and modified my diet. Eventually, all these once-challenging activities became routine, and then became habit. I had cleared a path for solid internal regulation, created an information exchange system, and began to communicate clearly with myself for the very first time. It was life-changing.

I cannot emphasize enough the importance of communicating well with yourself. A good internal communication system allows you to see all the choices that are available to you, with clarity and insight. Over time, identifying emotions gets easier, hearing your body signals becomes more natural, and regulating your response to the overwhelming nature of the world feels a little more under your control. For those of us on the autism spectrum, feeling a little bit more in control of our own lives is almost as welcome a relief as receiving our diagnosis.

## Dr. Michelle Garnett on communication

Becca provides many valuable insights about internal and external communication for women on the spectrum, and I love that she has included each type of communication in her discussion. Social communication difficulty is at the core of the diagnostic definition of autism spectrum disorder, including deficits in social emotional reciprocity, non-verbal communicative behaviors, and persistent difficulties in developing and maintaining social relationships.

However, social communication takes two, and one can argue that the reason social communication problems exist for a person on the spectrum is that the person on the spectrum is in the minority. The majority of people in our community use a different social communication system that presumes an innate capacity to understand when and what to say, emotional meanings in the eyes, faces, and bodies, how to use eye contact and body language, and how to understand social relationships. Not being born with this innate social communication capacity means that one can easily be misunderstood as being rude, strange, awkward, or very fond of oneself (i.e. too self-absorbed to bother answering). It is still the case in our society that judgment and punishment for social mistakes are severe, including character judgments as just described, but also rejection and cruel bullying.

I have met too many autistic adolescent girls who have chosen the solitary confinement and boredom of their bedroom rather than face being with people again and risk the cruel consequences of their social communication differences.

In my clinical experience I have found spectrum girls and women have the smartest coping mechanisms for their social communication difficulties. These mechanisms include using observation, research, and imitation to be able to emulate neurotypical social communication. A helpful analogy is learning a new language. If one moves to Japan where most people speak Japanese, but one insists on speaking English, there are going to be communication problems. To navigate a largely neurotypical community, it makes sense to learn the communication system of that community. It is effortful to do so. Girls and women become exhausted by the intellectual effort, not only of learning the system, but the need to use it on a daily basis.

Once a girl or woman discovers that she is on the autism spectrum, she can experience a strong grief reaction. She grieves for the person she could have been if she had not needed to mask her whole life. She may grieve that she does not have a social communication system that matches most people within the community in which she was born. Part of this grief reaction can include denial, anger, deal-making, and extreme sadness and depression. It is important that she resolves this very natural grief reaction to be able to accept her own communication style, and make an informed choice about how she will be in the world.

Rather than using masking and imitation, she may choose to be strongly her own person, to communicate directly and honestly, with no small talk and many neologisms, to speak about her own topics with passion, and to decide somehow to just bear any negative comments about her facial expressions, or lack thereof. She may choose largely internet and online friends as opposed to face-to-face friendship. The face-to-face friends that she chooses may be of her own neuro-tribe, where the same communication system is used and she does not have to mask.

In my clinical work with girls and women on the spectrum, we discuss these options. I have found that knowledge empowers people. Once people are aware of the differences between their own social communication system and others' and they realize that they have a choice, this social anxiety and fear of making a mistake often diminishes. I have worked with girls and women who have chosen the extreme of each option, as well as girls and women who have chosen a hybrid model. There is no right or wrong, but it is important that the person makes a choice, and feels that their own choice is congruent with who they are as a person.

Making a choice about masking social communication difference, being one's own person, or using both styles depending on the situation, does not take away the problem, but it does provide direction, a sense of empowerment, and, most importantly, self-acceptance.

**A word on selective mutism**

As Becca describes, one of the all-too-common experiences of girls and women on the spectrum is selective and elective mutism. Elective mutism is understood to be voluntary, where the girl chooses not to speak in certain situations—for example, at school with strangers. Selective mutism by contrast occurs out of the blue, and is involuntary, sabotaging the girl's capacity to communicate. Selective mutism occurs when the brain is overwhelmed with anxiety. The areas in the brain responsible for language literally shut down during the overwhelming anxiety, and speech is unavailable. The best intervention for elective or selective mutism is a therapy that reduces anxiety, such as CBT.

**The spoken Social Story™**

A powerful intervention for any social communication difficulty can be using a spoken Social Story™. Carol Gray invented Social Stories™ to both give positive feedback to people on the autism spectrum for their successes, and to teach them the hidden curriculum within social settings. The purpose of the spoken Social Story™ in this context is to provide the social communication partner the missing information they need to understand autistic communication. Some examples include:

- "I am the sort of person who needs to look away when you are speaking to me, so that I can truly concentrate on what you are saying."
- "I am the sort of person who does not do small talk, but I am very interested in what you think about things."
- "I am the sort of person who can take time to process social and emotional information."

- "I am a visual thinker. Sometimes it takes me time to convert the pictures in my brain to words."
- "I'm the sort of person who says what I think, sometimes forgetting to edit what I say."

## Internal communication

Becca eloquently describes a very common additional hidden difficulty for women on the autism spectrum—the difficulty in detecting your internal regulation responses, or interoception. I completely endorse Becca's encouragement to increase your capacity to sense your interoceptive cues. At first, like learning anything new, it is difficult. One is literally laying down new neural pathways, making new connections so that one's consciousness is available to hear what the body has to say. At the clinic we use the metaphor of a torch as an awareness tool. I encourage you to practice "shining the light" on messages of your body, including hunger, breathing, thirst, tiredness, muscle tension, relaxation, the early signs of anxiety, and so on. Initially, some of the messages of your body may be very loud, and others non-existent. I recommend that you continue to listen; they constantly change and all are important. A number of tools exist to help with this. Tony Attwood and I have recorded two awareness scripts, each only a few minutes long. These are on our respective webpages. Using these daily will be of enormous assistance. I can also recommend using body sensing; please see the Recommended Resources section at the back of the book.

## CHAPTER 13

# Emotional Regulation

*Renata Jurkévythz*

## Meltdowns and shutdowns

Identifying, filtering, and regulating emotions are a big challenge for autistics and a cause of frustration and misunderstanding between us and our non-autistic peers. When we fail to deal with our emotions, and we do so very often, we short-circuit. This malfunctioning comes in two forms—meltdowns and shutdowns—and even though they present differently, they have the same source. All our repressed or not properly identified emotions start gathering, slowly or quickly, depending on their intensity, until they become something big enough to get acknowledged.

Eventually, this gigantic emotional mass just runs over you, like a truck you fail to see coming down the road. By then the collision is unavoidable and all you can do is hope you will survive. This emotional build-up comes from little frustrations here and there—sensory disturbances, communication fails, and empathetic feelings—until your limit is crossed and the explosion or implosion occurs. Sometimes the trigger is very clear; other times you have to think hard and relive the whole day in your mind so you can identify what it was.

Meltdowns are the explosions, while shutdowns feel like imploding. Meltdowns happen when emotions take your body hostage and you simply lose control of it. The emotions can't be contained anymore in the space available in your body and burst out in a volcanic explosion, until they are all acknowledged and freed. When they come, it feels like all is over. It is a feeling of absolute desperation, of imminent death, and it is so scary. The emotions violate your body and mind in the most violent way, and you are unable to think or feel anything other than hate, hopelessness, and sadness. This triggers your survival instincts and you feel violent towards others and/or yourself as an automatic response to the invisible violence you are suffering. It is hell, it hurts, it terrifies you, but no one can see any of it.

For non-autistics, it is very hard to grasp, to imagine that such a horrible thing is going on inside that person. To them it looks just like a tantrum, because for someone who has the ability to identify and control their emotions, such a reaction could only be staged. Very differently from a meltdown, tantrums are a way to manipulate others to get what you want. They are usually seen in kids because they are going through a psychological phase of defiance and testing limits. They do so to establish the reach of their power and desires. An adult who does this may have been a kid who didn't have good established limits and now demands their wishes get fulfilled by coercive means. As you can see, it has absolutely nothing to do with meltdowns. A meltdown presents itself as a disease, much like a seizure. It creeps in suddenly and painfully, immobilizing the person, making it impossible for them to react. They just have to wait until it goes away.

Unlike meltdowns, shutdowns are invisible to outsiders. They happen just beneath the surface, and represent absence, not overflow. Instead of letting the emotions take over, your body shuts them all off before they can damage you. Just like a blackout would happen in your house when one outlet short-circuits, your whole emotional self stops functioning to prevent a greater threat. If feels like being dead inside. Suddenly, you stop feeling, caring, wanting, reacting. It is a big empty desert and you just feel so tired. Not only your emotions, but your overall energy is cut off. The whole world outside you looks like a movie you are watching on TV. You are not there, because you don't feel it. It is like being underwater. You can't move properly, everything around you looks distorted, and you can't hear what others are saying. You know that if you stay there long enough you are going to drown. A terrible anguish consumes you, and you feel dead even though you know you are alive. It is also terrifying but for different reasons. And once more, you have to wait until it goes away.

To outsiders you would simply look apathetic. People might think you are just not interested in them and are being rude. Some friendships might be broken or lost if others are not aware of your situation. I've seen it happen, many times. People might also think you are depressed, which is not necessarily true. I might be depressed before a shutdown happens, but I usually don't get depressed while it is happening.

Because, as I said, it feels like the absence of everything. So I don't feel sad, simply because I don't feel. It is a state of nothingness. Again, it is very difficult for people with functioning emotional regulation to understand this, because for every situation they have an emotion. They might get very angry, or very sad. They scream, cry, argue, and get emotions out of their systems in a more concise way. Unfortunately, we don't have such a balanced relationship with our emotions.

Another very important point to discuss is the aftermath. Unlike regular emotional outbursts that other people have, with meltdowns and shutdowns it is not over when they are gone. When they go, now comes the desolation and shame. The same way all the land would be destroyed after an explosion, and a building would crumble after it imploded, we get out of our internal fight in pieces. We emerge emptied of all our energy and feeling terribly sorry for whatever we have done, or, in the case of a shutdown, what we haven't done. It is a deep feeling of worthlessness and guilt.

## Regulation

We need to prevent these reactions happening as much as possible, and establish strategies to survive them when they come. About prevention, I consider two things key: recognize your triggers and indulge in your interests as much as possible. Triggers can be sensory sensibilities, excessive social exposure, or contact with specific people or specific situations. You need to learn to recognize what triggers you and organize your exposure to them.

By organizing, I mean avoid what is possible and don't let the rest happen all together or too close to each other. High temperatures are a big trigger for me, so I try to avoid social events in the open when it's summer, for example. Then there are your interests. They are vital for your survival, so don't let people bring you down because you are too involved with your interests. They are an emotional cleaner. The pleasure and safety you feel from engaging in them will erase part of your accumulated triggers and will naturally help you regulate. Try to fit them in your schedule or connect them with your daily routines whenever possible.

Even doing all I have said, an occasional crisis will happen because life is unpredictable. In the case of a meltdown, support from others is essential. Just like when a person is having a seizure, the approach should be to make sure they are safe and talk to them in a calm, reassuring voice, saying you understand why they are feeling that way and that you know it hurts and you are there to help.

Acknowledge their pain, show compassion. Some of us like to be hugged and some can't stand to be touched, so this is something to consider. Even though it is extremely hard, try to keep your calm as much as possible. Try to avert the person's attention to something else they would like, to take them away from their emotional chain reaction. When it is over, never shame them. When it's over, we have such a suffocating amount of shame coming from our own system that adding any more could just be a trigger for a new crisis. With shutdowns, the person needs isolation and rest. You can keep the person company, as long as you do not require any interaction on their part. Sometimes people we love are able to energize us just with their presence, so in this case it would help.

After both types of dysregulation are over, healing is vital. It comes in the form of love, support, and again a good deal of contact with your intense interests. They are battery chargers and can perform miracles. When I'm over a crisis, I like to hug and kiss my husband and kids to the point of being obnoxious. I love to rest beside them and engage in my interest while they are doing their thing. It warms my heart and replenishes my energies, until I'm able to feel whole again.

Emotional regulation is a big issue for autistics and also a big source of misunderstanding in our relationships with others. Our lack of it makes our reactions completely different, and because of that we usually are misinterpreted, but love and an opened mind can circumvent all of that.

## Empathy

Of all the autism stereotypes, lack of empathy must be the one that triggers me the most. It is such a poor and simplistic conclusion that I can hardly believe it came from and was perpetrated by people that considered themselves specialists in autism. There are many ways autistic people deal with their empathy and I'll discuss it a little further, but first I would like to analyze the basic meaning of the word and show why I see this notion of autistics as a lack of empathy in itself, and consequently as rather hypocritical.

According to the Oxford English Dictionary, empathy is "The ability to understand and share the feelings of another." While analyzing this basic definition, the first thing I want to point out is its ending: "of another." As we may notice, it does not say "of neurotypical people" or actually of any specific group or type of person. It just says "another." Taking that into consideration, we can clearly see that the ability to feel empathy relates to a human being understanding and perceiving another human being's feelings. Autistic brains feel differently; they interpret the word differently and demonstrate their feelings in a different way. When non-autistics say autistics are unable to recognize or feel other people's emotions because they don't do it their way, it is clear they are lacking the ability to understand and share the feelings of said autistic person, and therefore are lacking empathy themselves.

My point here is that obviously both sides are going to struggle to understand each other on many levels. Accusing one of the sides of being unable to empathize because they don't do things like their counterpart while both are going through the same difficulty to recognize each other is just hypocrisy, and, to be honest, it's rather cruel.

As you can see, meltdowns and shutdowns for people on the spectrum can be strongly affected by their emotions. Several examples of lack of empathy towards autistics are: when people say autistics are robots, that they don't have emotions; when we have meltdowns and people can only interpret it as a tantrum, because that is what it means when a non-autistic behaves that way; especially during meltdowns, when the person is crying, screaming, and visibly in pain, others are unable to realize that, are not touched by it, and simply ignore or punish the person for being disruptive. All of that is so painful, because our feelings are so easily misunderstood by the same people who accuse us of not being able to feel or to relate to them. In the end, the message we receive is: "You are defective because you don't feel like we do and you need to be fixed. You have to be like us and we don't have to be like you because you are just wrong."

It is also important to point out the consequences of telling a person that they are simply not capable of feeling or understanding other people's feelings. It is very damaging to someone's sense of worth, to their self-esteem. Stating something like "You will never be able to..." is already bad enough, no matter the ending of that sentence. But saying a person will never be able to relate to others, when they are struggling to do so and to make sense of themselves, might be just what it takes to close the bridge between their world and the outside one for good.

Going back to the definition of empathy, I would like to focus on the two different aspects of it: the ability to "understand" and "share." There are two different types of empathy called cognitive and emotional, the "understand" part being related to the cognitive kind and the "share" part to the emotional one. I will describe my experience with two empathic profiles I see the most in the autistic community: the ones who appear to not feel anything (who people like to refer to as robots) and the ones who feel too much all the time (who are prone to having meltdowns and therefore may be perceived as childish or too sensitive). I will call the first "shelled" (the ones protected by an invisible emotional shell that safeguards them from other people's feelings) and the latter ones "exposed" (the ones who don't have this shell and are completely affected by people's surrounding emotions).

During my childhood and my teenage years, I was predominantly the shelled type. I never cried (except in the case of physical pain and injury) and was completely oblivious to other people's emotions. My friends used to think I was so strange and they didn't understand how I could seem so detached from their feelings (and apparently also from my own). For me it just felt as if feelings were something hidden behind a wall and I just couldn't see what was happening on the other side. I felt a lot and very deeply, but just didn't understand these feelings. I couldn't properly label or deal with them, so in a way I was putting off the need to face them. It would come as no surprise that I had a lot of psychosomatic diseases and allergies. Hospital visits were commonplace for me. Now I know these were the effects of my feelings trying to manifest themselves somewhere, since I was not letting them out.

Everything changed when I met my husband (and even more so each time we became parents). I think the shock of falling in love with someone and being loved in return broke my shell, letting the feelings just come out, with all their repressed might. I don't want this to seem like a romantic description; it was just my trigger for getting out of the shell. It made me an extreme empath because now the wall had fallen. And, unfortunately, in many ways things became a lot worse than they had been.

I got rid of many previous health problems but then I started to feel too much. All the autistic extreme empaths will agree with me here that this is hard. I feel exposed and overly delicate, like a snail without its shell, and it is frightening. I often just wish I could have my shell back because now everything hurts. I can't see someone crying as I will also immediately cry. I don't even need to know why the person is feeling that way. I feel people's emotions all the time; then when they say something but are actually feeling something else entirely, I get very confused and overwhelmed.

Both my girl and my boy are on the spectrum and have always been extreme empaths. I must watch out for any cartoon or movie with people feeling sad, because it will make them inconsolable. Even when people are hitting the "bad guys," they feel very bad for them and start crying. They don't see the socially constructed idea of "antagonist"; they feel their emotions instead, their hurt, no matter who they are. A perfect example of how things are with us happened last month in my boy's kindergarten summer party. They had some activities that rewarded kids with stamps which, at the end, they could exchange for a prize. So, my boy was playing in a water race (you take water from a bucket to another, going back and forth with a glass, and whoever finishes first is the winner) at his own pace. But he notices the girl beside him anxiously running to catch up. He stopped in his tracks, waved to her and said "Come!", then followed as she outpaced him. He felt she was nervous, so he waited for her. He wasn't even aware of the competitiveness of the game. With all the craziness of the party going on around him, he focused on this girl's feelings and all he wished for was to make her feel good. And that is the true demonstration of empathy, right there.

There are so many examples I could give and so many intricacies regarding autistic empathy that it would surely need a whole book of its own to cover it all. But I hope that, with what I explained here, I have been able to change people's ideas about empathy and autism, even just a little. The way people currently connect the two is both sadly hurtful and damaging. The general approach to this theme needs to be re-evaluated. Let's all use empathy to relate to each other with care and respect. This cannot be a one-way street, not anymore.

## Dr. Michelle Garnett on emotional regulation

Renata communicates with such love and elegance. It is both delightful and so sad to read her chapter. As Renata describes, for a person on the autism spectrum, not only are emotions extremely difficult to understand and regulate, but so are other people's attitudes. There has certainly been a lot of misunderstanding about empathy over the years in the literature, and hence a lot of misunderstanding about autism in the community.

**Why do people on the autism spectrum experience difficulties with emotional regulation?**

As Renata describes so well, people on the autism spectrum tend not to have a "balanced relationship" with their emotions. Both extremes of and lack of emotion can occur, and both are distressing in their own way. There are a number of reasons for this.

- **Neurology.** Brain studies indicate neurological differences in the brains of children and adults with autism, both in the amygdala and in the pathways between the amygdalae and the frontal lobes. The amygdalae comprise of two almond-shaped structures contained within the limbic system, the emotional part of the brain that primarily exists to register threat. Once the amygdala is triggered, the body will react with fight, flight, or freeze. "Fight" can be recognized as a meltdown, "flight" can be recognized as avoidance, and "freeze" is a shutdown. Unfortunately, the person whose amygdalae have been triggered does not get a choice about which mode the body enters to process the emotion. As Renata describes, the emotional reaction is not manipulative, it is not chosen; it is a reaction.
- **Genes.** Genetic studies show a strong link in the genes between mood disorders and autism. This means that many family members of people on the autism spectrum experience unipolar or bipolar depression and/or anxiety disorders.

Therefore, genetically, a person on the autism spectrum is more prone to experiencing strong emotions throughout their lifetime.

- **Alexithymia.** The co-prevalence of the condition called alexithymia is also common in autism, affecting about 80%. Alexithymia is defined as a difficulty in being able to put into words one's own or another's emotions or thoughts. Not being able to express one's emotions in speech commonly leads to suppression of these emotions, and then, as Renata describes, psychosomatic diseases and allergies can emerge. For some, alexithymia is another reason for meltdowns and shutdowns since the emotions need to be let out, but there are too few avenues.
- **Exhaustion.** Another factor is exhaustion. Dealing with persistent anxiety, too much socializing, and overwhelming sensory experiences on a daily basis with no concession or understanding from others is a recipe for exhaustion. Exhaustion leads to depression and a lack of emotional regulation.
- **Lack of sleep.** Many people on the autism spectrum experience sleep difficulty, including sleep disorders. There is research to show that being able to get to sleep for most people on the autism spectrum takes between 30 and 60 minutes, instead of the usual 15–20 minutes. Sleep deprivation leads to depression and the lack of emotional regulation.
- **Unhelpful coping strategies.** Lastly, the two most common ways people on the autism spectrum deal with strong emotions are avoidance and suppression. While each of these coping mechanisms work in the short term, allowing a person to be more functional and to suffer less emotional pain,

they are not helpful in the long term. Excessive avoidance and suppression of emotion tends to lead to clinical levels of anxiety and depression, as well as an increased rate of shutdowns and meltdowns.

**What helps?**

In my work as a clinical psychologist I have found, as Renata suggests, that it is helpful to understand both your own emotional triggers and your emotional restoratives. I love Renata's description of the intense interest being "an emotional cleaner." Yes! As Nick Dubin says, "I have never met a person on the autism spectrum who is depressed who was engaging in their special interest" (Dubin, 2014, p.22). The intense interest can indeed be a wonderful tool for emotional regulation.

A good system for understanding both emotional triggers and emotional restoratives is to use an accounting system that was developed by Maja Toudl, an awesome spectrum woman, which she has labeled Emotional Accounting. Tony Attwood and I further developed these ideas in our book about managing depression when you are on the spectrum (Attwood and Garnett, 2016). Simply, make a list of all your emotional triggers—that is, those events and experiences that drain you of energy—and then list all of your emotional restoratives—the activities, people, and experiences that replenish you. Assign a numerical value to each activity from 0 to 100 in terms of how much that activity drains or restores you. Use this system to assist you to plan your day, week, and month, in terms of ensuring that you do not go into the "red" (i.e. too many withdrawals of energy and not enough deposits).

Lastly, the understanding of people around us through acts of love and compassion is vital, both to assist a woman on the spectrum to survive the shutdown or meltdown and, as Renata says, to heal afterwards. Tell the people who care about you the acts of healing that will be most helpful to you, so that they can act in the best way both during and after the shutdown or meltdown. Be prepared to offer the act of kindness to them. This reciprocity acts to keep the relationship happy, frees you from guilt, and serves as an insurance policy to militate against pain in the future.

### Empathy

Fortunately, professionals are becoming more aware of the intricate nature of the neurological circuitry in the frontal cortex that leads to the expression of empathy. This research and its ramifications for ASD are well described by Professor Simon Baron-Cohen in his book *Zero Degrees of Empathy* (Baron-Cohen, 2012). I highly recommend reading this book to many professionals. For example, we know that there are at least three different forms of empathy: the affective (to feel the emotions of others), the cognitive (to know how to describe these emotions), and the behavioral (to know what to do to help the person who is suffering).

Research indicates that women (and some men) on the autism spectrum very commonly experience hyperarousal of the empathic system—that is, they feel others' emotions too much. This is a very long way from the original old conceptions of "empathy deficits" of autism and needs to be understood and shared.

CHAPTER 14

# Executive Functioning

*Terri Mayne, Maura Campbell, and Kate Ross*

## Organizational skills—*Terri Mayne*

As a child, I was always aware that I was somehow different to the other kids at my junior school. I didn't understand the girls or their interests; my brain just seemed to think about different things to them. Unsurprisingly, they were wary of me; I had different interests. I was into cars, aeroplanes, combine harvesters (yep, my intense interest), riding my BMX bike, and fixing my model tank. Maybe I could have got on better with the boys, but that didn't happen either. Instead, I just went through each day getting picked on and not really understanding why. I wasn't just different socially; when it came to lessons, my brain continued to be obstinate and refused to conform. When given tasks by the teacher, my brain protested, often not understanding the tasks it was being asked to do. It felt pretty rough as all the other kids quickly got on and understood straight away; it was as if they had been given an extra instruction that someone had forgotten to give me.

I often found that I understood the concept of what was being asked, but what the first step should be and how to make my mind or body actually take it was overwhelming and just blew my mind.

Deep down, I knew I was bright but I felt so damn stupid watching everyone else just "get it" while I floundered or froze. I'd keep trying to process to the point of collapse and when the teacher eventually came round to check in, I would be distressed, have produced no work, and was unable to explain why. My brain would be finished for the day, just exhausted.

On a different day, the class would be given a math problem to solve. Although still hard work, this was easier for me and did not cause so much distress. I didn't get stuck in the same way because all of the numbers and information I needed were right there in front of me and that immediately made the whole situation more bearable. The sheer panic caused by not having all the pieces and not knowing how to start wasn't triggered, which meant that I was able to get on with the task. I could visualize the units so that they became more tangible in my mind. It used to take several pages of workings-out (even including some drawings), and I would almost always solve the problem, but so many times I got marked down because my workings were "not as expected."

Not that I knew it at the time, but this is an example of what a young autistic girl's executive function challenges look like. The teachers are puzzled by it; they know this girl is intelligent and yet she appears to be unable to manage the simplest task and does things in a way they don't understand. There are tears and behavioral outbursts, she doesn't fit in socially, and it's difficult for her teachers to know what to make of her.

Executive functioning is generally seen as a group of abilities that allow you to manage your thoughts, emotions, and actions in order to get things done. It is responsible for skills such as organizing and planning, initiating and managing tasks, paying attention, regulating emotions, and self-monitoring (keeping track of what you're doing and modifying your behavior accordingly).

As you grow up, the more skills you need, the more complex

the emotions become, and before you know it, you are expected to behave like a responsible adult! Things get tough! As more is demanded of your executive functioning ability, the number of challenges and risks of total shutdown increase at an exponential rate.

If you are new to your autistic identity or are still coming to terms with it, it is easy to become disheartened, to think about how many things in day-to-day life rely on these key skills, to wonder how you are going to manage, and to feel that the odds are unfairly stacked against you. When I learned of my own autistic identity at age 33, I went through those very same thoughts and feelings. Many autistic women say that their diagnosis was a positive thing and a turning point in understanding themselves, but for me the experience was different. I felt it was more like society telling me what I couldn't achieve or do. "You're autistic so you can't feel emotion, you can't make eye contact, you can't have friends." Fortunately for me, I didn't know that I wasn't supposed to be able to do those things, as I never did pay much attention to what was expected of me. For me, one of the benefits of being autistic is that I have never been restricted by any preconceptions or boundaries of how things were supposed to be done (mainly because I didn't realize it), but this allowed me to think and act freely to find solutions to problems I faced.

Remember the little girl who worked through the math problem? She may have done it differently to everyone else, including her teacher; it may have taken her longer, she may have used lists and pictures in order to process her thoughts, but she did it. Also, she innovated, creating her own method to reach the correct outcome; it's one thing to use a map to find a well-trodden path but it is highly commendable to build your own new path to reach your destination.

I was often asked why I insisted on doing things "the hard way," as if I was being deliberately awkward. If only they knew how hard it was for me to do things their way—I thought their way was "the hard way"! Regardless of whether or not the method looked clunky or awkward to the outside world, I knew that I had a strong ability to apply logic and find solutions.

There are some things that the majority of people would find easy that I'm not so good at: performing my morning routine correctly, handling something unexpected that might take a lot of energy, getting to work on time, organizing my finances, making sure I have food in the fridge, socializing, doing all of the above all at once, the list could go on... Over the years, I've often had that isolated and confused feeling where I'm alone in not understanding or being unable to perform these tasks or steps, feeling that I'm inferior because I can't do something that appears to be simple. The confusion increases when I'm feeling stressed, tired, overloaded, or overwhelmed. The confusion causes more stress and upset; seemingly insurmountable challenges continue to snowball, eventually leading to tears, shutdowns, meltdowns, loss of speech, and an inability to stand up or move, becoming stuck in a hideous loop, and eventually ceasing to function at all.

It doesn't take long to realize that these episodes are no fun, can prevent me functioning in life, and are things that I'd sure like to avoid—but is that possible? This is where I'm grateful for my ability to use logic. Although it's clear that I struggle with some things, I have other skills and talents that I can engage to make it easier to manage.

The simple desire to function drove me to perform some self-reflection—logically, honestly, and openly working through the things that challenged my executive functioning skills, determining what helps and what hinders. One of the challenges that can trigger a shutdown in executive function for me is if something unexpected occurs when I am already at full capacity; there is simply no mental energy left to process anything else. The fact that it's unexpected means it takes more capacity to handle, even if it's minor in the grand scheme of things. So, how can anyone really plan for the unexpected? Well, in truth, I'm not sure you can! But for me, I now work to ensure the rest of the tasks I am running are managed. I look for signals that I might be approaching full capacity and then rein it back a bit so that if something unexpected does land, it doesn't tip me over.

It is difficult to prioritize the things you need to do while you're trying to perform those tasks at the same time. It's a sure-fire way to overload my executive functioning as well as being inefficient. For example, when getting ready for work in the morning, if I try to think of all the individual items I need to take with me at the same time as I'm packing my bag, there's a high chance that I'll manage to leave the house not fully dressed or without brushing my hair.

The risk is starting too many tasks and not completing any of them. The solution for me is to use tools to plan in advance so that the "planning" stream of thought isn't trying to run at the same time as the "doing" stream! I prepare lists the night before to tell me all the things I need to pack for the morning. I then go through that list to make sure I can access all the things I will need. It's a bit like a piece of new computer software; you need to install it along with all its drivers before you can use it!

My job as Project Manager involves managing multiple priorities, unexpected challenges and pressures, client relationship building, as well as motivating and coaching members of the team when they need assistance managing their own priorities. I'm not sure that this is typically considered the type of role that an autistic woman with challenges in executive function should attempt. Luckily, I didn't realize that was meant to be a restriction applied to me!

In fact, it is my skills in planning that make me good at my job, skills that I probably wouldn't otherwise have if I hadn't been practicing them daily to manage my life already. As an autistic, I have an advantage when team members come to me when they're feeling overwhelmed by their task list and need help with getting going. Non-autistics rarely need to dig so deep in order to function in daily life, and they are unlikely to have had the same learning path as an autistic person in this area, so this is an example of where an autistic person could be at an advantage through consistent and necessary creation and use of tools to support executive functioning.

I am able to share my acquired skills of creating lists and diagrams to help my team. For my job, the lists are more complex than those for my daily life, so I use spreadsheets with formulae to help work out the priority of a task, although the same theory applies; it's the use of tools and strategies to do the executive function work for you and take the strain away. I can recognize when someone is feeling stuck, overloaded, and unable to proceed with their tasks, because I've faced and overcome this very challenge many times in my day-to-day life just to get by. I know only too well how an overloaded brain will respond, or not, and what support is needed to bring things back on track.

I am immensely grateful for the insight that my autism has given me; I am thankful that I have a logical mind that I can apply to solve problems and I am genuinely humbled by the opportunities I am given to share what I've learned with others.

I would challenge anyone to ignore others' expectations. If you think you can achieve something that you want to do, it doesn't matter how you get there—the more unusual the path, the more new ground you will break! You know yourself better than anyone and will have the best idea of what you can achieve. I'd encourage everyone to utilize their strengths in everything they do; use them to develop strategies and make tools to support yourself, use them every day, and share them with others wherever you can.

## The need for control—*Maura Campbell*

There are two phrases above all others that are guaranteed to strike fear into my soul: "Let's play it by ear" and "Let's just go with the flow." No, let's not. I like my spontaneity to be meticulously planned and executed with military precision. My husband once floated the idea of organizing a surprise party for me. I threatened him with divorce. I'm not even good at receiving presents—I struggle mightily to pretend to be grateful when I'm given something I don't like.

Despite having performed well academically and being well established in a good job with a high level of responsibility, my ability to deal with practical day-to-day issues fluctuates wildly and is highly sensitive to unplanned changes in my routine or environment. Interruptions are like a huge spanner that has been lobbed into a carefully calibrated production line. My monotropic mind makes it extremely difficult to change gears suddenly, and I frequently find myself staring at someone realizing I haven't processed a word they've said. Even worse, I may realize I've responded by saying "OK," without having a clue what they've told or asked me, as a device to make them stop talking so that I can return my attention to whatever I was doing before they interrupted me.

Some days I struggle to remember how to turn the shower on— the same shower I have been using for the past 13 years. When I cook, I have to lay out every ingredient and utensil in advance, and no one is allowed to speak to me. I recently ran out of fuel (both literally and figuratively) on the way to work. It happened because my routine was decimated the day before. Flinging my feminist principles aside, I had to call my husband because I simply could not process what I needed to do to deal with my predicament. I was useless for the rest of the day.

Another way in which my need for control manifests itself is in my tendency to hoard. For example, I often wear clothes until they literally fall apart, and when the time finally comes to let go, it feels as though I'm throwing away a part of myself. I grieve. I remember as a child having a major meltdown when I discovered my mother had thrown out a pair of jeans that no longer fitted me. I ran outside in a blind panic and pulled them out of the dustbin before tearfully begging her to let me keep them in a drawer.

I'm not sure why letting go of clothes or other belongings is so difficult for me; perhaps throwing things away is a reminder of the passing of time? The hardest part is getting started. It's best to plan it in advance. It helps if it's a bright day and I'm well rested. It's also easier to let things go if they're going to be reused, recycled, or repurposed, and a charity bag dropping through the door usually provides a good incentive to attempt a clear-out. I compromise by letting myself keep a few items, though. Being surrounded by familiar things is comforting and helps me to feel safe.

So why this constant need for control? Why did my childhood involve lining teddy bears up on my bed in exactly the right order and refusing to play with my younger sisters because they weren't doing it *right*? Like so many of our autistic traits, the need for control serves a practical purpose. When things are happening the way you expect them to and think they are supposed to, it promotes feelings of safety and security. It also allows you to anticipate better any likely sensory or social challenges. Conversely, when the unexpected or something you don't feel properly prepared for happens, it can feel as if things are careering out of control or that you are under sensory or social bombardment, engendering feelings of real fear and panic.

Needing to control and insisting on sameness can make us seem rigid, particularly if it extends to trying to control the actions of others around us. However, I have come to realize that my level of executive functioning is much better when I feel in control. I am more confident and relaxed, and I can give of my best. An autism diagnosis has allowed me to understand that and it has given me the vocabulary to explain it to others.

## Task inertia—*Kate Ross*

I'm not lazy.

Sometimes, it takes me a bit longer to figure out what I need to do or how I need to do it. Sometimes, my mind gets overwhelmed with so much information that I cannot function.

This is the perpetual conundrum with being autistic and having issues with executive functioning and task inertia.

Agony Autie (2017) put it brilliantly:

> You gotta remember I believed I was neurotypical all my life; I believed I was *a failing neurotypical*. All my life, I remember thinking, "Why can't I do this? Why can't I keep this together?" ... You feel like it makes sense, but at the same time, you then have to reimagine your whole life again.

I couldn't have put it better myself.

I was academically able, behaved myself, and permanently masked and camouflaged myself so I wasn't seen as "the weird kid" when I had difficulties starting on a project, assignment, or research paper. To the untrained eye, it would just appear that I was being lazy, when in reality my poor little brain couldn't organize itself. I'd end up panic-writing something a night or two before it was due because the adrenalin seemed to give me the focus I needed to get it together; luckily for me, my grades ended up being pretty good, but it very easily could have gone the opposite way.

As an adult, it's not about grades, passing or failing; rather it's about deadlines. The work I do exclusively revolves around deadlines and timescales; if these are not met, it has negative implications. When in a calm scenario, I can organize the information I need to do my job and work away quite nicely, feeling a sense of accomplishment when I complete something either on time or before deadline. However, the nature of my job does not always cater to this idealistic method of working. More often than not, I can have a happy little to-do list created and it gets scrapped before 9 a.m. when some sort of crisis arises and I have to drop everything to sort it out. In some crisis situations when I am unable to see the way forward or a possible solution (I like being solution-focused), I freeze, needing someone else to tell me what to do in small steps due to the overwhelm being too much for me to be able to process anything other than the absolute basics.

I could see clear signs of frustration in my managers' faces when they said, "We know you can do this." I know I can do it too! However, just because I can't on one day doesn't mean I'm completely incapable. Some days are better than others, and this rings true for all of us—neurodiverse and neurotypical alike. Because I've "worn the neurotypical mask" for so long and only since my diagnosis have I acquired the vocabulary to be able to explain *why* I'm having difficulties. I feel as if these are being interpreted as excuses rather than reasons, which makes me feel that I'm being gaslighted: you're not autistic, you're just lazy.

*Gaslighting* is defined as "a form of manipulation that seeks to sow seeds of doubt in a targeted individual or in members of a targeted group, hoping to make them question their own memory, perception, and sanity" (Wikipedia, 2017). When, as an adult, I came to recognize that I was autistic, I came to learn that these terms—executive functioning and task inertia—perfectly explained the difficulties that I experienced throughout my life and gave me the language to be able to better advocate for my needs and difficulties.

However, there are some individuals who will still cast doubt on these explanations and cause me to doubt myself all over again. Just a simple "I understand you and I believe you" from a friend or colleague can go a long way to minimize the effects of gaslighting and to promote understanding of how autistic people experience executive functioning and task inertia difficulties.

What would be even better is this: "I understand you and I believe you; *how can I help you?*"—rather than expecting us to just "get a grip," "snap out of it," or "figure it out." Offering practical strategies to assist us when we hit a mental roadblock would be infinitely more helpful than writing us off as useless and inept. I think this could contribute to the significant unemployment issues faced by a majority of autistic adults; it's perceived not to be in a company's best financial interests to expand human resources to support autistic employees, even though our unique neurology can bring exceptional skills to the business.

I'm not lazy; I have executive functioning and task inertia difficulties. How can you help me?

## Dr. Michelle Garnett on executive functioning

Research indicates that approximately 75% of people with a diagnosis of autism spectrum disorder Level 1 also have a diagnosis of attention-deficit disorder, with or without hyperactivity (ADD/ADHD), meaning that they have a full range of executive functioning difficulties (Holtmann, Bolte, and Poustka, 2005). Clinical experience shows that even if a formal diagnosis of ADD is not warranted, most people on the autism spectrum have fragments of ADD. These findings are not surprising given that ASD affects the frontal lobes of the brain and that the frontal lobes are responsible for our executive functioning. Terri, Maura, and Kate offer elegant and compelling explanations for the internal experience of executive functioning difficulties. I do hope that many teachers and employers read these descriptions.

Without these explanations, pejorative character judgments (e.g. lazy, defiant, passive aggressive, manipulative), confusion (e.g. "Why could she read that paragraph yesterday but not today?"), and questions about the person's intellectual ability are highly likely. The marked discrepancy between the intellectual capacity of a person on the autism spectrum and their adaptive functioning, or daily living skills, is not widely known and is even less well understood, even by health professionals. One of the biggest reasons for this discrepancy is poor executive functioning skills, and how these interact with other issues such as sensory processing disorder and emotion regulation difficulties.

Further executive functioning difficulties, in addition to the ones Terri described, are:

- poor ability to shift attention when required
- difficulty transitioning to a new problem or a new solution
- being easily distracted
- hyperfocus (over focus on one topic, activity, or detail)
- poor concentration, except when the topic is novel or of high interest
- difficulties prioritizing tasks or building a sequence
- problems getting started without a prompt
- impulsivity
- difficulties summarizing and discerning important information from less relevant information
- poor short-term memory (memory for what happened in the preceding seven seconds)
- poor working memory (ability to keep information in mind while working on it)
- poor self-reflection, including about one's own strengths and weaknesses, and how to improve next time.

Poor executive functioning skills contribute to the development and maintenance of specific learning difficulties, social skill difficulties, anxiety disorders, relationship difficulties, employment issues, and sexual dysfunction. Research shows that people with ADD/ADHD are more likely to develop addictions, either substance or behavioral, such as gaming or gambling.

Like any skill that is the weakest in our skill set, executive functioning skills are the first to "fall out" when we are tired, ill, stressed, or overloaded, either socially or sensorily or both. As each author in this chapter articulates, overwhelm or shutdown is the natural result.

**What to do?**

- **Assess.** The first step is understanding and awareness, both for the person on the spectrum and for the teacher and parent/carer or employer and partner. At my clinic, Minds & Hearts, we screen for executive functioning difficulties routinely, whether for a diagnostic assessment or for therapy. Psychologists use specific measures to determine exactly the type of executive functioning difficulties that may be occurring. It can be difficult for a young child to report exactly what is happening, so we ask both parents and teachers to complete questionnaires to understand their behavior. Warning signs that a young child may have underlying executive functioning difficulties include elective and selective mutism, frequent meltdowns, motor restlessness, sensation seeking, frequently losing items, and learning problems at school. Older children and adults tend to have much more awareness about the exact difficulties they are experiencing.

- **Manage.** Unfortunately, there is no cure or "fix" for executive functioning difficulties. The approach is management and finding ways around. The following strategies can be helpful:
  - **Psychoeducation.** Borrow from the literature on ADD/ADHD to explain what is happening to the people

who need to know, including advice about what they can do to help. There are good resources for parents (Moraine, 2015; Moyes, 2013) and adults (Hallowell, 2015; Hallowell and Ratey, 1995).

- **Ensure a healthy mind.** Choose a lifestyle that supports a healthy body. A healthy body means a healthy brain. A healthy brain means better executive functioning and an easier life with fewer problems. Make sleep, healthy food, and lots of water non-optional. A good fish oil as a supplement has been shown to assist with executive functioning. Start the day with some protein for breakfast. Avoid or minimize junk food and recreational drugs, including alcohol.

- **Manage anxiety.** Many people on the autism spectrum who also have executive functioning difficulties do best with a routine and structure to their lives because it helps with anxiety. The more aspects of daily living that can be embedded as being on automatic pilot, the more energy is left for dealing with the unexpected aspects of life and new learning. Include physical and relaxation activities as part of your daily schedule. Many people on the autism spectrum have found their life transformed when they take up a regular yoga, dance, martial arts, gardening, musical, meditation, running, weights, painting, or gym routine. Employ both people and technology to help.

- **Exercise your frontal lobes.** We now know that we can increase neural connectivity through the activities we choose to do on a regular basis. The activity that has the best research evidence base for increasing the connectivity and therefore functionality of the frontal lobes is meditation. People are finding that meditation has huge applicability to people on the autism spectrum. When you take up meditation, remember that it is a practice not a performance. You cannot be bad at meditation; all you can do is practice it. When we do this, we reap the benefits.

**Strategies.** Read the Recommended Resources section at the back of the book to find out more strategies to "scaffold" your day. These may include, as has been described, making lists, including a list of who to ask for help; also use daily, weekly, monthly, and yearly planners. Utilize technology to give you messages and alarms as needed to remind you what you need to do. Take regular movement breaks though the day. My own two best are starting the day with yoga, which helps me to notice when I become overwhelmed, and then when I notice, reminding myself to "Breathe and sequence" and asking myself, "What do I need to do next?"

## CHAPTER 15

# General Health

*Kate Ross and Anita Lesko*

## Hygiene and personal care—*Kate Ross*

Health professionals would agree that not keeping yourself clean is bad for you—but you may ask yourself, "Why?" Taking a shower could be sensory overload waiting to happen—how the water feels hitting your skin and scalp, the temperature of the water never being "just right," the slippery texture of shower gel or soap, the artificial fragrances of shampoo and conditioner. It's a wonder anyone can tolerate keeping clean at all!

Washing regularly removes dirt, dead skin cells, and oil (sebum) from your skin; if you don't wash enough, bacteria will quickly accumulate and cause body odor—this can become a sensory nightmare for you and for those around you, both neurotypical and neurodiverse. Dirty skin equals itchy skin; while scratching can feel good, if you scratch too hard, you may break through your skin, which can lead to infection—nobody wants that! Believe it or not, dry skin from over-washing (i.e. showering too often) can lead to the same outcome, so it's about washing often enough without inadvertently causing yourself further problems.

There are plenty of unscented body washes available if you don't like fragrances, and vice versa if you don't like the lack of scent (or can detect the subtle scent of unscented soaps). If showering is too much sensory overload, perhaps using a washcloth with your choice of soap to clean the areas most prone to bacteria growth—at minimum, underarms, vulva, and buttocks—and be sure to use a clean washcloth every time; otherwise you're just washing yourself with the same bacteria over again.

Now that your body is clean, you need to help keep yourself fresh between washes. This is generally achieved with antiperspirant deodorants (especially helpful if you're a "Sweaty Betty" like me) and making sure you're wearing clean clothes—especially fresh undergarments daily.

There are many types of deodorants available, but one variety that has been recommended is crystal deodorant, which suppresses bacterial growth and doesn't clog your pores; this type of deodorant is good also because it's fragrance-free, so if you're sensitive to smells or have sensitive skin, this could be a brilliant alternative for you.

With clothing, even though an item of clothing may pass "the smell test" after a day of wear, you need to be mindful of external factors; on a hot humid day, you are likely to be sweating more than usual (despite deodorant use), and as the day progresses, bacteria will no doubt start to reside in your clothing. This isn't meant to gross anyone out—it's just fact! Washing clothing after wearing gets rid of these bacteria so it doesn't ruin your clothing and make you smell bad; wearing dirty clothing on a clean body negates the shower/bath you've just had, and while products like Febreze may get rid of smells, it does not make your clothes magically clean. In short: a clean body with appropriately applied deodorant adorned with clean clothes makes you look, smell, and feel great!

Another component of personal care is hair removal—more

specifically from one's legs and underarms by shaving, waxing, or creams. However, you're no cleaner by shaving, nor are you more dirty because you choose not to shave. I know plenty of women who do not shave for a variety of reasons; it's Western society that has ingrained the mentality that a woman is "gross" if she doesn't shave. Men have hairy legs and underarms, right? Ultimately, it's your choice whether you do or not; you may be surprised how many within the autistic sisterhood do not either.

## Puberty and menstruation

Your body is capable of so much, including the potential to grow a new life (if you so choose). Puberty brings on a whole set of challenges—growing breasts, widening hips, hair growth, and the onset of menstruation or "periods." Puberty is difficult for everyone, but can present a whole multitude of additional difficulties for autistic girls—sensory differences, disruption to routine, a higher level of personal hygiene (see above) required, mood swings, and a general societal attitude that women should just get on with it silently without complaint, despite discomfort experienced.

Puberty is also the stage at which our differences may become more apparent; the social demands increase as we get older, and navigating this figurative minefield can be very difficult for autistic girls. When it comes to our emotional maturity, our peers may surpass us quite quickly, leaving us feeling left behind if we don't develop similar interests at the same pace (e.g. stereotypically "girly" things—make-up, clothes, shoes, dating, etc.), especially if we end up retaining our interests which are deemed socially "childish." Our bodies are maturing faster than our minds are, which can make us feel even more out of place than we did before.

For some crazy reason, we're restricted to talking about our periods in hushed tones away from anyone we might offend by discussing this natural process. I'm changing that up. Please note that I'm *not* a medical professional and I'm purely sharing my opinion and personal experiences—if you have questions or concerns, talk to your doctor or other health professional.

I was quite fortunate during puberty in that I did not have severe acne (just very oily skin), nor did I experience painful or unpredictable periods; they came regularly as expected and that was that. However, I seemed to be caught off guard whenever they would actually start—I'd know the day, but the time would always be different—especially if it was while I was at school, and more than once I needed to be excused from class to waddle to the girls' room, hoping that I didn't stain my clothes.

My periods started three months before my 12th birthday, just before I started 7th grade. My mother wasn't overtly ceremonial about it and I wasn't freaked out when it happened. My class had "the talk" in 5th grade—all the girls were shown a video and given a period starter pack. I was given pads to start, but I hated them—even though they were a far cry from the foot-long, inch-thick cotton pads which my mother had to use in the 1960s; to me it felt like wearing a diaper. I eventually took to using tampons, but when I read the insert slip from the box, the toxic shock syndrome warning and crude demonstration diagram put me off trying for a long time. If anything, it was the growing dislike of pads that eventually led me to use tampons. I'm not embarrassed to say I used a mirror (and awkward acrobatics in my locked bedroom!) to have a look "down there" in order to figure out how I worked like the diagram in the booklet that I was given at age 10. Once I became familiar with my own anatomy, I felt comfortable with tampons, which then led to me becoming a BIG FAN of menstrual cups (more on that later).

In my opinion, tampons are better than pads, but they're still not without their flaws. My main issue with tampons and pads is they create so much waste—the plastic packaging is not biodegradable and can take anywhere from 450 to 1000 years to decompose!! Think of how many tampons or pads a woman could use in her lifetime, then think of how many women that applies to—that's a LOT of plastic! I'm an environmentalist and felt awful at the thought of my contribution to the ever-growing waste issue, so I looked into menstrual cups.

I came across testimonials from women saying they would never go back to pads or tampons once they got used to their menstrual cup. There are several brands and designs, but I decided on the Lily Cup by Intimina. I liked how it was designed to be more ergonomically designed to fit the female anatomy and could be rolled up as small as a tampon for insertion. I won't lie: it took me a few tries to get used to it; however, I cannot imagine having my period without it now. Personally, I think menstrual cups are great for autistic women because:

- they hold more menstrual blood than a tampon or pad
- they only have to be emptied (up to) every 12 hours (depending on flow), thus less disruption to routine
- they're easy to keep clean
- when inserted correctly, you don't feel them at all
- they're eco-friendly!

Using my menstrual cup has massively improved my period experience and I do not dread its arrival anymore; if anything, I feel more connected to my body and experience my period not as an inconvenience, but as just another routine. I know I'm quite lucky that I only experience mild issues with breakouts, cramping, headaches, or mood swings (some months better than others), but having something which means that my period is less of a disruption to my routine makes a noticeable and beneficial difference.

## Visiting doctors and hospitals—*Anita Lesko*

It is a known fact that individuals on the autism spectrum avoid seeking healthcare for a variety of reasons. This would include all the sensory violations one encounters when visiting any type of healthcare facility. There are typically bright lights, over-crowded waiting rooms with numerous people talking, a television with a news channel playing and never-ending commercials coming on.

There are sounds from cell phones of text tones or gaming, phones ringing behind the reception counter. There are typically chairs adjacent to each other so one must sit right next to others, who may be wearing strong perfumes or colognes, or who have strong body odor.

There is lack of privacy, not only due to sitting in such tight quarters with others, but a nurse or assistant will come into the waiting area and holler out the next person's name, so that everyone sitting there hears the name being called.

Once it is your turn, you are taken back and placed in yet another waiting room, with bright lights. At least you are generally alone at that point. Your blood pressure, oxygen saturation, heart rate, and temperature are obtained and charted. The nurse/healthcare provider will then question you regarding the purpose of your visit. They may talk fast, or ask in such a way that you don't understand. You may have just been setting in the main waiting area for an hour or longer and on the verge of a meltdown. Your thinking may not be so clear at this point and you might not be able to process what you are being asked. You might need time to respond, or need to respond in a way the provider is not used to. They may not understand why you are taking so long to respond, or not responding at all.

You also will be touched by strangers—the one getting your vital signs and then the doctor who comes in to examine you. Let's face it, the whole process is a massive sensory overload and violation, *especially* if the visit is for embarrassment-provoking reasons such as pap smears and mammograms. I've never heard of a neurotypical liking it, so *we* surely won't.

In addition to the sensory issues, equally important are the communication issues. As a healthcare provider for over 30 years now, I can safely say that, in general, most healthcare providers lack understanding of autism and how there might be various ways this population must be cared for.

Here is my big opportunity to come galloping in on a white stallion in my coat of armor to save everyone! I am in the extremely unique position of being a healthcare provider who's also autistic! Seeing the desperate need to help this situation, I wrote the book *The Complete Guide to Autism and Healthcare* (Lesko, 2017). I wrote it to educate *all* healthcare providers about autism and how to provide quality care to us. It is a first-of-its-kind. I was also sure to include a very detailed chapter on women's issues. It starts out by discussing the environmental factors that need to be changed, and how staff can help provide a positive experience for the autistic patient.

The healthcare system must change. There are some tips that can be given to the ASD patient ahead of time, such as what to expect. I have recommended that all healthcare facilities make websites that have photos of the environment and different areas the patient will see, and brief video clips showing procedures such as getting vital signs taken, getting an IV started, and various procedures. It is also helpful that they include photos of the staff the patient will encounter. All of that, when it can be viewed ahead of time, multiple times as necessary, will help the ASD patient to feel comfortable and as if they have been there before. I also suggest that healthcare facilities allow ASD patients to visit the facility ahead of time to see it in person and meet some of the staff they will encounter. This is particularly important prior to having surgery.

It is helpful to make a list of questions you'd like to ask your healthcare provider. It's best to have that list with you when you go, as otherwise it's easy to forget them when you are overwhelmed.

After that, you need to be your own advocate and help your healthcare providers understand autism and how they can best serve you. We all deserve quality healthcare just like everyone else. It's up to us to make that happen.

## Surgery and physical changes

Going for surgery and anesthesia are a frightening thing for anyone, even more for us. In my book I have plenty of information on not just how you can prepare for surgery, but everything that the healthcare team needs to do for *you* to have the best outcome possible.

The type of surgery you are having will determine what physical changes will be present *after* the surgery. Even if it's something like "just" a scar, that could be very emotionally challenging. I had surgery on my right shoulder for a very rare type of cancer back in 2009. The incision was about 12 inches long, going right over my shoulder. To me, it looked as if I had been attacked by a shark! To this day I avoid looking at it and touching it. For one thing, due to the depth of the surgery there was a lot of nerve damage, and when that area is touched, it makes a very unpleasant sensation that freaks me out.

For females, any type of breast cancer surgery will leave either scars or total body changes as in a mastectomy. Of course, there are surgeries to reconstruct the area, but it will never look or feel the same. There are support groups in most hospitals or communities to help patients get through the recovery phase and emotional trauma.

Any type of surgery that changes a person's body will create an emotional scar. It can even impact on how the body functions. A person cannot get through that alone. You would need a support person if you have one; if not, don't be afraid to ask the healthcare provider where you can find one.

Recently, I completed another book, about Temple Grandin— *Temple Grandin: The Stories I Tell My Friends*—and one of the things she shared with me during our many interviews was about when she was in her 20s and had surgery for a cancer on her eyelid. She talked about how unpleasant the surgery was, which was done under local anesthesia. She was able to see the surgeon's hand with the scalpel coming towards her eye. Afterwards, the area developed an infection which took nearly four weeks to heal. During that time, she was worried she might go blind. She had a friend who had something similar happen with her eyes, and that friend provided Temple with emotional support, encouraging her to get through that period of time. Everyone needs support. Never be afraid to seek it out.

## Pain threshold

It is not uncommon for individuals on the autism spectrum to have very high pain threshold levels, meaning they can withstand far greater pain than the average person. Pain is defined as an unpleasant sensory and emotional experience associated with actual or potential tissue damage. While some ASD individuals are insensitive to pain, others are unusually vulnerable to it. Sensory sensitivities—exaggerated reactions to certain sounds, lights, touch, or other stimuli—affect most ASD individuals. Pain may emanate from autism-related health issues such as gastrointestinal problems. Additionally, difficulties with sleep, anxiety, and perseveration (the tendency to fixate on a particular thought), all common features in people with ASD, may intensify pain (Lesko, 2017, p.43).

The ASD patient may not know how to convey their pain to the healthcare provider. Again, there is a dire need to educate all healthcare providers about how an ASD patient might exhibit pain, and how they can elicit the type and location of the pain.

**Anesthesia and autism**

As a Certified Registered Nurse Anesthetist who spends 40 hours a week doing anesthesia, I feel it is my duty to provide you with a bit of information about getting anesthesia as an ASD person. It is not uncommon for ASD individuals to have mitochondrial dysfunction. Other than going for genomic testing, there is no way to know you have it except by recognizing the symptoms. There are potential complications resulting from general anesthesia if a mitochondrial deficiency is present (Lesko, 2017, p. 93).

There are numerous things that can be done to help prevent complications from occurring. To help further understand mitochondrial disease, you can read more on this from the Cleveland Clinic (2017).

**Suggestions for anesthesia for the ASD patient**

Following is an excerpt from my book *The Complete Guide to Autism and Healthcare* (2017, pp. 93–94).

Chances are that the anesthesia provider will not be able to order all of the lab work you may require. It might be wise to treat every ASD patient as if they have a mitochondrial dysfunction, going along the same lines as using Universal Precautions for each and every patient. You never know which one might have a transmissible disease, so simply protect yourself at all times. The same applies here. Why take risks when the safest approach is simply to do the following:

- ASD patient to be first case of the day to limit NPO[1] time (as well as stress of waiting)
- Avoid nitrous oxide

---

1    NPO—nil per os/nil by mouth.

- Avoid Lactated Ringer's, since it contains lactic acid, and patients with mitochondrial dysfunction generally have elevated blood lactate levels. Normal saline should be fluid of choice
- Avoid succinylcholine
- Maintain normal blood glucose, body temperature, and acid-base balance (Szakacs and Davi, 2017)
- Be generous with fluid replacement. Dehydration is the major cause of post-operative nausea. Instead of administering multiple drugs to prevent nausea, why not simply give the ASD patient appropriate fluid replacement so they don't have to contend with polypharmacy to metabolize
- Suggest to the parent ASD patient to take a B-vitamin complex (B6, B12, Folate) a few days prior to the surgery/anesthesia

**A word on good health**

We all know too well about living with anxiety. It's a normal part of daily life for most of us with ASD. By taking some simple basic steps, you can help yourself maintain good health. Eat a healthy diet rich in vegetables, grains, fruit, lean protein, yogurt, nuts, healthy fats such as avocados, and eat a balance of it all. Getting enough sleep is extremely important. Exercise is another absolute *must* to keep you healthy. Walking is the simplest thing you can do. Whether you go for an after-dinner stroll around your neighborhood or walk on a treadmill, just get moving. It doesn't need to be fast, just a nice pace to spark up your metabolism. It will make you feel better not only physically, but mentally as well.

My mom was a huge fan of *The Dr. Oz Show*. Most people are familiar with his show and the experts he has on each day who provide the audience with the latest information about food, sleep, exercise, sexual health, and every possible topic related to healthy living. She loved when I'd sit there with her to watch the show, and if I wasn't home or simply couldn't spare the time, she'd fill me in on whatever she learned that day. What *was* clear is that you have the power to take care of your mind and body by just following some basic steps.

## Dr. Michelle Garnett on general health

I love this book! Where else have you read a chapter on general health that discusses, in detail, topics as important and diverse as the advantages of menstrual cups over tampons and pads, to a checklist for surgical staff to safely use anesthesia with someone with ASD? Such is the diverse and detailed wisdom of women on the spectrum.

In my clinic, three of the uppermost presenting concerns we see regarding general health for women on the spectrum are issues with personal hygiene (usually in adolescence), poor general physical health affecting mental health, and challenges in health communication.

### Personal hygiene
As Kate discusses, one of the major reasons girls and women can stop (or not start) washing themselves or not use deodorant can be sensory pain, usually tactile or olfactory. There are certainly some good accommodations to be made to ensure that smelling good and being clean happens daily. However, we have found that another big obstacle for many on the spectrum, including women, can be difficulty understanding the purpose of washing oneself and wearing deodorant.

Some men and women on the spectrum very much like the scent of their own body odor—the more pungent the better! When I broached the subject with one of my clients, he told me that his odor was an indicator of his pheromones, and therefore made him more sexually attractive to the opposite sex. Unfortunately, the smell was so obnoxious and overpowering that I had to use an odor-neutralizing spray in my clinical room and the waiting room after he had left.

When personal hygiene is an issue for clients in the clinic over and beyond sensory processing difficulties, we explain that it is a social issue. While we may like our own smell, it is very commonly the case that others do not like it, especially as the smell becomes stronger through the day. We eliminate the smell through washing and deodorizing for the sake of others, not for ourselves. The way this will benefit us in the long term is that we are more likely to make and keep friends, win and maintain a job, and generally have a higher chance of achieving social acceptance if we do not exude a strong body odor.

Sometimes this spoken Social Story™, with its aim to educate about the unwritten rules of social conduct, is not enough. In this case, I quite like to use a different Social Story™, one written by my dear friend and colleague, Professor Tony Attwood. It goes like this:

> What is body odor? Body odor occurs in the following manner. When we do not wash, we develop pockets of old sweat in our armpits and groin area. Old sweat is a wonderful breeding ground for bacteria. When bacteria feed on old sweat in our armpits and nether regions they poop and fart. Body odor is the smell of the bacteria pooping and farting.

This story mostly helps the person understand the problem.

### Physical health and mental health

Poor physical health for the person on the autism spectrum can be the result of heritable health problems such as an autoimmune disorder or gut disorder, or could be the result of lifestyle factors, such as eating an unhealthy diet and/or not incorporating physical and relaxation activities into their lifestyle. These latter problems are often secondary to poor executive functioning skills, poor interoceptive skills (the ability to sense bodily signals), and sometimes to mental health problems such as depression or an anxiety disorder. Regardless of how the physical health problems started, inevitably there is a negative effect on the person's mental health, where they feel more pessimistic, gloomy, anxious, numb, foggy, and/or stressed.

The mind and the body are intimately connected. One truly does influence the other. One of the best ways a person on the autism spectrum can increase both their well-being and functionality is to look after their physical health. I fully endorse Anita's recommendation to follow some simple basic steps to increase your physical health.

## Health communication

Women on the spectrum have specific physical health needs and are often looking after children with healthcare needs, so they often independently represent themselves and others in healthcare. Recently, I was involved in a pilot study in Brisbane that investigated perceptions of healthcare experiences for women with and without ASD (Lum, Garnett, and O'Connor, 2014). Women with ASD reported greater challenges in experiencing anxiety in the healthcare setting, significantly reduced communication due to emotional distress, anxiety relating to waiting rooms, not being assisted by support and information offered during pregnancy, and problematic communication during childbirth about pain, needs, and concerns. They described that self-disclosure of their autism commonly led to negative responses by medical staff, and 75% of the women with ASD said that they would not disclose. Problematic lack of ASD awareness by healthcare providers had been experienced by 100% of the sample.

Such challenges raise the risk of significant delays in seeking treatment due to anxiety-related avoidance, misdiagnosis due to underreporting of symptoms and distress, and resultant misguided treatment plans. These issues are all concerning, especially considering the higher mortality and morbidity rates of individuals with ASD, and the poorer health and social outcomes.

I heartily endorse Anita's book recommendations in this chapter, as well as the information contained in her new book (Lesko, 2017). In addition, I recommend for women on the spectrum:

- increased awareness that both anxiety about healthcare communication and problems with healthcare communication are common for women on the spectrum
- increased awareness that early detection and treatment are paramount for ongoing good health, including well-being
- a firm commitment to self to face medical and health issues
- a plan for the resultant anxiety, including seeing a psychologist if needed for anxiety management
- developing a good relationship with your GP and educating that person over time to your own expression of ASD and best methods for communication
- developing greater awareness of interoceptive cues via meditation or mindfulness techniques to become more adept at detecting physical discomfort or changes in the body that need investigation
- many women find that they can express more accurately what is going on in their mind and body by typing or writing
- if being able to communicate personal health issues to a stranger seems impossible, ask a good friend or family member, with whom you can communicate, to attend the appointment with you and take notes.

# CHAPTER 16

# Autism and Co-Occurring Conditions

*Anita Lesko*

A number of medical conditions frequently occur with an autism spectrum disorder (ASD). These co-occurring conditions include anxiety, depression, attention-deficit/hyperactivity disorder (ADHD), gastrointestinal (GI) problems, sleep disturbances, epilepsy, autoimmune disorders, Ehlers-Danlos syndrome, mitochondrial dysfunction, dyspraxia, dyslexia, dyscalculia, sensory processing disorder, sensory integration issues, and eating disorders. The general public is used to associating many of these with children on the spectrum, but those children grow up to become adults. Other conditions that can occur in adulthood include hypertension (HTN), diabetes, sleep apnea, chronic obstructive pulmonary disease (COPD), sexual dysfunction, anxiety, and mental health issues.

An autistic individual can have none of the above, but most likely will have several conditions, with anxiety being one of the biggest factors that can manifest in numerous other issues.

As I look at the list above, it looks rather depressing and daunting. Individuals on the autism spectrum face any number of these afflictions as part of our daily lives. It hardly seems fair. It can take so much out of a person to struggle with any one of them, let alone having multiple problems. Neurotypicals (NTs) might look at us as the weakest link. I choose to look at it differently. Instead, we are the stronger ones, for we have the fortitude to forge through life *despite* having these afflictions.

I have been in the medical profession for more than three decades thus far. Graduating in 1983 with my Bachelor of Science in Nursing, I went on to Columbia University in New York City from 1986 to 1988 to earn my Master of Science in Nurse Anesthesia. I then took my Board Exam, passed that, and have been working full-time ever since as a Certified Registered Nurse Anesthetist.

Because I didn't know I was on the autism spectrum until age 50, I spent those first 28 years as a healthcare provider with a very different approach! When I was younger, I had difficulty interacting with other staff and patients as well, but I didn't let it deter me. I tried to use each social blunder to teach me better for the next interaction. Recently, I did a calculation to determine how many times I've interacted with people. I based it on five days a week at work for 9–10 hours a day, times the number of cases per day, and people I must interact with. The number came out to more than *one million* social interactions. I've done over 55,000 cases, meaning that I've done the anesthesia for that many surgeries.

Just recently, I had a new book come out, *The Complete Guide to Autism and Healthcare* (Lesko, 2017). I combined my 34 years as a medical professional with my autism to bring this much-needed book into the hands of healthcare providers, parents of autistic children, and all individuals on the autism spectrum. There is no one more uniquely qualified to present this information, as it's coming from an autistic healthcare provider.

The following will look at each of the co-existing conditions.

## Anxiety

Anxiety is a real difficulty for many on the autism spectrum. It can affect a person psychologically and physically, producing a range of symptoms. These symptoms of anxiety are very closely connected, leading to a vicious cycle which can be difficult to break (National Autistic Society, 2017).

Because anxiety affects so many autistics, I will go into a bit more depth. The National Autistic Society has a lovely list for this, and is as follows.

The psychological symptoms of anxiety include:

- easily losing patience
- difficulty concentrating
- thinking constantly about the worst outcome
- difficulty sleeping
- depression
- becoming preoccupied with or obsessive about one subject.

Physical symptoms include:

- excessive thirst
- stomach upsets
- diarrhea
- frequent urination
- rapid heart rate
- muscle aches
- headaches
- dizziness
- numbness
- tremors.

Autistic people can sometimes have extreme difficulty in minimizing or eliminating their anxiety. There are things you can do to help relax. When we have extreme anxiety, it can easily evolve into a meltdown, no matter your age. I'm 58 and have had my share of them! Most of us know when we need that quiet time or have developed ways to lessen the degree of anxiety. I know it's easier said than done. Make a list of things you enjoy doing that bring you comfort and peace. When anxiety starts to build, do one of them, if possible. If not, at least *think* about those things. Physical activity can also help reduce stress. So too can deep breathing exercises, a calming bath, listening to your favorite music, aromatherapy, or whatever works for you.

It is imperative to work at decreasing your anxiety. Another critical point is that stress weakens the immune system. There is a field of psychology—*psychoneuroimmunology*—which proves that the state of mind affects one's state of health (American Psychological Association, 2006).

There is not much information specific to *adults* on the autism spectrum, least of all specific to *females*. The information provided is mostly recommended for children, but these problems obviously continue into adulthood. This, in fact, is being addressed by a research project on which I am project co-lead. You can learn more at www.autistichealth.org.

## Depression

With everything we face in society, and also having other issues as shown here, it's easy to understand why a person would get depressed. Please refer to Chapter 17 of this book for more on depression.

## ADHD

About 75% of children with autism also show signs of attention-deficit/hyperactive disorder (ADHD), a rate that's significantly higher than it is in the general population (Attwood, 2008).

## Gastrointestinal (GI) problems

The most common complaints in autism are constipation, diarrhea, and gastroesophageal reflux or GERD. Recent research shows that more than 50% of children with autism have GI symptoms, food allergies, and maldigestion or malabsorption issues (Breaking the Vicious Cycle, 2017).

## Sleep disturbances

Researchers estimate that between 40% and 80% of children with ASD have difficulty sleeping. The biggest sleep problems among these children include:

- difficulty falling asleep
- inconsistent sleep routines
- restlessness or poor sleep quality
- waking early and waking frequently.

In adulthood (and often childhood) sleep apnea becomes a problem. A sleep study is necessary and use of CPAP (continuous positive airway pressure) is necessary.

## Epilepsy

According to Dr. Megdad Zaatreh, Medical Director of the Comprehensive Epilepsy Center at Centrastate Medical Center in New Jersey, research has found that adults with epilepsy are more likely to show signs of autism and Asperger syndrome. Nearly one-third of people with autism spectrum disorder also have epilepsy. The connection between the two conditions was made in a study that showed that epileptic seizures short-circuit the neurological function that affects socialization in the brain (Zaatreh, 2014).

## Autoimmune disorders

There is a long list of autoimmune disorders that affect the general population (too long to list here).

## Ehlers-Danlos syndrome (EDS)

The Ehlers-Danlos syndromes are a group of connective tissue disorders that can be inherited and vary both in how they affect the body and in their genetic causes. They are generally characterized by joint hypermobility (joints that stretch further than normal), skin hyperextensibility (skin that can be stretched further than normal), and tissue fragility. The ED syndromes are classified into 13 subtypes, most of which have the connective tissue disorders. Life expectancy can be shortened with the vascular EDS, due to organ and vessel rupture. The other EDS varieties typically do not affect life expectancy (Ehlers-Danlos Society, 2017).

## Mitochondrial dysfunction

Mitochondria are the powerhouse of every cell. They turn sugar and oxygen into the energy the cells need to work. When the mitochondria are not functioning properly, cells cannot work correctly. There are many types of mitochondrial disease, and they can affect different parts of the body: the brain, kidneys, muscles, heart, eyes, ears, and others. Mitochondrial diseases can affect one part of the body or can affect many parts. They can affect those parts mildly or very seriously. Not everyone with a mitochondrial disease will show symptoms (Centers for Disease Control and Prevention, 2017).

In adults with autism, mitochondrial dysfunction can manifest simply by the person becoming suddenly exhausted to an extreme degree. Vision may become blurry at times when the person feels exhausted. The presence of mitochondrial dysfunction increases the risk for potential damage to the brain, which is dependent on oxidative metabolism. This risk is more pronounced in procedures that require general anesthesia (Lesko, 2017, p.91).

## Dyspraxia

A form of developmental coordination disorder (DCD), dyspraxia is a common disorder affecting fine and/or gross motor coordination in children and adults. It may also affect speech. DCD is a lifelong condition, formally recognized by international organizations including the World Health Organization. It occurs across the full range of intellectual abilities. Individuals may vary in how their difficulties present: these may change over time depending on environmental demands and life experiences. An individual's coordination difficulties may affect participation and functioning in everyday life skills in education, work, and employment. Children may present with difficulties with self-care, writing, typing, riding a bike, playing, and other recreational and educational activities. In adulthood many of these difficulties will continue, including in learning new skills at home, in education, and at work, such as driving a car (Dyspraxia Foundation, 2017). Researchers suggest about 7% of adults with ASD have dyspraxia (Autism Research Institute, 2017).

## Dyslexia

Autism and dyslexia are both linked to the way the brain processes information. For this reason it is not unusual for people on the autism spectrum also to have a diagnosis of dyslexia. People with dyslexia have difficulties with reading, writing, and spelling, as well with as interpreting maps, graphs, sequences, and patterns. For people on the spectrum, the additional frustration of not being able to read or write can lead to feelings of even greater isolation and frustration. They may even become angry and uncooperative (Autism Spectrum Australia, 2017).

## Dyscalculia

Dyscalculia is defined as a failure to achieve in mathematics commensurate with chronological age, normal intelligence, and adequate instruction. It is marked by difficulties with visualization, visual-spatial perception, processing and discrimination, counting, pattern recognition, sequential memory, working memory for numbers, retrieval of learned facts and procedures, directional confusion, quantitative processing speed, kinesthetic sequences, and perception of time. Dyscalculia is known by several terms:

- specific learning disability/disorder in mathematics
- math learning disability
- developmental dyscalculia
- acalculia

- Gerstmann's syndrome
- math dyslexia
- math anxiety
- numerical impairment
- number agnosia
- non-verbal learning disorder.

It is very common for adults on the autism spectrum to have this problem to some degree (Dyscalculia.org, 2017).

## Sensory processing disorder (SPD)

This is a neurological disorder causing difficulties with taking in, processing, and responding to sensory information about the environment and from within an individual's own body. The senses include visual, auditory, tactile, olfactory (smell), gustatory (taste), vestibular (balance and spatial orientation), and proprioception (or kinesthetic—the sense of one's own limbs in space).

While SPD is a condition separate from autism, 90% of autistic individuals also have SPD. A child with SPD will either act out or withdraw in order to manage the overwhelming stimuli of their environment (Autism Key, 2017).

## Eating disorders

Some estimates hold that as many as 20% of people with enduring eating disorders have autism. Because autistic girls are frequently underdiagnosed, it's often an eating disorder that first brings them to clinical attention—although autistic men and boys can and do develop eating disorders, most of the research and clinical attention has focused on girls and women. This gender bias has led some to refer to anorexia as "the female Asperger's" (Arnold, 2016).

Eating disorders frequently occur in conjunction with autism spectrum disorders. The comorbidity of anorexia nervosa and Asperger's syndrome is a significant clinical complication (Dudova, Kocourkova, and Koutek, 2015).

There are several types of eating disorders, the most common being the following:

- **Anorexia nervosa.** A disorder in which a person will not sustain an average weight. The person is typically terrified of gaining weight, even though they are underweight. They see themselves as overweight. A female with anorexia typically loses their menstrual cycle due to low body weight. They restrict food intake or stop eating altogether. In addition to the mental health problems, they will develop physical problems as well.
- **Bulimia nervosa.** Characterized by binging followed by self-induced vomiting, excessive vomiting, or misuse of laxatives, diuretics, or enemas. Numerous medical complications occur from these activities, compromising the individual's health.

Psychotherapy is needed for these eating disorders. It is highly recommended also to seek medical care and a nutritionist.

## Hypertension (high blood pressure)

This is a common condition in which the long-term force of the blood against your artery walls is high enough that it may eventually cause health problems, such as heart disease. Blood pressure is determined both by the amount of blood your heart pumps and the amount of resistance to blood flow in your arteries. The more blood your heart pumps and the narrower your arteries, the higher your blood pressure. You can have high blood pressure for years without any symptoms. Uncontrolled high blood pressure increases your risk of serious health problems, including heart attack and stroke. It can be easily detected and treatment immediately initiated (Mayo Clinic, 2017b).

## Diabetes

Diabetes is a chronic condition associated with abnormally high levels of sugar (glucose) in the blood. Insulin, which is produced by the pancreas, lowers blood sugar. The absence or insufficient production of insulin, or an inability of the body to properly use insulin, causes diabetes.

The two types of diabetes are referred to as type 1 (insulin-dependent/juvenile) and type 2 (non-insulin-dependent/adult-onset).

Glucose is an essential nutrient that provides energy for the proper functioning of the body cells. Carbohydrates are broken down in the small intestine and the glucose in digested food is then absorbed by the intestinal cells into the bloodstream; it is carried by the bloodstream to all the cells in the body where it is utilized. However, glucose cannot enter the cells alone and needs insulin to aid in its transport into the cells. Without insulin, the cells become starved of glucose energy despite the presence of abundant glucose in the bloodstream. The abundant, unutilized glucose is excreted in the urine. However, excess glucose will still remain in the bloodstream, leading to numerous dangerous problems, even death, depending on the level of glucose (Conrad Stöppler, 2017).

## Sleep apnea

This is a serious sleep disorder that occurs when a person's breathing is interrupted during sleep. People with untreated sleep apnea stop breathing repeatedly during their sleep, sometimes hundreds of times a night. This means the brain—and the rest of the body—may not get enough oxygen. There are two types of sleep apnea:

- **Obstructive sleep apnea (OSA).** The most common type, caused by blockage of the airway when soft tissue in the back of the throat collapses during sleep.
- **Central sleep apnea.** Unlike OSA, the airway is not blocked, but the brain fails to signal the muscles to breathe, due to instability in the respiratory control center (WebMD, 2017b).

## Chronic obstructive pulmonary disease (COPD)

COPD is a chronic inflammatory lung disease that causes obstructed airflow from the lungs. Symptoms include breathing difficulty, cough, mucus production, and wheezing. It's caused by long-term exposure to irritating gases or particulate matter, most often from cigarette smoke. People with COPD are at increased risk of developing heart disease, lung cancer, and a variety of other conditions (Mayo Clinic, 2017a).

## Sexual dysfunction

In the autistic population, there may be numerous factors for difficulties in this arena, such as sensory issues, social issues, medication issues, anxiety, or depression.

## Mental health issues

Up to 70% of autistic people experience mental health conditions such as anxiety and depression. A lack of acceptance can significantly impact the mental health of an autistic individual (Cage, 2017).

In conclusion, there is very little information available specifically to autistic adults, let alone autistic females. The majority of conditions are those the general population acquires. As we all know, living on the autism spectrum carries with it often unusual health issues with which we must deal. Life with autism is stressful enough. Top it off with one or more of these conditions and it becomes a truly stressful day-to-day struggle. Only we know what it feels like to be in our bodies. The outside world could never understand how we experience this world in which we live.

The scope of this chapter has not allowed for remedies/therapies/ treatments related to each issue. I will provide my own advice to my fellow members of the autism community. There are things that *do* require medications, but more often than not conditions can be treated by natural avenues such as diet, exercise, proper sleep, and good hydration. Everyone knows how to use a computer to Google topics. Use it. So many medications come with side-effects, some of which are even fatal. Our bodies don't metabolize drugs the same way others do. For that reason alone, try first to investigate alternate ways to treat the condition. Sometimes there are none, so then there is no choice.

I am giving each of you an assignment: healthcare providers *don't* understand individuals on the autism spectrum. How then could they provide you with proper care? *You* must educate them about autism and how to communicate with us. In my book, I very clearly map out how this can be done. I want to change healthcare around the world with this book. *You*, my friend, can help make this happen! We deserve excellent healthcare just like everyone else. That can't happen until healthcare providers understand autism, how to communicate with us, and how to make medical exams better.

Finally, get outside, go for a walk, enjoy watching some birds, watch a beautiful sunset. Decreasing your anxiety is your first step in getting healthy and enjoying life!

## Dr. Michelle Garnett on autism and co-occurring conditions

Certainly, the list of conditions that may co-occur with autism is long and can initially appear daunting. At the Minds & Hearts Clinic we find that it is rare to meet a girl or a woman who has only ASD, and it is the co-occurring conditions that need treatment. To be clear: we do not treat ASD at Minds & Hearts. We do treat the psychological sequelae of living in a world of social zealots who do not understand ASD. We also make many referrals for the medical conditions that co-occur due to genetics or epigenetics, where there is a genetic propensity for the condition and environmental trigger/s for its onset.

Unfortunately, as Anita states, the long list of conditions that co-occur with autism has absolutely nothing to do with fairness. If fairness came into it, whoever decided this would no doubt consider that autism alone would present enough challenges for anyone to deal with. While the "not fair" outlook is accurate, and a common initial reaction to further diagnoses, staying with this thought is not particularly helpful as it tends to lead to a sense of victimization and disempowerment.

In my clinical work, as I explore the strengths and challenges for women on the autism spectrum in their search for self, it is most often the case that the list of strengths far outweighs the list of challenges.

In other words, being on the autism spectrum brings gifts as well as challenges, and, as Anita rightly points out, the fortitude, inner strength, tenacity, and perseverance that come along with being on the autism spectrum adequately equip them to face their challenges.

Having "ASD plus" has nothing to do with fairness, but everything to do with neurology and genes. We know, for example, that both mood disorders (depression and anxiety) and autoimmune disorders are genetically linked to autism. We also know that there is under-connectivity in the neural networks of the frontal lobes in autism spectrum disorder, attention-deficit/hyperactivity disorder (ADHD), and sensory processing disorder. Differently functioning frontal lobes are a likely explanation for these common co-occurring conditions.

My own advice about having co-occurring conditions is to face the problem as if you were a scientist—that is, dispassionately and with curiosity. Accept that your first response is likely to be emotional; you may experience a sense of outrage, stress, anxiety, and/or grief. Accept and allow this emotion. Offer yourself compassion for your situation. Seek support from others who care about you. Seek professional support from a psychologist or counselor. Use the wisdom in other chapters of this book to deal with the anger, anxiety, and grief. Then allow yourself a second response: the scientific response.

Consider each label as a signpost pointing you in the direction of gaining more knowledge and wisdom about the mind and body you inhabit. Research each condition; consult specialists. Beware of quackery; it is bountiful in the field of autism. Use your hard-won knowledge and wisdom to empower yourself to treat your mind and body in ways that give you the energy, equanimity, and good health you need to fulfill your life goals.

Unfortunately, too many adolescent girls and young women on the spectrum have collected many mental health labels prior to being accurately diagnosed with having an ASD. These labels may include, but are not limited to, major depressive disorder, bipolar disorder, borderline personality disorder, dissociative disorder, schizotypal disorder, social anxiety, generalized anxiety disorder, obsessive-compulsive disorder, etc. An unfortunate consequence of this experience can be to align with psychopathology and to interpret one's self only in the context of dysfunction.

A long list of psychiatric labels is indicative of confusion and lack of understanding of ASD by health professionals, not dysfunction and psychopathology in the young woman. Aligning with psychopathology can seem attractive to a young woman who is confused about her self-identity and suffers paralyzing anxiety when she is out and about in the world. Avoidance is reinforced by the consequent relief from anxiety and negative tension in the short term, but leads to paralyzing depression in the long term. In this case, exploring each psychiatric label would not be helpful; instead, I recommend psychological sessions to treat the paralyzing anxiety and to explore the person's sense of self in terms of their qualities, abilities, and interests. The overall goal of therapy is self-acceptance to allow the person to design a life that suits their perfect spectrumness as well as their authentic sense of self.

## CHAPTER 17

# Considering Autistic Life and Mental Wellness

*Dena Gassner*

This chapter will consider those challenges related to managing and supporting mental wellness for autistic girls and women (G/W).

## Our journey

Some women report grieving their diagnosis and others report no regret whatsoever. But most autistics report some wistful thinking about the years between their first symptoms, their diagnosis, and the integration of their sense of self embracing autism.

I am no exception. I remain grateful for my diagnosis. Tony Attwood, Stephen Shore, Cathy Pratt, Valerie Paradiz, and Liane Holliday Willey hold precious space in my heart as those most directly responsible for me understanding and embracing my diagnosis. Becca Lory is a daily touchpoint for me as we navigate this world in our sisterhood. For those more arts- and/or visually driven people, Karla Helbert's *Finding Your Own Way to Grieve* (2012) may be a good place to start. It has only been in the last three years that I have even had regular contact with supportive peers. This should not be the case for autistic G/W. We need one another. Supports should happen for us all.

Some 20 years from my diagnosis, I've learned to use my logical brain to override the emotional, moving forward with gratitude and joy for my integrated identity. I choose no longer to give cognitive space to what was unknowable. We must find our own way to process, find what works, because however we process and release our past, move in the present, and anticipate our future, in doing so it becomes the foundation of stable and consistent cognitive and emotional wellness that ultimately helps to protect our mental and physical well-being.

I have found that experience of integrating my diagnosis and the resultant processes I've used (for myself and on behalf of my son) as we navigate these measures and the associated systems have helped people secure needed services and supports.

This chapter is a combination of my own journey as an autistic woman, as a mother, as a social work professional, and now, as I maximize my potential, as an autistic researcher. You may notice a more academic tone to my writing—this is my authentic voice—so I will write with the voice that has evolved in this final chapter of my journey. But I promise to make the information regarding mental health and autism usable and send you with "take home" ideas to help you on your journey.

## Coming to diagnosis

Many autistic women come to their diagnosis when experiencing crisis. Some of it is cumulative. It involves the layering of cognitive processing differences, constant pressure to prove disability for support, never-ending sensory and social demands, and what appears to be ensuing poverty. Before diagnosis, we find ourselves at the doorstep of community mental health providers, social workers, homeless shelters, post-secondary disability services offices, and treatment centers for chemical dependency and/or domestic violence. These are sometimes mistaken as the primary issue when the underlying autism is the *real* and unaddressed/unidentified issue. Few providers are fully prepared to "see" and address the complex and ongoing nature of difficulties experienced by autistic women.

Autobiographical accounts of autistic women note that very late diagnoses and challenges including sexual abuse, homelessness, poor partner choices, and other forms of increased vulnerability that bound to unidentified autism can result in co-occurring mental health issues (Fling, 2000; Gassner, 2012; Lawson, 1998; Miller, 2003; Paradiz, 2002; Prince-Hughes, 2004; Holliday Willey, 2014 and 1999; Zaks, 2006). Even after diagnosis, some continue to fight anxiety, depression, and general fatigue that are difficult to manage.

Many women report difficulty with the unnecessary skills and information required to seek out support programs. They cite communication limitations, anxiety, hopelessness, and disenfranchisement from resource-knowledgeable groups as just a few of the barriers. Daily challenges remain.

Generally speaking, autistic people experience significant barriers to mental and physical health support (Nicolaidis *et al.*, 2013) and women, particularly, are most likely to experience an unreasonable delay in obtaining a diagnosis (Lai *et al.*, 2014). As a result of delayed, missed or misdiagnosis, unresolved and/or mismanaged co-occurring mental health concerns can happen. Even after diagnosis, it is very difficult to find support to help us process our shift in understanding ourselves that is needed to reframe the past.

## Our current status

Sadly, our story has to begin with the darkness this chapter seeks to escape. Our current status is improving but we must look honestly at where we are right now, as a community and as women.

Jones *et al.* (2014) find that anxiety, mood swings, and relational difficulties are among the top reasons why autistics seek a diagnosis. These studies say that when people address autism with general practice professionals (in the UK), they face "narrow and stereotyped views of ASD and the range of ways that ASD could manifest" (p.3041).

White, Ollendick, and Bray (2011) note that up to 70% of autistics have one or more mental health issues. Roux and Kerns (2016) say, "When mental health issues go undiagnosed and unaddressed, their effects can accumulate over the life course. Mental health issues can impede follow-through on recommendations and can affect acquisition of life skills."

Stress and coping are escalated in autistics (Hirvikoski and Blomqvist, 2015). And we experience shorter life spans, also according to Hirvikoski *et al.* (2016). Croen *et al.* (2015) with Kaiser Permanente noted five times the number of suicide attempts and multiple co-occurring issues that are often co-existing or that result from service failures for autistic persons including immune disorders, gastrointestinal issues, sleep disturbances, obesity, hypertension, and diabetes. From Canada, Burke and Stoddart (2014) report higher mortality rates, delays in treatment, and increased complications upon presentation for treatment largely resulting from barriers to care.

This chapter does acknowledge trauma as part of the mental health difficulties we experience, floundering in a treatment community with insufficient providers who are unqualified or not sensitized to treating trauma and helping us unpack the old history for reframing. As a result, we suffer needlessly. And these needs contribute to the increased frequency and incidence of co-occurring mental health concerns. All of these things accumulate and make proactively preventing or surfacing from an established mental health issue more than difficult.

This is being covered brilliantly by another author; however, we can't address anxiety and the status of autistic G/W without mentioning gender fluidity. This is highly common among autistics (Kristensen and Broome, 2015). The newest phenomenal book about a couple's journey through gender transition is by Wenn and Beatrice Lawson and is called *Transitioning Together: One Couple's Journey Through Gender and Identity Discovery* (2017).

Regardless of where we are on our life journey, we can and do survive, and even thrive if we seek out contacts, support, and resources.

## Anxiety

Anxiety is an inherent experience reported by most autistics. Roux and Kerns state that "Anxiety, in particular, is known to add to functional impairments in those with autism" (2016). They share a laundry list of potential triggers which provoke anxiety, including fears of rejection, phobias, sensory issues, and even "ordering food" as reasons that autistics may find themselves increasingly more isolated. Sensory challenges, the unpredictability of expectations and other people, anticipation of activities with prior negative histories, planning, organizing, and just coping can raise anxiety for autistics.

Some anxiety is triggered by simply entering family environments, school, work, or community. Others can experience anxiety in response to a reminder of a past traumatic situation that may include interpersonal rupture or even a setting that reminds us of that situation. Smells, sights, sounds can trigger us. In my own personal opinion, I believe we are experiencing a post-traumatic experience worthy, possibly, of a secondary diagnosis of PTSD. My anxiety is provoked by unpredictability and multitask demands of work and family.

Poverty, the fear of poverty, and housing relocations are at the top of a list of possible significant life events, along with interpersonal disruptions and changes in routine as anxiety triggers (Milovanov *et al.*, 2013). Sadly, women (autistic and non-autistic) are particularly vulnerable to stay in poor situations for financial survival—especially where children are involved. The loss of income may be a result of a lack of employment support or needing to be a stay-at-home mother, managing school meetings, therapies, and advocacy training for an autistic child. Predictability, consistency, and peace of mind are key to our continued wellness, but these factors of poverty and childcare can make doing that very hard.

## Depression

Anxiety can reduce one's capacity to engage in the world. Isolated from social engagement and its attached resources, isolation and loneliness can become sadness and depression. This can manifest as physical pain, fatigue, confusion, brain fog, or panic. Depression compounds processing difficulties including working memory issues, processing speed, co-occurring learning difficulties. This has an impact on coping and strategizing.

In my case, PTSD from sexual assaults, depression, and anxiety manifested more "loudly" than the ASD symptoms, so I was trapped for years with ineffective therapists bastardizing the sexual abuse without considering the underlying vulnerability that allowed assaults to continue to occur, more than once. They didn't know cognitive behavioral strategies (see below) that were much better suited to my extremely logical brain. The medical maltreatment and overmedication nearly killed me.

A starting point for me that may help many is learning anxiety-provoking triggers. We've been programmed and socialized to repress these needs, so playing detective and re-engaging awareness of our needs may take time, but processing the sources of anxiety and developing plans before they're needed can be helpful. Without meaningful help and counseling from qualified providers, many autistic women sink into a very deep hole, but even more are finding their own way out.

## Self-harm

I am not an expert on self-harm. However, in my research I've learned that I do engage in a non-suicidal form of self-injury (NSSI—cuticle biting and tearing). This type of deliberate injury joins trichotillomania (hair pulling), self-marking, picking at small wounds, and other behaviors that are not pathological in themselves, but do physical damage and act, in fact, as coping mechanisms directly related to stress and anxiety by releasing intruding thoughts and fears.

In my personal experience, self-harm provides a kind of paradoxical calming experience and, at times, enhanced focus. Infection, negative social feedback, and disfigurement occur. I work hard each day to find alternative coping strategies to manage, but it's still a challenge. For me, too, this behavior increases with the use of stimulant medication for attention. This is not uncommon.

Outcomes are not good for those who engage in this behavior.

In one study, at least 50% of those studied affirmed engaging in NSSI and the numbers were higher for women (Maddox, Trubanova, and White, 2016). Whitlock *et al.* (2013) explain that NSSI prior to suicidal behaviors can serve as a "gateway behavior for suicide and may reduce inhibition [to suicide] through habituation to self-injury" (p.486). This means that the more you engage in the behavior, the easier it could be for you to consider and/or execute a suicide.

The good news? Whitlock *et al.* further state that "Treatments focusing on enhancing perceived meaning in life and building positive relationship with others, particularly parents, may be particularly effective in reducing suicide risk among youth with a history of NSSI" (p.486). Using the strategies described below can help us find the authentic self that exists within all of us and engaging others in our process can help us through to the other side.

## Eating disorders

As far as my research shows, no one has looked at a possible connection between eating disorders (ED) and self-injury in autism specifically. However, in my practice experience, they tend to serve similar purposes, which is to foster a barrier to outside and the multilayered pain we experience from the world. It is important to note that many autistic girls and women are diagnosed with ASD after a diagnosis of ED, and treatment is less than successful.

We can confirm that there are many forms of eating disturbances in ASD ranging from food aversions, texture selectivity, pica (eating non-food items), rumination (allowing previously consumed food to come back up), and simply avoiding food in public places. Autistic G/W often have histories of food phobias or restrictions (Rastam, 2008). Certain colors, textures, sounds of eating, or combinations are simply intolerable. ASD and ED share dually matched issues of perfectionism, seeking predictability, and rigid thinking. Some report that the mental fog of malnutrition dulls sensory stressors and anxiety. Relief found in this physical silence can be seductive.

But the costs are high. The harsh truth is that restrictive eating and full-on eating disorders can cause great harm and even death. Recovery is possible but, like all other mental health support, it is dependent on the providers identifying the co-occurring autism and adapting treatment accordingly. For example, socially demanding "group work" may not be useful and may, in fact, escalate anxiety. The key is to identify the value of the condition to the individual and treat accordingly.

## A starting point

Seeking out resources requires networking, engaging, and navigating the healthcare system and support group agencies to identify trustworthy local providers. It requires socialization and executive function. It requires us to be brave and find our worth so we can ask for help. And it requires resilience and persistence when resources don't initially work out.

Our autism family is far-reaching and can be quite helpful in understanding how hard it is to pick up the phone and who, as providers, will be understanding toward us. Podcasts, books, and lectures are all helpful resources. But if I were the "Queen of Support Services," I would wave my wand and demand partnerships with allies (autistic and allistic) who could act as "translators" and "system navigators" for us. Just living our lives is demanding enough. In my magic world, none of us would deal with any school meeting, post-secondary setting, or social service environment without support. We'd have "Our Person" who would know the systems we must navigate and would teach us the hidden curriculum. Other disabled persons have such support—it's time for us to have this as well.

## Ideas and resources for mental wellness: Getting to the other side

For any autistic to achieve maximum wellness, it is key that we first set aside a time for (1) understanding autism, (2) understanding our experience of autism and how, through that lens, we see the world uniquely; then (3) through the solicitation of gentle feedback, we can learn how others perceive our autism, and (4) through disclosure (informal and formal), scripting, collaborative advocacy, accommodations, modifications, and supports, understand ourselves as whole and complete including our autism. This is the foundation that allows us to maintain personal wellness while achieving our maximum potential. Books to help include all of the previously mentioned autobiographical accounts and logic-driven books that help with this process by Valerie Paradiz (2009) and Stephen Shore (2004; Antony and Shore, 2015) are listed in the references.

The "Connection Process" (for integrating one's diagnosis) as I call it has no time or season. The sequence can be arbitrary. But seeking to know—reframing misinformation and reworking our lives not to overcome autism but to fully integrate it into our identities—this is where we all must start.

## Physical health

Looking at one's physical state should always be the first stop. Are you like the vast majority of autistics with sleep disturbance?

Do you need a sleep study? Do you need medication to help with sleep? How's your vitamin D level? Are you eating properly? Could you have co-existing visual processing issues and require intervention with Irlen filters? With my clients, this is always the first place we start.

## Books

There are many options to help us manage ASD. Even though some of us may feel we've aged out of books written with younger autistics in mind, revisiting strategies and applying them to our adult lives can be helpful. Check out Jed Baker (2015), Valerie Gaus (2017, 2011), and Zosia Zaks (2006), who remain some of my all-time favorites, addressing social skills, daily chores, and personal management. Although I know he's controversial, Phil McGraw's earliest book, *Life Strategies: Doing What Works, Doing What Matters* (2001) helped me to see the ineffectiveness of rumination and angst and how logically to reframe my life to move forward.

## Mindfulness and nature

Mindfulness has become a new construct that many autistics report as successful. Meditation, yoga, tai chi, art, reading, or repetitive quiet activity such as walking, running, swimming, music, and quiet baths can help. Music can be in either category.

I have to be honest and say this never works for me. My mind is extroverted in that it draws its capacity to perform from the energy of others, so this isn't a fit—and that's OK: we're all different. But many can and do enjoy solitude and peaceful settings. I would be in

Starbucks in headphones! And recently (as I write) I've found some release and focus using apps like Brainwave Binaural Programs. I have no idea how, but it has massively helped my sleep disturbances and focus with work. (Note: Those prone to seizure should consider this with caution.)

## Work

Some autistics can work without accommodations or disclosure; others can work using these supports. But another reasonable option is self-employment. When you look at the most successful autistic role models, we often see self-employment as their home space. Yes, they may be affiliated with a university or a shop, but even these opportunities are quite autonomous. It must be viable. You must be able to identify support to close the gaps in your own skills (for me, it was the bookkeeping), but in the US it's possible to receive funding for self-employment enterprises through Vocational Rehabilitation agencies.

## Cognitive behavioral therapy (CBT)

Dr. Phil's first book helped dip my toe into a cognitive behavioral mindset. He uses black-and-white logic to process life's challenges and that spoke to me. While I never saw a therapist who used CBT, my research has suggested that this is a viable option for many autistics—especially if a more "talk therapy" approach without action steps has been unsuccessful or unsatisfying. Although it's geared toward providers, I learned about CBT through Gaus's book *Cognitive-Behavioral Therapy for Adult Asperger Syndrome* (2007).

## Medication

Are you one of the many for whom a biochemical difference cannot be supported sufficiently by these options? Then, yes, medication may be a choice. I have found that my noisy brain requires nightly low doses of sleep medication. I keep the dose low by supporting this one tablet with supplements, but for me this was a deal breaker. Sleep issues when my children were babies nearly brought me to my knees, and medication will always be a necessary support in my case. Know that you'd not be alone in needing this. There's nothing wrong with it. It can be challenging as we all respond differently and trials can be exasperating. But when you find the right mix, it can be life-changing.

## Finding peace

This chapter has looked at the current status of mental health in the autism community. It has discussed the implications of late diagnosis. It has examined co-occurring mental health conditions and some of the layering of issues that create difficulties. We've looked at books, resources, and interventions that may help. I hope that somewhere in this effort you've found ideas for moving forward in your most authentic, meaningful life.

## Dr. Michelle Garnett on mental wellness

Like Dena, in considering autistic life and mental wellness, it has been my extensive clinical experience that, for many women on the spectrum, a critical turning point toward mental wellness has been accepting their diagnosis of ASD. This acceptance paves the way for integrating the diagnosis as an explanation for the past

("I am not defective, I am different") and understanding the authentic self for planning a meaningful life ("I can now accept who I am and plan my life for my own interests, needs, and values"). This process of acceptance takes time and has important stages. I agree with Dena that Stephen Shore (2004; Antony and Shore, 2015; Overton *et al.*, 2005) is one of the best authors to guide this work.

Involving others in this process, whether professional or personal, can be difficult for many women on the spectrum because of past trauma, as Dena describes. Being abused in the past, including being rejected and/or bullied at school, can lead to the generalization that people are not safe and therefore not to be trusted. This is an understandable position to take because it is self-protective and minimizes the chance of future pain. Unfortunately, over-learning the lesson that some people can be abusive can lead to further social isolation and poor mental health. No one can take this journey toward wellness and self-realization for you, but it is also the case that you do not have to take this journey alone.

**Trauma**
Seeking treatment for past trauma can be an important first step in feeling safe and grounded enough to explore who you are. The incidence rate of ASD and PTSD is unknown, but it is widely recognized that individuals with PTSD are at higher risk for development of PTSD because of neurological, cognitive, and psychosocial vulnerabilities. For example, under-connectivity between the amygdala and prefrontal cortex leads to emotional overactivity and more difficulty processing strong emotions. A tendency toward "black-and-white thinking" can prevent adaptive cognitive processing of adversity leading to ongoing high levels of distressing emotions (Kerns, Newschaffer, and Berkowitz, 2015). It is widely recognized that children on the autism spectrum are also at higher risk of abuse than children not on the spectrum (Berg *et al.*, 2016).

**Self-harm**

There are many reasons why a girl or woman on the spectrum may turn to self-harm. These include:

- seeking physical pain to block out the emotional pain
- seeking to feel something—anything—because of physical numbness
- becoming addicted to the rush of endorphins that can occur just prior to cutting
- as an outward expression of intense emotional pain where words fail
- as a cry for help.

If self-harm is occurring, it is important to seek professional help. Self-harm generally is an indication that the person is suffering from a lack of strategy to cope with strong emotions. Suicidal ideation may or may not accompany self-harm. Self-harm does not always lead to suicidal thoughts or intent. However, it is important to assist that person to discover different strategies for their psychological pain and distress.

**Anorexia nervosa**

Personal risk factors for developing anorexia nervosa (AN) include having the trait of perfectionism, overuse of "black-and-white" thinking, having an anxiety disorder, ineffective emotion regulation strategies, and having a poor sense of self. Unfortunately, these factors are all typically present for a girl or woman on the autism spectrum. Consequently, the co-occurrence of ASD and AN is high. Different research suggests that around 16% (Wentz *et al.*, 1999) or as high as 28% (Gillberg *et al.*, 1996) of adolescents with AN have signs of Asperger syndrome or a full diagnosis. In AS, anorexia nervosa is not always a disorder of body image; instead, an underweight body can be purposefully chosen to prevent becoming feminine or because the person may overvalue the experience of feeling light or hungry, due to a sensory processing disorder. Diet, exercise, and food rituals may be employed to prevent feelings of being out of control, and to eliminate disabling anxiety. Their intense interest can be nutrition and calories, with fascinations occurring in measuring food and calculating the body mass index (BMI).

### Gender dysphoria

In my experience, people on the autism spectrum generally, and women in particular, are far more likely than the general population to experience gender fluidity. They may wish to be the opposite gender, either in personality characteristics, body form, or social role. This wish can come on suddenly during adolescence while they are exploring the answer to the question, "Who am I?" It can reflect a genuine confusion in overall identity and a seeking to resolve poor peer relations—for example, not feeling accepted by peers, or getting along better with boys compared with girls. There can be a feeling that social and emotional difficulties would be resolved if the girl was a boy. Sometimes this confusion and yearning causes considerable distress. If this is the case, I recommend embarking on a course of therapy to explore self-identity with a psychologist who understands ASD.

I have found that a common therapeutic resolution for girls on the spectrum is to consider themselves gender-neutral, or non-binary. They resist social gender stereotypes and decide to be their own person, adopting a gender-neutral form of dress or vacillating between male and female dress, equally comfortable with both. As one teenage girl recently said, "I wish I was a shape shifter. I would like the experience of being male some days and female others. I would not choose to undergo gender reassignment surgery because I cannot see that the advantages of being one gender outweigh the advantages of being another to that extent."

Equally, for some girls and women, gender reassignment surgery is a serious consideration and may end much suffering, also placing them firmly on a pathway to authenticity of self-expression and meaning in life. I cannot stress enough the importance of ongoing non-judgmental support and counseling through the experience of gender fluidity.

## Cognitive behavior therapy

Like Dena, I find cognitive behavior therapy (CBT) to be a good match for a person on the autism spectrum who is suffering anxiety, including trauma-related anxiety, depression, self-harm, and/or anorexia nervosa. CBT is a good match for a person who has sound verbal intelligence, the capacity for insight, and a logical mind, and who is a truth seeker. It is action based and provides structure. Professor Tony Attwood and I have written a book for people on the autism spectrum who also experience depression, which is based on the CBT model (Attwood and Garnett, 2016).

There is good evidence that using mindfulness and CBT can be a better match when the person also has trauma-related anxiety and/or depression. I can highly recommend the use of Integrative Restorative Yoga (iRest®) as an adjunct to CBT for the treatment of trauma. iRest® was developed by Dr. Richard Miller, clinical psychologist and yoga teacher, to treat PTSD in war veterans (Miller, 2015). I find iRest® well suited to women on the spectrum because it is highly structured, introspective, well founded in research, and experienced as being safe and grounding. It does not rely on the capacity for putting thoughts and feelings into words, or using non-verbal communication or social skills in therapy.

CHAPTER 18

# Self-Care

*Becca Lory, Catriona Stewart, and Kate Ross*

## What is self-care?—*Becca Lory*

The concept of self-care has been a pillar of mindfulness practice since its inception. Yet, for centuries, self-care was far from integrated into our daily lives. These days, self-care can be found in almost every aspect of life. We see it in medical settings, mental health blogs, and productivity podcasts. As yoga and meditation make their way into the mainstream, we continue to hear more about self-care. But what is self-care and why is it so important?

### Self-care: The info dump

Self-care is often confused with being selfish, egocentric, or some other such negative implication. Often described as insubstantial and indulgent, self-care is treated as an optional courtesy. This could not be further from the truth. The medical profession tells us that self-care is any *necessary* human regulatory function which is voluntary, deliberate, and self-initiated. Simply, self-care is any activity that you do intentionally which helps you preserve your physical, mental, or emotional health. Although this definition may not tell us the what and where of self-care, it does tell us that self-care is an essential component of living a successful and fulfilling life. In fact, self-care has saturated our world. There are self-care blogs, self-care apps, self-care podcasts, self-care classes, self-care books, self-care meditations, self-care groups, and self-care retreats. There is currently no shortage of information on self-care in sight. Worry not: you are but one internet search away from an endless supply of ideas regarding self-care, how to do it, when to do it, and where to do it. You will find that acts of self-care come in all shapes and sizes, from eating your favorite snack without guilt, to adopting a pet or relocating. It covers the essentials of daily living too, such as eating well, sleeping well, and exercising. If you simply throw "self-care activities" into your internet search engine of choice, you will get a plethora of results ready to inspire your very own self-care routine. Take in all the choices, pick some good ones, and add them to your schedule. Self-care that supports your overall well-being will make you feel good, help you to think clearly, and supply you with the fuel not just to get through your day, but to enjoy your day.

An act of self-care can be big or small, long or short, simple or complicated. The only requirement is that it must be an "intentional" act with the goal of "preserving" some portion of your overall well-being. It sounds simple and yet we must constantly be reminded of its importance. For example, every time you fly on a plane you get the safety lecture from your smiling flight attendant. They stand by the cockpit and run down the rules for safety in an emergency. Eventually, the oxygen mask comes out and they give you instructions for its proper use. The last thing they always tell you about that mask is that if you are traveling with somebody else, you must put your mask on first before you help them. Why? Because if you suffocate and die, you cannot help anybody.

This scene plays out less dramatically in our daily lives too. How many times have you said to yourself, "I'm hungry but let me just do A and then I will eat"? Or, "I have to go to the bathroom but let me just do B and then I will go"? In both of those instances, self-care is not the priority. Instead of taking care of your essential needs, you do A or B or both. Do that enough, and not only are you failing yourself, but whatever else you are doing is suffering too. Success will always be "just" out of reach as you incrementally become impatient and rush, and the quality of what you are doing suffers, as do the people around you. A little bit of "me time" can make doing what you need to do a whole lot easier and whole lot more effective. A good self-care routine makes you feel healthy, relaxed, and ready to tackle your responsibilities. It recharges your personal batteries, giving you extra energy to accomplish your goals and help others accomplish theirs. Self-care keeps you focused and feeling emotionally balanced, keeping the communication line open between your body and your mind. Lastly, self-care feels good. It allows you actively to incorporate pleasure and happiness into your life. If you take the time for self-care, everybody wins.

**Not that: The autism side of self-care**
Wondering why self-care is being included in a book about spectrum women? The answer is simple: spectrumites are horrible at self-care. The good thing is, as with most aspects of spectrumness, there is a logical reason for that. As we already know, people of the spectrum have unique needs and partake in different activities to the rest of the inhabitants of the human bell curve. We also do activities with varying forms of intensity that is not necessarily under our control. What this means is that when you begin to look at popular self-care programs, you are not going to find an abundance of spectrum-friendly activities. But do not fear: we can,

as always, accommodate for that. The best self-care activities are the ones that you decide to give that label. If you love to read, schedule an hour of reading time for yourself every day. If you like listening through your headphones while walking, schedule that in. If you simply like lying quietly with your thoughts, make time for that. Those are the activities you should seek to incorporate more intentionally in your life. Let's bank on our love for routine. Don't create a self-care program; create a self-care routine. Schedule an hour of something you enjoy every day at the same time. Do the same thing every day or something different each day. Eventually, this new routine will become second nature and you will find comfort in your recharge time.

Another roadblock for spectrumites on the way to self-care is our compromised sense of self; meaning, individuals on the spectrum have figured out that who we are, not just the way we are, is different. We are also taught that different is bad. Very early on, those lessons are put together to tell us that who we are in our natural state is bad. We are taught not to trust ourselves, our gut instincts, or our core emotional responses. Our sense of self-understanding, self-control, and self-compassion is distorted by our early teachings. Our needs are complex, unique, and often ignored or rejected. To implement self-care routines, you must first evaluate your sense of self. Get to know your needs and wants. Spend some time listening to your own voice without the judgment of others. Find out what you really get recharged by and give yourself the gift of that time. You deserve it.

### Like a lady: Women and self-care

Besides spectrumites, you know what other group is even worse at self-care? Women! We are "natural caregivers" and that is a self-care trap. We worry about everybody, and I mean *everybody*, before we let ourselves bask in the glory of self-care. We are filled with guilt for every "supposed to" that has us putting ourselves last. We are "supposed to" work, be mothers, be wives, and do chores. We don't get to be selfish because doing things for ourselves is not on the "supposed to" list. But what if it were?

What if the women of the world decided to make self-care a priority? Would the world fall apart? Not immediately. Would we stop breathing? Not likely. Will anyone die? Illogical. So, what would happen if women deposited self-care into their energy bank? I'd venture to say we would see happier women doing more for the world at large, calmly, responsibly, and enjoying every minute of it.

**Know thyself: Self-care**
Mastering self-care is no easy task. I've been at it for years and I still have days where I forget to tend to my needs. But here are some keys to my success:

- Spend time with yourself. Make time to get to know yourself. You change over time and so do your likes, tastes, skill sets, and interests. Are you sure you still hate Brussels sprouts? Check in and find out. You could be missing out on greatness… just probably not in your vegetable drawer.
- You must know *yourself* to know your needs. This may seem repetitive, but even so, it bears repeating. You cannot know your needs if you don't spend time listening to your body, mind, and emotions.
- Let your needs guide your activities, in quantity and quality. Listen to your body and mind; they will guide the duration, frequency, and method of self-care. More is not always better.
- Schedule your self-care. Commit the time to do nothing but take care of yourself. Even if that means doing nothing. Resting is not doing nothing.

- Hold yourself accountable. Check in with yourself. Did you create a self-care routine? Did you stick with it? Answer yourself honestly.
- Take care of your emotions, your mind, and your body with the same intensity that you take care of your collections, enthusiasms, and pets. Make sure your mind, emotions, and body are being cared for with the same effort and energy that you are giving to other activities. They are just as valuable.
- Have fun. If you are not enjoying yourself, it is *not* self-care.

## Knowing yourself—*Catriona Stewart*

Self-care is a such a broad term; it ranges from the practical aspects of personal grooming and health to less tangible aspects of our lives, such as being able to assert our needs or the making of major life choices. It includes toenail cutting, eating well, and being confident enough to apply for that great-sounding job.

There are issues for many of us around aspects of what is described as "Executive Functioning Theory." In practice, that means it can be challenging just to get out of bed and organized in the morning, to implement plans, to get through a day's tasks, or take part in activities we want to. Another concern for many of us is getting enough sleep, which Kate Ross writes about later in this chapter. Many of the sensory issues involved in autism can make supposedly simple tasks such as having a shower or shopping for food highly complex and tiring. Which means that we have to be motivated in some way to do these things.

When I was young, I had three main motivators to action. One was curiosity; like a cat (I was called Catti, or The Cat at school) I was driven by a very energetic inquisitiveness, a need to "know stuff"—all sorts of stuff. That meant voracious reading and hours spent watching films or going to the theater, but it also meant being curious about people, what makes them tick, why they are what they are. My very active brain needed to be occupied, and if it wasn't occupied positively, it got itself into trouble.

The second was a genuine love of the physical—walking, dancing, creating beautiful things. When I was in a good place, I did all these things, energetically and with pleasure. Having realized as a child that keeping clean was a function of both staying healthy and being acceptable to others, I also learned that long soaks in hot baths were actually soothing and calming, and so they became part of my essential self-care regime. I've always liked being fit and active, so I try to find things that help with this and also that I enjoy. (I don't like gyms, for example, but I do like being outdoors in the countryside, so I have a dog I have to walk. She also makes me laugh, which is a bonus.)

The third of my key motivators, however, was fear. From about the age of 11, I was stalked by a nameless dark thing that sat just behind my shoulder, never quite catching up but sometimes getting very close. As well as being curious about people, I was frightened of them, but I didn't realize that until I was much older. Once I had left home at 18 years of age, though, what I was most frightened about was failing, of becoming trapped, dependent, losing my autonomy (as many autistic people do). That was a powerful motivator to keep going in the social world, to get out of the door in the mornings, to create work, to get to wherever I needed to go. I was very fortunate; I was determined and capable and got by, more or less, most of the time.

But I was also frightened of finding out I didn't really exist. I carried this unacknowledged motivator with me for years. Somewhere at the center of my being was a big black hole where I should be, with the fear that if I ever decided to look into that hole, there would be nothing, I wouldn't be there. Years of "pretending to be normal" (thank you, Liane Holliday Willey) or, at least, "pretending to be real," of fudging and busking it and copying other people (badly), had made not being myself an ingrained habit. I tried on a whole lot of different identities, none of which seemed sustainable (except being a mother, which I took on in my 30s and still have!).

Maslow's Hierarchy of Needs (Maslow, 1943) is often referred to when people are discussing human needs. Maslow created a kind of layered pyramid, with each layer representing a set of needs that have to be fulfilled before the individual is motivated to fulfill the next one "up." The first layer is physical needs (e.g. food, sleep, warmth, rest), and the second one is security needs (safety), and only when all of these needs are taken care of can we think about emotional needs such as "belonging" (e.g. relationships, friendships) and self-esteem (and then, finally, self-actualization, self-fulfillment).

That's where the more subtle aspects are of what we mean by self-care, in the roles of identity and self-esteem in our daily lives. If many of the daily activities of life require extra effort for autistic people, then the motivation to carry them out needs to be more powerful than for others, or perhaps just more clearly defined. We often need to have conscious awareness and understanding of what motivates us and why we need to complete the many tasks involved in looking after ourselves. It can be almost impossible to address self-esteem needs if we have little, and if we have spent so much of our lives trying to "fit in" that we don't even really know who we are.

Self-identity and self-esteem impact on every aspect of our lives, from the motivation to look after our physical needs, to the life choices we make, to our abilities to keep ourselves safe or resilient, or to pursue our dreams and desires, to our whole life trajectories. We need to be able to care enough *about* ourselves to care *for* ourselves.

My key motivator these days is a need to share what I've learned in the hope that autistic girls will grow to adulthood knowing who they are and confident in their self-esteem. If I ruled the world, I'd have every girl (not only autistic) given assertiveness training. I'd have all young people, especially autistic young people, undergo at least some form of martial arts training, including tai chi, for example. Martial arts training really is a training in balance, emotions regulation/anger management, and confidence. Assertiveness training is also about balance and confidence and, first and foremost, about knowing who you are, with the ability to assert your needs with clarity and confidence.

That might mean knowing when you have had enough of other people's company and you need to leave or turn down an invitation; it might mean asking for accommodations at work or telling your family about your autism (and being able to stay calm in the face of their reactions, whatever they may be!). It might mean asserting yourself against the wee voice inside that tells you it doesn't really matter if you don't eat well or get enough exercise or make space in your life to do the things that bring you joy, because you don't really matter. Because you do. You are real and you do matter.

## Sleep—*Kate Ross*

I love sleep, but it does not always come easily. As a newly identified aspie (relatively speaking), I managed to figure out how to help myself sleep a few years before my aspie-ness was discovered and confirmed.

Growing up, I had a "waveless" waterbed (i.e. you really had to throw your whole body into it to get it to move). I wasn't entirely sure why my parents bought it for me, but I loved my waterbed... It provided pleasant proprioceptive feedback any time I rolled over during the night, as the gentle waves would rock me peacefully back to sleep.

In my early teen years, I would end up staying awake late into the night and sleeping late into the day, especially during summer, because the lack of structure and regular activities made me feel very disengaged and provided no motivation to maintain a normal sleep schedule.

At university, my erratic sleep pattern continued because there were always far more interesting things going on with my hall mates, so again I'd survive on only a few hours of sleep. Ah, the days of being a carefree college student! However, by the time I made it to grad school, I needed to have far more discipline with my sleep routine, as classes were more regularly scheduled and work and internship patterns were more consistent. I found having a fan on in my room helped to provide white noise which blocked out random noises overnight.

In the US and Canada, melatonin is available to buy without a prescription, and I started to take this, finding it helped my sleeping patterns significantly. When I found out it was only available on prescription in the UK, I panicked, until I found a supplement called 5-Hydroxytryptophan (5-HTP) which worked for me for ages...that is, until I found out that one should not take it when prescribed certain anti-anxiety or antidepressant medication. It ended up making me a borderline insomniac because I was unintentionally overdosing myself on serotonin. Long story short: *Talk to your doctor before taking supplements.*[1]

I've requested a melatonin prescription, but I feel as if I'm not being taken seriously and don't want to be prescribed sleeping pills; I know that melatonin helps me fall asleep without feeling

---

1   Guidance on dosage and usage, as well as availability of melatonin and 5-HTP, varies between countries, so speak to your doctor first.

groggy or drugged in the morning. Research has been done and it is suggested there is a link between autistic individuals and low melatonin production; however, it's a rather niche subject for general practitioners to take on board, especially if they don't have many identified autistic patients.

Since 2010, I've been using a white-noise app to help me get to and stay asleep. My brain is constantly running, thinking about anything and everything. Because of this, I cannot get to sleep in an absolutely quiet room, so I need white noise to drown out my internal running commentary. I set the timer on the app to turn off when I want to wake up, and I've naturally been able to wake up like this with no backup alarm, only setting one when oversleeping would lead to missed appointments.

I prefer sleeping with the window on the latch and a fan on to move air around the room; otherwise, I wake up with a headache from stuffy stale air—even during winter. Also, I like to sleep with the sheet/duvet tucked up under my chin, because I hate the feeling of breathing on my skin; any occupational therapist will tell you that the tickly sensation is an alerting one, rather than calming.

My Kindle Paperwhite has been invaluable to me; it allows me to read in the dark without having a light on. The adjustable backlight allows me to dim the screen gradually as my eyes adjust to the darkness. Because it illuminates the screen and doesn't shine the light into your eyes, your brain is not being affected the same way it would be by blue light generated from other devices such as phones and tablets. I honestly don't know how I managed before I had my Kindle.

Another sensory tool I use is a weighted blanket. When I had my diagnostic sessions with the occupational therapist, trying the weighted blanket was a complete revelation. I never understood how something heavy would be relaxing, but within five minutes of having it on my lap, I felt noticeably calmer and focused, and was able to participate in the appointment in a productive manner. Having one to use at home helps me unwind when I've had a particularly stressful day.

Ultimately, sleeping habits are as unique as each of us. Yes, all humans sleep, but we all have different preferences for how we do this. Soft or firm pillows or mattresses, warm or cool rooms, wearing pyjamas or nothing at all. I hope this helps you think about what will help you sleep better. Pleasant dreams!

## Dr. Michelle Garnett on self-care

While the logic of self-care is hard to dispute, especially when described so expertly by Becca in this chapter, it can be surprisingly difficult for girls and women on the spectrum to put into place. The reasons for this include, as each of the authors of this chapter wonderfully describe:

- the difficulties someone on the spectrum has in truly knowing themselves and their values and needs, as well as executive functioning that make it difficult to prioritize, plan, initiate, and maintain new habits
- poor self-esteem ("I am not worth it")
- poor self-concept ("I am not real, I do not really exist, therefore I do not matter")
- paralyzing anxiety leading to avoidance of meaningfully engaging with the world
- presence of co-occurring conditions, including depression and anxiety
- lack of motivation
- being a woman and therefore often a natural caregiver
- lack of sleep.

I suggest making a list for yourself of the reasons that you consider may prove barriers to establishing good habits of self-care. Use the wisdom in this chapter to assist you to overcome these barriers. Enlist the help of someone who cares about you. Even if you are not convinced that you are worth it, or that you have the capacity to care for yourself, or even that it is worthwhile caring for yourself, my strong advice is to do it. Research evidence and clinical experience suggest that the more we care *for* someone or something, whether it be a person, an animal, a garden or ourselves, the more we care *about* that someone or something. In other words, the feelings of caring grow with caring actions.

Whenever I am engaged in discussion about self-care, I am always reminded of the stark difference between Western culture and that of Tibetan Buddhists. According to the Dalai Lama, Tibetan Buddhists are raised to believe absolutely and totally in their own self-worth. They are worthy because they exist. The Dalai Lama described his great confusion in understanding the concepts of low self-esteem, self-doubt, and low self-concept that are so prevalent in Western society (Goleman, 2004).

Through my study of yoga philosophy, which is not far away from Buddhism, I believe that one of the major differences between Western and Buddhist cultures is the definition of self. In Western culture we are taught to believe that we are our thoughts, feelings, and actions, including our achievements and failures. We are taught that our choices of societal roles (e.g. mother, daughter, friend, professional, student) and our choices of possessions (e.g. the type of car we choose, how we dress, whether we wear make-up or not, whether we wear designer clothes, the area in which we live) define us. We thus become overly identified with many aspects of our experience, as we are taught that this is what we are.

In Buddhist culture there is not this over-identification of self with thoughts, feelings, actions, societal roles, or possessions. We are none of these things because we are separate from them. We can observe our thoughts and feelings as internal experiences, but these internal experiences do not define us. The essence of self is our true nature; it is life, and life is worthy.

I have found in my clinical experience that it is helpful for women on the autism spectrum to learn to watch and observe their thoughts, feelings, and bodily sensations but not to over-identify with them. By observing ourselves, we give ourselves self-agency, which is the capacity to act outside of these experiences. For example, if we observe ourselves being overly caring of others, this observation gives us the choice to draw boundaries and create space in our lives to care for ourselves.

### Sleep

Kate's story is insightful and gives good examples of how, even with chronic sleep difficulty, it is possible to find ways to have enough sleep. I cannot overemphasize how important enough sleep is for self-care and emotional management. If sleep is an issue for you, I do encourage you to prioritize finding solutions. Included below are more ideas and there are some excellent resources to assist.

### Potential barriers to sleeping well

- **Sensory issues:** sounds are too loud, the bed is uncomfortable, problems with temperature regulation.
- **Motor/muscular problems:** restless leg syndrome, difficulties relaxing the body to allow sleep.
- **Busy mind:** too many thoughts in the mind, or racing thoughts, no particular focus.
- **Anxiety:** where it is difficult to get to sleep because of a particular focus of anxiety, for example money worries, anxiety for the future, health anxiety, relationship problems, being able to get to sleep, worried about the next day, etc.

- **Excessive alcohol consumption:** where two to three standard drinks are consumed regularly per evening, leading to early-morning awakening and increased anxiety.
- **Excessive caffeine consumption:** where consumption of tea, coffee, and/or caffeinated soft drinks is leading to wakefulness through the night.
- **Inactivity:** where daily life contains little to no physical exercise and the body is not tired for sleep.
- **Overtiredness:** where sleep has been delayed or missed too often, and the mind feels "wired" and unable to "switch off."
- **Fear:** where sleep has been associated with trauma, and therefore it does not feel safe to go to sleep.
- **Vitamin D deficiency:** either as a result of lack of sunshine, or a difficulty with the body processing vitamin D.
- **Unhelpful thinking patterns:** "I am just a hopeless sleeper," "I can never change."

**Potential solutions to allow better sleep**
- Addressing sensory issues by exploring and discovering solutions for auditory and tactile sensitivities, and/or temperature dysregulation.
- Addressing motor/muscular problems by learning physical relaxation strategies to allow the body to let go of tension and rest.
- Addressing "busy mind" problems by learning effective strategies to manage a busy mind at night-time such as getting up and engaging in a low-key activity (e.g. reading a slightly boring book), then going back to bed.
- Addressing anxiety problems by learning effective strategies to manage anxiety.
- Modifying alcohol or other drug consumption by addressing any problems with addiction.

- Modifying caffeine consumption, addressing any problems with addiction.
- Increasing physical exercise to wear the body out, allowing deeper sleep.
- "Easing the mind" activities to counteract the problems of overtiredness and a mind that feels "wired"—for example, yoga nidra.
- Therapy to address unresolved trauma that is affecting sleep.
- Addressing vitamin D deficiency via medical consultation and either increasing time in the sun or taking regular vitamin D supplements.
- Addressing low melatonin issues with use of melatonin supplements.
- Cognitive restructuring to recognize and challenge unhelpful thinking patterns.
- Attending a sleep clinic to identify problems with architecture of sleep or presence of a sleep disorder, such a sleep apnea.

## CHAPTER 19

# Intense Interests

*Christine Jenkins with Renata Jurkévythz*

Some of us believe we have to be productive, to justify our existence by what we do "for a living." This chapter is about what you do "for life to be well lived."[1]

## Why interests and passions matter

My intense interests are a matter of survival, not mere subjects of curiosity or recreation. When I fully engage in a pursuit, I am completely myself. Conversely, when I try to mimic an ability in an area outside my realm of mastery, I can fail miserably. High- and low-functioning labels are counterproductive and hurtful. It took decades to realize I either play to my strengths or I don't play at all.

I was identified by a psychiatrist at age 48; I regret that it took so long to celebrate my way of being.

---

1    Note: These may variably be termed affinities, talents, hobbies, passions, preoccupations, specializations, or extreme enthusiasms, but I avoid the term "obsession" unless in a quotation. I have chosen positive terms—for instance "collecting" versus "hoarding."

To help autistic women, I would start by asking:

- "What makes you tick?" List your pastimes, strengths, skills, affinities.
- "What makes you light up inside?" Beliefs, topics, people you admire.
- "What makes your heart beat faster?" Go with your gut instinct; don't censor yourself by thinking it doesn't make money or seem acceptable or age-appropriate to others. You are the expert on your talents.

It took me nearly 30 years to undo the damage of a high school guidance counselor stating I couldn't work in the music business (I started classical voice training at 32 and teaching music in my mid-30s).

Autistics show an extreme degree of involvement in their interests: "overarching," "all-encompassing," "immersive," "engrossing" are some words I use (Schaber, 2014a).

Although spectrum women lead rich interior lives, they can be more interested in people and ideas than things—joining a knitting club rather than doing their craft alone. The internet allows shared activity in the privacy of home. We teach ourselves online through education modules or via books (bibliotherapy, as my friend Dr. Kevin Stoddart terms it), and skip the oft-turbulent life on campus.

## Collections and hobbies

Why do we collect and even hoard? I surmise it's a form of systemizing to create order in an otherwise chaotic world.

In a way, organizing ideas or things is a rehearsal for life experience. Collecting and repeatedly reading Jane Austen books or watching movie adaptations becomes a way of emulating her characters. This form of restricted (or rigid) and repetitive behavior (RRB) is overlooked in Section B of the DSM-5 (*Diagnostic and Statistical Manual*), as it lists traits of boys. The stereotype of autistic men collecting train timetables, model cars, or sports statistics contributes to the male bias in ASD diagnosis and research, and in recent studies has been linked to the skewed gender ratio in autism rates. This impedes timely female identification—the women I've known are multifaceted and have several co-existing interests. I collect facts and love the sound of words; someone once called me an information packrat, which was spot on.

Having to be good at something or even have a special talent is a slippery slope, as there is a danger of equating usefulness to society with humanity (Malaquias, 2017). A 2014 advertising campaign promoting the rights of Down syndrome children (trisomy 21) was canceled in France over this debate (Malaquias, 2014).

It should be emphasized that the current criteria see RRBs as deficits rather than differences, undesirable traits to be treated rather than unique neurology. Female autistic authors such as Rudy Simone, in her classic *Aspergirls*, and later Samantha Craft, have more accurate female characteristics outlined. A recent medical article, "Learning when to treat repetitive behaviors in autism" (Harrop and Kasari, 2015), highlights the current state of research (very few studies on adults, and, as usual, few adult females). Even using the word "treat" is problematic; most of us thrive on our repeated behaviors!

Currently, I am a detective with acute interest in research on female (mis)diagnosis. Dr. Will Mandy at University College London is the best researcher on autistic females to date. His study "The experiences of late-diagnosed women with autism spectrum conditions: An investigation of the female autism phenotype," co-authored by autistic advocate Robyn Steward, appears in the *Journal of Autism and Developmental Disorders*, October 2016, Volume 46.

Collecting a lot of clothes (I took up sewing to afford a wardrobe), hats, recordings, and/or books (my earliest friends) can be fine as long as it doesn't turn into obsession. I used to keep lists of songs heard on the radio. I still make lists in my head or in long-hand. This helped at my late-life assessment to provide evidence of repetitive behaviors, since my parents were long gone.

My sphere of expertise is in the arts, so I'm pleased to have co-author Renata giving her insights on gaming.

## Technology and gaming—*Renata Jurkévythz*

Games are my safe haven. They have always been for as long as I can remember, since my childhood in the 1980s, and I want to offer an insight into why I love them so much, and why they are incredibly important to me. They have been a major part in sheltering and healing me in more situations than I can count, and they still continue to do this on a daily basis. To begin, I divide my experience into two different types: my emotional connection with the games that are story-based, and the puzzle games that provide mental stimulation and relaxation.

The emotional experience is when I really dive into another world and remove myself from reality. It is very similar to reading books, but the difference is I am directly responsible for the actions in that world. This completely hooks me. I cry, laugh, and feel so connected with some of the stories and characters that I just don't want the game ever to end; I don't want to say goodbye.

Very important in this type of world is the ability to try again and again, to fail multiple times until I reach what seems like that impossible goal. My brain is working hard, and the feeling I get when

I overcome these challenges is magical. It has also proved with time to be amazing training for all the difficult things I need to face in the outside world. I can overcome the impossible in this fantasy world where I learned that there are no impossible tasks. Coming back to my daily world, I see every challenge as a difficult stage to traverse or a huge "boss" to defeat. It gives me strength. It motivates me in a way my brain understands and pushes me forward, facing my fears.

My other type of gaming experience comes with the basic brain stimulation provided by solving puzzles. Puzzle games, especially mathematical ones, have the ability to heal me instantly. When I'm playing them, the stimulus is undoubtedly strong but soothing. The sensation feels as if all my brain's "lights" are lit at the same time, making me feel extremely energized but also calm, in balance. It is a primitive feeling of satisfaction and comfort. In these moments, I feel like everything is in its place, and all the anxiety and excessive thoughts just melt away for a while. This is heaven.

When I feel overwhelmed, I resort to gaming and all the comforts it gives me, at least until I can restore my strength and be able to come back. With time, I have learned I can avoid being overwhelmed by actively making some free time for gaming. When I'm feeling restored, I can face life and give it my best. So, for me, gaming is about connecting with myself, refilling my energy and preparing for the battle that awaits me outside. Escaping to my gaming worlds assists me in living a parallel life, one in the fantasy that helps me to cope with the real world.

## Immerse yourself in nature—*Christine Jenkins*

### Take back something worth remembering
So much has been written about the beauty of the outdoors and the healing power of nature. I shall only highlight some wonderful resources.

The Germans are way ahead of us with their outdoor kinder-
gartens or Waldkitas. The forest bathing movement known as
Shinrin-Yoku (basking in the forest) in Japan is slowly catching on in
Canada and the US. I have also walked outdoor labyrinths and found
peace in gardens. A pioneer of restorative walks was Sierra Club
founder John Muir, and recent advocates of gardens for inspiration
and soothing include the autistic gardener Alan Gardner in the
UK and the developer of Quebec's Les Quatre Vents, Frank Cabot,
who also founded the Garden Conservancy. Another wilderness
influence was Ernest Seton Thompson, who inspired Lord and Lady
Baden-Powell to found the Boy Scout and Girl Guide movements.
His writings inspired many Canadian wilderness camp directors.

## Walking on water

All the women in my family are naturally rubenesque and buoyant.
My Swiss grandmother was an early adventurer, the first woman to
swim across Lake Geneva, so I consider the dolphin my avatar. I'm
also a water baby, averse to getting wet, but once in, I stay in.

The canoe is the next best thing to being in the water, balanced
between waves and sky. The aboriginal people called it *Waterwalker*,
a term which my mentor Bill Mason utilized for his autobiographical
film. I never took canoe lessons from him but I heard enough tales
at his home. He was a quirky guy who escaped family life for months
of the year to paint in the wilderness. We shared a common faith
and an insatiable curiosity.

Being Canadian, I take open spaces for granted. My city of Ottawa
is cradled on three sides by a greenbelt that has slowly been eroded
by development since the plan of Jacques Gréber, a Paris-born
landscape architect, to set aside lands, starting in 1956. I live near
two of our nature reserves, the Mer Bleue peat bog and Green's
Creek Conservation Area. In 15 minutes by bicycle, I can be in the
woods or on the Ottawa River, the second largest in Eastern Canada,
whose fate is watched over by a full-time riverkeeper. When I go

backcountry canoe camping, I like to take photos, especially sunrises and sunsets. They help me deal with our long Canadian winters and remind me "this too shall pass."

## Talk to the animals

For many of us, the thought of life without animals is unbearable. The joy of a furry wake-up call, the steady companionship, and their carefree existence are all gifts to me. Friends call me the "cat-charmer" or "whisperer"; I know all the names of animal neighbors and tend to forget their humans. Perhaps I am half feline—I understand them and they get me. I make long eye contact where I can't with most people. One cat at a time usually suffices; for a four-year period I had a second, a stray; one brother warned me not to turn into the "crazy cat lady." I hesitate to say I "owned" Minuette, as she chose me.

I begged for a cat until I was seven. Tinker the tortoiseshell inspired my first piece of prose, published in the school paper when I was eight. She was rather aloof but most nights ended up on my bed. Cats have sat with me through deep sorrow, joined me in a happy dance, given comfort by their presence. They don't notice my lack of social skills. They are the perfect housemate—living side by side, mostly quiet, not demanding much, content with simple necessities—food, water, the occasional playtime or cuddle, and a place in the sun.

Cats socialize of their own free will, sort of like aspies. I feel honored when one spends time with me. There is their softness, of course—I prefer longhairs for tactile stimulation. There is the purring which I find so calming. I try not to think about moving to an apartment or long-term care residence where pets are not admitted. I hope the rules will have changed by the time I have to move.

If I start with the arrival of Tinker, I've averaged about eight years together per cat. I took in several no one wanted because they were older (4–7 years); with my tender care, most have lived past 18 years. No surprise, then, that my favorite show-and-tell book is *All Cats Have Asperger Syndrome* by Kathy Hoopmann (2007).

Autistic children who are drawn to animals can enrol in animal therapy, especially equine, where they learn compassion, care habits, and responsibility. Some teens and adults have started businesses such as dog walking, grooming, and in-home pet sitting. Some become vets, therapists, or zoo animal specialists (e.g. Dawn Prince-Hughes). Some receive service dogs specially trained to calm autistic anxieties. The fixed routines of animal care provide interaction, stimulate oxytocin production, and may create an income.

Here in Ottawa the Humane Society adopts out spayed and neutered cats, and the rescue service uses the Feline Café to showcase them, a win-win proposition. My women's support group Asperfemme has several pet volunteers who meet at the café. As with any intense interest, I can go overboard: I'm addicted to cat videos.

## The arts

### My life is a song (more than one at a time!)

My intense interests may come and go, but music is the undercurrent of my life, the wellspring of reassurance and contentment. It's my two-way street. John Elder Robison, Daniel Tammet, Leith McMurray, Rudy Simone, Stephen Shore, and Tim Page have all gone on record (pun intended) with their strong ties to music. Described eloquently by these older aspies who were usually identified in their 20s or later, their musical journeys strike a deep chord.

Music both allows me to express my emotions and distracts me from everything else. It helps me find my voice, soothes me with repeated lines, then traps me in an earworm.

Not everyone with perfect (or absolute) pitch is autistic, but research shows many on the spectrum have perfect pitch. Dr. Laurent Mottron was the inadvertent catalyst for my self-diagnosis. Pitch recognition is a form of systemizing that gives order and serenity. I was shocked to find most others lack it. To me it was as natural as breathing; others thought I was a freak or a show-off when I named a note, or gave the starting pitch out of the blue at school or choir.

This made me seem odd, so I learned quickly not to stand out. Children in the 1960s were expected to be seen and not heard. I sang alone whenever I could, then I self-calmed after school at the piano, playing by ear from the playlist in my head. (One of my high school nicknames was "the human jukebox" as I could identify most songs on the hit parade after a few notes.) At the rare parties I attended, I hovered near the turntable putting on records (a talent I used as a college radio music host), or took requests at the piano, momentarily popular. At dances I was the wallflower standing next to the loudspeakers.

Until my early teens I could not play in front of anyone but family. Playing piano in front of people seemed too intimate, but I soon realized, like any performer, I could don a persona and socialize on my own terms. Although my acting involvement has been limited to musicals, radio hosting, and some recitation, I understand how autistic actors and comedians feel about controlling the stage—for a short time we are in charge and everyone pays attention. Music helps me do just that: it grounds me in the present.

**Music on the brain**
Most of my earliest memories involve music. Even when I found it challenging to get words out, I was singing inside or "tuning," often from the moment I awoke. My godmother, Helen, played "Moon River" while I, unknowingly at age two, lived through the Cuban

Missile Crisis. The piano, which moved around Canada with us, became my mouthpiece from toddler age. Some people mimic dress, accents, mannerisms; I mimic tunes. My brain was never silent, although I appeared to be (selective mutism). If people would not come into my world, music would become the portal for me to enter theirs, my own personal TARDIS.

A few years after my ASD diagnosis I was assessed for sensory processing disorder (SPD). I brought in a checklist to the appointment of all seven senses of which I was aware. The two main findings were that I am auditory overresponsive and tactile defensive. It has been both a blessing and a curse to be a slave to my acute hearing and perfect pitch.

My interior playlist continues to provide the backdrop to my daily activity. Episodes in my life will always link to my musical past. Some people use "scripting" from books, comic strips, movie or TV scenes (Schaber, 2014b); I rely on "tuning" repeatedly to song lyrics. Awake or asleep, I am truly singing for my life.

## Sharing your interests

With whom do I share my interests? No one person, even a romantic partner or spouse, can engage with all of my jewel facets at once. The way I handle my diverse enthusiasms is to find different comrades (or persons online) for each. This keeps me from wearing out the relationship. If people shame you for your interest, find new people, not new passions!

As the self-styled Mother of Reinvention, I would caution about talking too long about your (latest) field of expertise—some people consider it bragging when you list off your skills, or that peculiar fact discovered after an immersive period of study, where you may forget to eat, sleep, perform hygiene, or do chores.

## Avoid info dumping—respect your listener

Carrying on a reciprocal exchange of ideas in the throes of a new passion is nearly impossible. Start with a short comment of a general nature, to see if your companion responds, then add more detail. Because of my unique wiring, my brain tends to flow from the specific to the general, so it is harder to think otherwise. The aim is not to insert an anecdote every time a topic arises, or it becomes always about you. Just because I have a personal opinion doesn't mean I should share it. I often learn more by listening, although it took years to keep quiet, and I still interrupt excitedly on occasion.

Some interests have waned with time, perhaps when I exhausted my curiosity. Sadly, this boredom occurs in relationships too— novelty is the spice of life, and crushes can be addictive (Davide-Rivera, 2013). When I am tempted to take up with a person, or explore a topic, I flip back through the "life inventory" in my Rolodex brain, and decide how it worked out before. If I remember losing my boundaries or neglecting my self-care (the so-called tortured artist effect), I will pause and reflect on the cost.

## Changing interests

With intense pursuits, some are needed to blend in or survive; others are a source of endless delight.

| Constant/enduring | Intermittent/passing |
|---|---|
| Books (several at once) | Swimming/lifeguarding |
| Piano by ear/tuning | Travel (limited due to cost) |
| Cats | Domestic management |

*cont.*

| Constant/enduring | Intermittent/passing |
|---|---|
| Rock music/musicians/concerts | Marriage and relationships |
| Sewing | Cycling safety (only full-time job) |
| Contemporary music radio host | Motorcycling (pillion) |
| Writing and correspondence | Opera (certified to teach), choirs |
| Tea (managed a tea house) | Fashion and make-up (pre-menopause) |
| Canoeing | Theology/small group leader |
| Perfect pitch/singing | Cancer, environmentalism, justice |
| Social anxiety, later Asperger's | Grief therapy, healing from suffering |
| Advocacy and public speaking | Genealogy |
| Researcher/interviewer | Registrar/exam proctor |

As it is, we autistic women can spread ourselves too thinly—as parents, lovers, friends, and workers, we don many personas. Professor Brené Brown (2016, p.232) quotes a schoolchild who cautions against too much compromise:

> Belonging is being accepted for you. Fitting in is being accepted for being like everyone else.

## Major on the majors

I could envy the social prowess of others and attempt to mimic it, in a world where groupthink is encouraged, even expected. I would rather rejoice in my strengths. If I concentrate on my skill and not my limitations, I won't feel jealous of what others have, and thus be content in my own skin. Vive la différence!

Don't walk through the world looking for evidence that you
don't belong, because you'll always find it.

Don't walk through the world looking for evidence that
you're not good enough, because you'll always find it.

*Our worth and our belonging are not negotiated with other
people. We carry those inside of our hearts... I may fit in for you,
but I no longer belong to myself.* (Brené Brown, 2017, p.158,
my emphasis)

## Dr. Michelle Garnett on intense interests

"Interest, pah! How British! [understated] My painting for me is like
oxygen!" said Carmen, a local artist and woman on the spectrum
when asked about her intense interest. Stella, another woman on
the spectrum I had the pleasure of meeting recently, said that she
was confused by a question from a family member about why she was
always alone. She went on to explain to me that she was fascinated
by the film script she had been writing for ten years to the extent
that the characters in the film were always around her; she never felt
alone. When a personal interest is present, it is vividly, passionately,
and intensely present.

Women on the spectrum often differ from men in that they
do not always have intense interests, but when they do, these
interests may be similar to those who are not on the spectrum. For
example, many non-autistic girls love cats and horses, but a girl
on the spectrum believes she *is* the cat or moves outside to live in
the stable. Intense interests bring joy, relaxation, a sense of identity
and fulfillment, friendship with like-minded people, and can lead
to a satisfying, successful career. It is more common for women
than men to, as Christine describes, have multiple interests at the
same time, and to cycle through interests. This presentation is
not described in the diagnostic manuals, leading diagnosticians

who do not understand the female presentation of ASD to miss the diagnosis.

Common intense interests for women on the spectrum include literature, words, music, animals, nature, the arts, psychology (including self-exploration), and the autism spectrum. However, this list is not at all exhaustive, and some of the interests that are considered more "male"—for example, in IT, the sciences, aviation, and mathematics—also commonly occur for girls and women. Two of the most unusual interests I have come across are for windsocks at airports and potato mashers.

Certainly, as Christine describes, one of the downfalls of the definition of ASD being presented in a psychiatric medical textbook is that repetitive behaviors can be considered a disorder to "treat." While there are times when repetitive behaviors require treatment (e.g. when the behavior turns into an obsession, or morphs into obsessive-compulsive disorder, or is unsafe), for most people their intense interest is the "silver lining" in the cloud, and is an outlet for part of their set of strengths and abilities, which can be used to overcome their challenges.

I like Professor Tony Attwood's and Carol Gray's definition of Asperger syndrome, "The Discovery of Aspie," which can be found in our book (Attwood and Garnett, 2016) and on Professor Tony Attwood's website (www.tonyattwood.com.au). The premise for this article was the idea that Asperger syndrome is something to be discovered, in the same way as artists are discovered, rather than diagnosed. Section B in DSM-5 describes the restrictive and repetitive behaviors in ASD. In "The Discovery of Aspie" Tony and Carol describe these behaviors in the following way:

Cognitive skills characterized by at least four of the following:

- strong preference for detail over gestalt
- original, often unique perspective in problem-solving
- exceptional memory and/or recall of details often forgotten or disregarded by others, for example: names, dates, schedules, routines
- avid perseverance in gathering and cataloguing information on a topic of interest
- persistence of thought
- encyclopedic or "CD ROM" knowledge of one or more topics
- knowledge of routines and a focused desire to maintain order and accuracy
- clarity of values/decision-making unaltered by political or financial factors.

Our goal at the Minds & Hearts Clinic is to assist a person to utilize their strengths and abilities to overcome the challenges. I strongly encourage you to find out your strengths and, as Christine and Renata say, rejoice in them! Focus on your skills, rather than your limitations. Be your own version of yourself, embrace your passions, do what you are good at, be quirky and eccentric. Enjoy yourself!

# CHAPTER 20

# And Another Thing...

## Maura

When Barb and I were discussing the structure of this book, she proposed there should be 19 chapters. I cajoled her into adding one more. I don't think she realized I was serious when, at an earlier stage, I said we needed an even number or a multiple of five. I was in fact deathly serious. Once she confirmed there would indeed be 20 chapters, all was well with the world.

When my husband and I are watching television, we have matching remote controls. He flicks through the channels and I control the volume. I can focus on what we're watching so much better if the volume is at (yes, you know where this is going) an even number or a multiple of five.

Why should this be? I don't recall how or when it started, but for me multiples of five seem more solid and give me a sense of security. As for even numbers, well, they just seem...*friendlier* somehow. They're softer. I know it doesn't make much sense but it's one of many harmless quirks I've come to recognize in myself as an autistic female. I am so grateful to Barb for indulging me!

## Michelle

Once upon a time there was a little girl who lived in a happy, safe home in a faraway land full of color. While she was still young, her family moved to a new land; this one was only gray. In the gray land her family broke apart. She lived in many different houses. The girl was still much loved but she started to become a mouse. She became quiet, afraid, and gray, and she matched her new, ever-changing, always gray environment very well. Although she did not know it at the time, the girl had a fire within her and this was her compassionate heart and her love of learning. She traveled, she learned, she loved, and she grew into a mouse-woman. She did not know it but she was following her heart. One day, no different to any other day, she looked around and she recognized all the gifts in her life and she knew, deep in her compassionate heart, that these gifts were reflections back to her about who she was. She didn't like all the reflections, but she loved most of them because she recognized in these reflections her most heart-felt values of compassion, kindness, family, friendship, community, truth, achievement, courage, and most of all love. The world was vibrant, vivid with color, and she was no longer a mouse; she was a woman.

## Samantha

Recently, my three sons (ages 16, 19, and 21) and I ventured on a cruise to Alaska. Our family—gifted with a quirky sense of humor—came back with many joy-filled moments. One of the funniest instances was when my eldest son and I were volunteer participants in a cruise ship challenge game. The cruise director dared a group of audience members to go on center stage and give someone a wedgie (the act of yanking a person's underpants up from the backside). My son and I, and a handful of other folks, happily volunteered. Of course, as a person who often takes things literally, once on stage, after hearing the instructions, booming through the ship's loudspeaker, "Pull the underwear up and over the person's head," I didn't comprehend the jest and impossibility of the statement. Thusly, there I stood, red-faced and exhausted, yanking and yanking my eldest son's underwear, to no avail. By the time the over-stretched briefs settled up to the middle back area, my son stood chuckling wildly, and I remained, still determined, and quite perplexed about how to stretch them over his head.

## Jeanette by Mr. Kitty

My name is Mr. Kitty and my human is a writer called Jeanette. As far as I understand it, "writer" means spending long periods of time looking at a computer screen and typing really quickly. She talks to herself while she writes. Often I hear her say "Awesome!" or "I think that is probably a bridge too far, but what the hey?"

I sit next to her chair for hours and she often puts her hand down and scratches me behind the ears. "You are beautiful and I love you, Mr. Kitty," she says and then gets back into her busyness.

Sometimes she is so focused I can't get her attention to communicate important things, like the need for cat food or cuddles. When that happens, I jump up on the back of her big black CEO chair and gently bat her on the head with my paw or stand on her computer. Both of those strategies are effective at getting her attention.

When she edits, she reads out loud. This is punctuated with an exclamation of "Idiot!" when she sees a typo. She says "Idiot!" quite a lot. When she has finished what she is writing, she says, "Awesome.

Let us do this thing!" really loudly and then she picks me up and holds me and I purr and purr. I'm glad my human is a writer.

## ARtemisia

It's no secret among my followers that I travel a lot. More than most people. I fly from Rome to Athens to New York and back again with many other little stops in between. It might appear from the outside as if I am fearless, unstoppable, unflappable. Nothing could be further from the truth. When I first arrive somewhere, I usually clean and arrange my room so that it looks virtually identical every time, and then I begin to make small forays into my environs. People in Athens asked each other, "Who is this woman walking up and down the street every day?" I find what I need, where to get groceries, where to drink tea and hear good music, etc., and settle into a routine, my routine, ever unchanging with only minor variations. Until very recently, even if I wasn't particularly welcomed somewhere, I would return to the devil I know rather than trying something new. When I get bored, feel overexposed, or when duty calls, I move on. I was born a stranger in a strange land, elegant and clumsy (just dropped my tablet on floor with loud clatter while typing), wise and foolish, brave and scared.

## Terri

I'm grateful to be me. At the age of 38, I am just about starting to piece together this thing called life. I think back now to the sheer amount of effort I put in to fitting in over the years, and, perhaps more importantly, realizing that it really wasn't necessary; I'm sure I caused more problems than I solved. As I got older, I started to identify my negative behavior patterns and began to work hard to remove toxic things from my life—people, habits—some of which were terribly hard to lose, but now I have come out the other side so much stronger and what I value the most is living my own truth. Learning of my autistic identity at age 33 certainly challenged me to do that and, to be honest, I'm still processing it. I have learned to accept that it's OK not to have all the answers, to not yet know how you feel about something, to not have reached a conclusion, to not conform if it's not right for you. In 2018, the world is starting to become a place more tolerant of difference. The wheels of change are starting to turn; this book is part of that. I'm glad this is happening in my lifetime and that I will be around to see it.

## Kate

I've been a Beatles fan for as long as I can remember. I loved studying album artwork, staring at photographs, and memorizing printed lyrics. Listening to their discography in chronological order (anything else is sacrilege) immersed me in their music.

My family had a LaserDisc player—my husband loves teasing me because it's now obsolete, even though I was watching HD video before HD existed!—and we had the Beatles' films, *A Hard Day's Night*, *Help!*, *Magical Mystery Tour*, and *Yellow Submarine*, on LaserDisc; I would frequently scan back ("rewind") my favorite lines repeatedly to pick up their subtle, brilliant British wit.

What disappointed me was not having anyone else as intensely interested in the Beatles as I was. I learned to suppress my geekiness and stop waffling on about it because no one would like me; this was very tricky to suss out. Thankfully, my three cousins loved watching the films with me during sleepovers.

Of all the non-essential information out there that could occupy the precious real estate of my brain, there are definitely worse things to have in there than the lyrics to all of their songs, emblazoned in my mind forever.

## Liane

Years ago my father told me as long as I stayed in college, he'd pay all my expenses. Being a good literal thinker, I took his promise through 11 years of college until I earned a Doctorate of Education in psycholinguistics and learning style differences. I'd have loved to go on to law school, but Dad convinced me it was time to release him from his promise. I spent years teaching at university level until I was diagnosed with Asperger syndrome. I like to share my experiences of living with autism to audiences worldwide, bringing to each presentation some humor and positivity along with the real and not so happy memories surrounding my life as an autistic. My autism advocacy goals revolve around helping others understand the importance of learning from one another through shared experiences, flexible environments, and open hearts. My passion is anything equine, and if I had my druthers, I'd live in a barn stall next to my horses, dogs and cats, and maybe a fainting goat, and a bearded lizard. My hope is that someday humans learn to get along as well as different species of animals do.

## Christine

I went to a huge high school of 1300 students at the end of the postwar baby boom. After four years in the gifted program, I knew practically no one and did not fit in well.

What saved me was the academic life and the camaraderie of teachers who took an interest in a short, gawky, misfit girl. We talked outside of class. I remember my biology teacher Mr. Borland loaning me Kurt Vonnegut, feminist Ms. Lomas lending me books *not* on the English list, and Frau Kraus patiently coaching me for the provincial German contest. Each saw something worth encouraging.

Later I read the part of Sophocles' Antigone in English class and discovered my voice moved people. No one dreamed I would someday be on stage singing and speaking.

Before I graduated, I recorded a version of "In Flanders Fields" for broadcast on Remembrance Day, which the school aired annually for many years.

Those teachers who invested in me set me on the path to being the communicator I am today. I've used my languages for travel and work, embraced my geekiness, and regularly reinvented myself. This socially awkward, unidentified aspie became a creative force in the world. I thank all the other adults who've mentored me; their faith has been rewarded. I hope I inspire my own students even half as much.

## Anita

I came from a very poor family. My grandfather was a coal miner. I learned at a very early age that whatever I wanted to accomplish I'd have to work very hard to achieve it. I graduated in 1988 from Columbia University in New York City with my Master's in Nurse Anesthesia. I had to take out over $100,000 in student loans which took me ten years to pay back. I've been working full-time for the past 30 years as a Certified Registered Nurse Anesthetist. I always felt ashamed that I came from such humble beginnings. I've just completed a book about Temple Grandin, *Temple Grandin: The Stories I Tell My Friends*. I spent over 60 hours interviewing her. Temple shared with me how it bothers her when people bash her online because she came from a wealthy family, claiming that's how she got to where she's at. I confided to her I came from a very poor family. "You are proof that a person with autism can become successful despite coming from a poor family!" Temple stated. She made me realize just how much I *have* accomplished! I now am truly proud of my life, thanks to Temple!

## Catriona

I consider myself fortunate, born in a lovely part of the world with parents who taught us how important, and sanity-saving, our natural environment is. I was lucky nature gave me other things too—health, determination...

There were ways in which I wasn't lucky. I was an oddity. In a family of oddballs, I was different again. Being different isn't bad luck at all; being different in a context where "being normal" is valued above all else isn't great. Being a strange in-between thing in a binary world, a different thinker, not one of the girls, can be lonely.

It can build resilience, though—a controversial term for autists, maybe, when demands for resilience are so high—and strength. I had that autistic "unrealistic" perspective on my own capabilities (detect a bit of irony?). I had poor sense of identity, poor self-esteem, but I did go for some stuff, followed my passions, because there was no medicalized, deficit narrative of my being telling me I couldn't. I've had a lot of fun, met challenges and some great people, raised children. I've experienced failure, pain, and grief too; that just makes me human.

## Dena

I am a wife, mother, grandmother, and PhD candidate in Social Welfare, finishing ABD (all but dissertation) in May 2018. I will be getting this "bucket list" degree just six months after my beloved son will get his Bachelor's degree at age 29, from Marshall University. The emotional rollercoaster of joy and externally driven struggles while I am autistic parenting two children, one of whom is autistic, will begin a new chapter.

While focusing on helping PK develop more autonomous (less structured) decision-making, I will be helping him into employment. This, as I too "begin" my own career as an autism researcher, trying to leave a legacy in the few remaining years left in my viable time for work.

One might be remorseful or frustrated at the years spent being my son's "program" or because I relocated four times, each time further away from my husband, daughter, and daughter-in-law (and my delicious grandson), but I have found my new life in New York. It is a non-stop challenge and a cognitive delight that fills my soul. I miss them all dearly, but I feel complete here, embedded in a vibrant and dedicated community of researchers, providers, and family. Onward and upward!

## Becca

As is the case with many autistics, I am a lover of routine. I take great pleasure in keeping things organized and staying on schedule. I've heard it can be very annoying. One of the longest-standing routines that I keep is to eat dinner while watching *Jeopardy* every weekday at 7 p.m. This leaves me some wiggle room on the weekend to be flexible, but on weekdays, it's me, dinner, and Alex Trebek, as it has been since I was about 12 years old. I used to do really nerdy things like keep track of my score and the number of Final Jeopardy questions that I got right. I was never good at numbers, so I don't know why I tried to keep my stats. I guess I have always liked to challenge myself. I also love that for 30 minutes straight I get to have fun with my brain. I get to test out my filing system and make sure I'm still able to access quickly the ridiculous amount of factual information stored in there. Metaphorically, it is always fun to dust off an old file drawer and find that it still slides right open as if you opened it yesterday. But my favorite part of all is that there is still the occasional day that I manage to get the Final Jeopardy question right, while all the contestants have drawn a blank.

## Jen

As I sit here on a freezing cold Canadian cliché of a winter afternoon, like the elusive hermit I am, I cannot help but reflect. It is hard to find ideal words to illustrate how astonished and honored I felt upon learning I would share some thoughts from my oft idiosyncratic mind with the world in actual book format (thanks, Barb!) and contribute alongside a collective of amazingly talented women, some of whom I even cited in my college research papers.

When I began to learn more about autism, much of the journey began with reading the stories of other women on the spectrum. These were revelatory times in my life, seeing others' narratives so closely mirror my own. I began to feel a bit less isolated in the social world, finding much solace in their words, and thus wanted to share some of my own.

Sitting in a dim room, loud classic rock playing, I think about how challenging it was to share such personal information about myself, but I am glad that I partook in the undertaking. It is my most sincere hope that this book encourages readers to find self-acceptance in their own stories too.

## Barb

Ron "Strom" Burgundy...my savior, my sanity, my love. Now, you would think I was talking about a significant person in my life; well, I am. It is just that he is composed of metal, rather than the usual flesh-and-blood types. The metal steed I ride, Ron (insert Bon Jovi in the background—"on a steel horse I ride, I'm wanted dead or alive..."), has an innate wisdom and ability in knowing what quells the anxious mind, to lift the depressed spirit and to satisfy my need for vestibular stimulation: that acceleration factor...of course, within the speed limits, mind you...

Ron has often been my solace, talking to him on sad days, catching a glimpse of the twinkle in his headlight eyes indicating to jump on, let's go for an adventure, to moments of giving him warm arms around his tank to thank him for saving my sanity, for quietly listening, understanding, and for keeping me safe.

Living in our own world, within this world, Ron and me, navigating this journey together—life, the roads, the adventures, the good and the bad, as combined observant souls—ever seeking and considering our reality and where the next chapter will begin...

## Renata

And so this game begins with a strange red-haired girl found in the woods and raised by a caring family in a nearby village. She spent her days in the village doing her best to fit in, but always felt something was missing. She was too different and always asked herself where she could have come from and, most importantly, if there were others like her... Time passed and she grew up. One fateful day brought to the village an incredible warrior on her beautiful black horse. She was traveling through all the lands to find her people.

They came from a special magical village lost in space and time. Nobody could return to it, but she was determined to gather everyone she could find so they would not feel alone anymore. The red-haired woman had her lifelong question answered, right there. Her people: they existed. So she left to join the mystery rider's group of incredibly skilled warriors in a special mission. A mission to share their stories with their people, so that they would not feel alone, so that they too would have their questions answered. Together they would create a magical book, whose powers, combined with all the other magical books already brought to the world, would accomplish the mission of reuniting their people, making them strong again. Off they went on their quest, determined and happy because they knew they had each other. And even without a land of their own they could stand proud, together.

# About the Contributors

**Barb Cook**

*Sunshine Coast, Queensland, Australia*

Formally identified with Asperger syndrome in 2009 at the age of 40, Barb is founder and editor in chief of *Spectrum Women Magazine*. Barb is a highly committed autism/Asperger's advocate, writer, speaker, and keen motorcyclist, making a variety of appearances on Australian radio, television, in newspapers and magazines, and appearing in the Australian television documentary *The Chameleons: Women with Autism*. She is Co-founder of Bikers for Autism Australia and Community Council Member of AASET (Autistic Adults and other Stakeholders Engaged Together).

Barb currently rides a Suzuki V-Strom DL1000 called Ron "Strom" Burgundy and implements a combination of her passion for motorcycling and her dedication to autism advocacy, creating acceptance and pushing for action to improve the lives of all on the autism spectrum.

Barb was awarded a Special Commendation in the 2017 Autism

Queensland Creative Futures Awards by the Queensland Governor, his Excellency Paul De Jersey. Barb is currently pursuing a Master of Autism at the University of Wollongong.

*www.spectrumwomen.com*

### Dr. Michelle S. Garnett, BPsych (Hons), MPsych (Clin.), PhD (Psych.), MAPS, FCCP
*Brisbane, Queensland, Australia*

Michelle is a clinical psychologist and founder and Director of Minds & Hearts: A Clinic for Asperger's Syndrome and Autism. The clinic was born through her passion for understanding autism spectrum conditions (ASC), and her strong desire to be part of positive change for people who have ASC and their families. Michelle thoroughly enjoys working in this area as a diagnostician, therapist, consultant, mentor, clinical supervisor, workshop presenter, student, and researcher. She has specialized in autism spectrum conditions for the past 24 years, developing expertise in all subtypes of autism across all ages. Michelle created the first screening instrument for Asperger's syndrome, the Australian Scale for Asperger's Syndrome (ASAS) in 1993. She obtained a PhD for her research into ASC, diagnosis, and families in 2007 from the University of Queensland, Australia. She provides training in ASC for postgraduate clinical students for four Australian universities. Michelle implements yoga as an adjunct to cognitive behavior therapy (CBT) for ASC. She has been an invited speaker at many national and international conferences and workshop events.

*www.mindsandhearts.net*

Photo courtesy of BBC

## Maura Campbell

*Killyleagh, County Down, Northern Ireland*

Maura Campbell is a features writer for *Spectrum Women Magazine* and lives in the countryside with her husband, Stephen, her son, Darragh, Ash the assistance dog and Baz the cat. She is a senior manager in the Northern Ireland Civil Service and served as a board member of Specialisterne NI from 2014 to 2016. Maura has spoken publicly about autism in both a personal and professional capacity and guest lectures at the University of Ulster. She was diagnosed with Asperger syndrome in 2011 when she was 44 years old. Like many adults on the spectrum, she sought the diagnosis after learning that her son had autism. Maura has also written on autism and learning disability for a number of other publications and performed at the 2017 Edinburgh Fringe Festival as part of the BBC Ouch storytelling event—*Tales of the Misunderstood*.
***www.neurodizzy.blog***

## Jen Elcheson

*Prince George, British Columbia, Canada*

Jen was professionally identified as autistic (Asperger's) at age 17, although she did not come to terms with this aspect of her multidimensional identity until age 26. That moment of knowing occurred when she entered a room full of autistic children for a college practicum, immediately realizing there was no denying who she used to be anymore, and that she very much still was/is one of those kids herself.

Jen has vocational training in social service work and school support. She works as an Education Assistant supporting students with a variety of neurocognitive differences.

Writing always came naturally to Jen, and she found it a perfect outlet to share her experiences as an autistic person. Jen currently writes for *Spectrum Women Magazine*, is on the board of directors of My Spectrum Suite LLC, and is involved with the International Aspergirl® Society. She is highly introverted and loves animals, coffee/tea with friends, psychology, list making, reading, documentaries, and music.

*www.facebook.com/jen.elcheson*

### ARtemisia—formerly Rudy Simone

*Planet Earth, Galaxy: Milky Way*

Author, Performer, Composer, Actor, Lecturer, Consultant.

Help 4 Aspergers is one of the top autism resources in the world and contains the first "Table of Female AS Traits," created by ARtemisia, which is now widely used by health professionals to help identify AS in women and girls.

She is founder and President of the International Aspergirl® Society; their mission is to bring women on the autism spectrum together for mutual empowerment, understanding, education, networking, and support via public global events with exclusive member benefits of videochat groups, consultations, and support.

ARtemisia gives presentations for professional and personal development around the world.

ARtemisia is also a composer, musician, recording artist and engineer, actor, and playwright. She has released three albums as Rudy Simone (*Gothic Blues*, *Thief of Dreams*, and *Penny Dreadful*) and performs regularly. American by birth, she has lived in many countries and currently resides in Athens, Rome, and New York. Her play *Dying Star*, a one-woman show featuring her music and script, premiered in Athens in 2017 and will be further developed into a full-length spectacle.

*www.aspergirlsociety.org*

### Dr. Catriona Stewart, PhD, MSc, PGDip BA (Hons)
*Dunblane, Stirlingshire, Scotland, United Kingdom*

Catriona's PhD research (2011) focused on girls, leading to the founding of SWAN: Scottish Women's Autism Network (2012). SWAN's autistic volunteers run peer-support groups across Scotland and online chat forums, and are involved in conferences and consultations such as the Cross Party (Scottish Government) Group. Videos from SWAN's ground-breaking learning events are on their website. Catriona presents/speaks nationally and internationally, including Autism Europe Congress Edinburgh 2016, Meeting of Minds Copenhagen 2017, Advancement in Women's Studies Toronto 2017. She has been a member of National Autism Project's (NAP) Autistic Advisory Panel since its inception, one of the project's "autism experts," and is a member of NAP's future project, the National Autistic Taskforce (NAT). She currently works as an advisor for Scottish Autism for whom she developed the online resource Right Click for Women and Girls, with SWAN's input into planning, research, and content. She's trying to find time to write her book!

*www.facebook.com/swans.scotland*

### Anita Lesko, BSN, RN, MS, CRNA

*Pensacola, Florida, USA*

Anita Lesko is an internationally recognized autism advocate who was diagnosed at age 50. Anita earned her Master of Science in Nurse Anesthesia from Columbia University in 1988. She's been working full-time ever since as a Certified Registered Nurse Anesthetist. Anita was a guest speaker at the United Nations Headquarters in New York City for World Autism Awareness Day 2017. Recognizing the need to educate all healthcare providers about autism, Anita combined her 30 years as a medical professional with her autism to write *The Complete Guide to Autism and Healthcare*, which has been selected by the Autism Society of America for the Temple Grandin Literary Award. Anita is a great friend of Professor Temple Grandin. From over 60 hours of personal interviews with Temple, Anita wrote *Temple Grandin: The Stories I Tell My Friends*. Working on this book was a life-changing journey. Anita and Temple realized just how much they have in common. Anita is married to her soulmate Abraham, also autistic.

*www.anitalesko.com*

### Dr. Liane Holliday Willey, EdD
*Michigan, USA*

Liane Holliday Willey is the author of several internationally bestselling books that explore her personal and professional experiences with autism. When she isn't working as an adjunct professor in English or as an equine education specialist, Liane provides seminars and private consulting in the fields of autism and developmental delay supports with individuals and academic communities around the globe. Dr. Willey has a doctorate in psycholinguistics and serves on many autism advocacy and research boards.
*www.aspie.com*

### Samantha Craft, MEd
*Olympia, Washington, USA*

Samantha Craft (aka Marcelle Ciampi) is best known for her prolific writings found in her well-received blog and book, *Everyday Aspergers*. She is the founder of Spectrum Suite LLC, Lead Job Recruiter and Community Manager for an innovative technology company with a neurodiversity hiring initiative, a professional educator, and Community Achievement Award Recipient at the 2017 ANCA World Autism Festival. Sam has served as a volunteer tutor, an advocate for children with exceptional needs, and a voice for individuals on the autism spectrum.

A former schoolteacher, with a Master's Degree in Education, Sam has been published in peer-reviewed journals, been featured in autistic literature, and has completed several graduate-level courses in the field of counseling. Some of her works, especially *The Ten Traits*, have been translated into multiple languages. Her list of traits for females on the autism spectrum has been shared in counseling offices around the world.
*www.myspectrumsuite.com*

### Jeanette Purkis

*Canberra, Australian Capital Territory, Australia*

Jeanette Purkis is an autistic author and public speaker, and is a passionate advocate for autistic people and their families. Jeanette is the author of four books on elements of autism and is a regular presenter on the *Talking Disability* program on Canberra Radio 2CC. Some of the events Jeanette has presented at include TEDx Canberra in 2013, as a keynote presenter at a number of major autism conferences and alongside Professor Temple Grandin in 2015. Jeanette facilitates a support group for women on the autism spectrum in Canberra. Jeanette has received a number of awards including the 2016 ACT Volunteer of the Year and finalist in the 2017 ACT Woman of the Year award. Jeanette has worked for the Australian Public Service since 2017.
*www.jeanettepurkis.com*

## Renata Jurkévythz
*Eriskirch, Baden-Württemberg, Germany*

Renata was born in Curitiba, Brazil, and moved to Germany in 2016 with her husband and three children, two of whom are on the autism spectrum. Renata's journey with autism began in 2014 when her two-year-old son was diagnosed. After immersing herself reading books on autism to learn more about her son, it became apparent that she too related to autism, and two years later she received a diagnosis of Asperger syndrome, followed by her ten-year-old daughter.

In 2003, Renata majored in International Business, working in this field until 2011.

In Brazil, Renata was a blogger on parenting and in 2016 she joined the writing team of *Spectrum Women Magazine*, changing her focus to autism, from her personal perspective and that of being an autistic mother of children on the autism spectrum.

Renata is passionate about video gaming, movie history, and psychology.

*www.spectrumwomen.com/?s=renata+jurkevythz*

## Becca Lory, CAS, BCCS
*Denver, Colorado, USA*

Becca was diagnosed on the autism spectrum as an adult and has since become an active autism advocate, consultant, speaker, and writer. With a focus on

living an active, positive life, her work includes autism consulting, public speaking engagements, writing a monthly blog called *Living Positively Autistic*, and the bi-weekly podcast that she co-hosts, *Spectrumly Speaking*. Becca sits on the Advisory Board of the Nassau-Suffolk chapter of the Autism Society of America, the Board of Directors of Different Brains and the Foundation for Life Guides for Autism, as well as the Community Council of AASET (Autistic Adults and other Stakeholders Engaged Together). Becca is also an animal lover, with a special affinity for cats. Becca spends most of her time with her partner, Antonio Hector, and their emotional support animal (ESA), Sir Walter Underfoot.
*www.beccalory.com*

## Kate Ross, MSW, CAS

*Gloucestershire, England, United Kingdom*

Originally from Buffalo, New York, Kate studied Psychology and Social Sciences and earned her Master's Degree in Social Work from the University at Buffalo before relocating to England in mid-2008. She changed careers in 2013 from social care to special educational needs, where she quickly developed a personal interest in autism and Asperger syndrome. After being recommended Rudy Simone's book *Aspergirls* in July 2015, her perception and understanding of herself changed and "everything suddenly made sense." Kate received a diagnosis of autism spectrum condition in August 2016. Since then, Kate has become an Ambassador for the International Aspergirl® Society, a contributing writer to *Spectrum Women Magazine*, an associate collaborator with

Aspiregers (Cheltenham-based autism organization), and a moderator for Agony Autie's Safe Space Facebook group. She lives in Gloucestershire with her husband, Kevin, and their cat, Blossom. She enjoys reading, crocheting, and going to concerts of her favorite bands (with earplugs, of course!).

*www.IAmMyOwnExperience.com*

### Terri Mayne
*Nottingham, England, United Kingdom*

Terri is not your typical girl. Born in Essex, United Kingdom, she went to her first motorbike race at age two. Maybe her parents knew they were sowing the seeds of a lifelong love of engines and motor racing. It perhaps became clearer when confronted by a smoky, two-stroke race bike, out from under the hood of Terri's pram came the words "Cor, Mum, smell that Castrol-R." Terri is never bored. She likes cats, motorbikes, aircraft, Dungeons and Dragons, heavy metal, more cats, *Star Wars*, *Harry Potter*, and *Lord of the Rings*. Oh and cats! Over the years she has also had a variety of what some may call "intense interests": combine harvesters, umbrellas, London Underground, New Kids on the Block, rotary engines, and the Mazda RX-7. Many of these interests remain until this day (I'll let you guess which…). Terri currently adults as an associate director in project management for a global pharmaceutical consulting firm.

*www.facebook.com/theautistrix*

## Dena L. Gassner, MSW, PhD candidate

*Long Island, New York, USA*

A wife, mother, and grandmother, Dena is a PhD candidate in Social Welfare at Adelphi University after spending 20 years navigating systems for her autistic son. Dena has spoken on various autism topics in Russia, Geneva (UN), Scotland, and at Cambridge, and has provided key testimony to multiple groups in Washington, DC. She has contributed articles and chapters to multiple publications. Her current research is on reframing identity using resilience theory for successful outcomes for autistics by maximizing supports rather than overcoming the condition.
*www.denagassner.com*

## Christine Jenkins, BJ, RMT (A.Mus-Voice)

*Ottawa, Ontario, Canada*

After self-identifying and trying to get assessed for eight months, Christine was diagnosed as Asperger's on Hallowe'en of 2008, aged 48⅔.

In 2011 she co-founded Asperfemme in Ottawa, "a forum to validate adult women with self/official diagnosis of Asperger syndrome... It exists for members to inform and support each other in areas of mutual interest and to foster friendships and social contacts." A chapter has since been founded in Toronto.

Christine is the author of *The Ottawa Bicycle Book* (1982). A Carleton University journalism graduate, she is a researcher, writer, and correspondent for *Spectrum Women Magazine*. She has been on the board of the Asperger's Society of Ontario, a panelist at Woodview's Stages of Autism conference in 2012, the first Asperfemme conference (which she helped organize) for women in 2013, and the Autism Opportunities Conference, Guelph, Ontario, in 2014.

Christine serves on the Policy Advisory Group for Girls and Women with ASD of CAMH/Autism Ontario in Toronto, assisting esteemed neuroscientist and researcher Dr. Meng-Chuan Lai, whom she met while interviewing Dr. Will Mandy about female diagnostic criteria, her current intense interest, in June 2017.

She is a private singing and piano teacher with absolute pitch, an avid reader, concertgoer, and cat lover.

*www.facebook.com/CJenkinsMusic*

# References

## Chapter 1

Rutherford, M., McKenzie, K., Johnson, T., Catchpole, C. *et al.* (2016) "Gender ratio in a clinical population sample, age of diagnosis and duration of assessment in children and adults with autism spectrum disorder." *Autism 20*, 5, 628–634.

## Chapter 2

Ormond, S., Brownlow, C., Garnett, M.S., Rynkiewicz, A. and Attwood, T. (2018) "Profiling autism symptomatology: An exploration of the Q-ASC Parental Report Scale in capturing sex differences in autism." *Journal of Autism and Developmental Disorders 48*, 2, 389–403.

## Chapter 3

Attwood, T. (2008) *The Complete Guide to Asperger's Syndrome.* London: Jessica Kingsley Publishers.

Bulhak-Paterson, D. (2015) *I Am an Aspie Girl: A Book for Young Girls with Autism Spectrum Conditions.* London: Jessica Kingsley Publishers.

Simone, R. (2010) *Aspergirls: Empowering Females with Asperger's Syndrome.* London: Jessica Kingsley Publishers.

## Chapter 4

American Psychiatric Association (1994) *Diagnostic and Statistical Manual of Mental Disorders*, 4th edn. Washington, DC: American Psychiatric Association.

Camneurodiversity (2017) From the transcript "Autistic People, Not Gendered Minds." Retrieved 9 December 2017, from http://camneurodiversity.tumblr.com/post/139681836318/talk

Coleman, M. and Gillberg, C. (2012) *The Autisms*, 4th edn. Oxford: Oxford University Press.

Grinker, R. (2008) *Unstrange Minds: Remapping the World of Autism*. New York, NY: Basic Books.

Silberman, S. (2015) *NeuroTribes: The Legacy of Autism and How to Think Smarter about People Who Think Differently*. St Leonards, Australia: Allen & Unwin.

Singer, J. (2016) *NeuroDiversity: The Birth of an Idea*. Australia: Judy Singer.

Stewart, C. (2011) "Hermeneutic Phenomenology: Experiences of girls with Asperger syndrome and anxiety" (PhD thesis), Napier University, Edinburgh.

Stewart, C. (2012) "Where can we be what we are? The experiences of girls with Asperger syndrome and their mothers." *Good Autism Practice 13*, 1, 40–48.

Wing, L. (1981) "Asperger syndrome: A clinical account." *Psychological Medicine 11*, 115–130.

## Chapter 6

Attwood, A. and Garnett M.S. (2016) *Exploring Depression and Beating the Blues: A CBT Self-Help Guide to Understanding and Coping with Depression in Asperger's Syndrome*. London: Jessica Kingsley Publishers.

Croen, L.A., Zerbo, O., Qian, Y., Massolo, M.L. *et al.* (2015) "The health status of adults on the autism spectrum." *Autism 19*, 7, 814–823.

Richdale, A. (2017) "Adults with autism: What do we know and what are the implications for psychology?" *InPsych 39*, 2.

## Chapter 7

Bear, G.G., Mantz, L.S., Glutting, J.J., Yang, C. and Boyer, D.E. (2015) "Differences in bullying victimisation between students with and without disabilities." *School Psychology Review 44*, 1, 98–116.

Brown, D. (2013) *The Aspie Girl's Guide to Being Safe with Men: The Unwritten Safety Rules No-one is Telling You*. London: Jessica Kingsley Publishers.

Holliday Willey, L. (2011) *Safety Skills for Asperger Women: How to Save a Perfectly Good Female Life*. London: Jessica Kingsley Publishers.

## Chapter 10

Australian Bureau of Statisitics (2017) "ABS Survey of Disability, Ageing and Carers: Summary of Findings, 2015." Retrieved 15 September 2017, from www.abs.gov.au/ausstats/abs@.nsf/Latestproducts/4430.0Main%20 Features752015?opendocument&tabname=Summary&prodno=4430.0&issue =2015&num=&view=it

Australian Public Service (2017) "Myths and stereotypes." Retrieved 24 September 2017, from www.apsc.gov.au/_data/assets/pdf_file/0010/80875/Myths-and-stereotypes_web.pdf

## Chapter 11

American Psychiatric Association (1994) *Diagnostic and Statistical Manual of Mental Disorders*, 4th edn. Washington, DC: American Psychiatric Association.

Kumar, S., Tansley-Hancock, O., Sedley, W., Winston, J. *et al.* (2017) "The brain basis for misophonia." *Current Biology 27*, 4, 527–533.

Middletown Centre for Autism (2017) "Strategies According to Sense: Proprioceptive." Retrieved 21 December 2017, from http://sensory-processing. middletownautism.com/sensory-strategies/ strategies-according-to-sense/ proprioceptive/

## Chapter 12

Mahler, K. (2015) *Interoception: The Eighth Sensory System.* Shawnee, KS: AAPC Publishing.

Merriam-Webster (2017) "Communication." Meriam-Webster Dictionary, online. Retrieved 27 March 2018, from www.merriam-webster.com/dictionary/ communication

## Chapter 13

Attwood, T. and Garnett, M.S. (2016) *Exploring Depression and Beating the Blues: A CBT Self-Help Guide to Understanding and Coping with Depression in Asperger's Syndrome.* London: Jessica Kingsley Publishers.

Baron-Cohen, S. (2012) *Zero Degrees of Empathy.* London: Penguin.

Dubin, N. (2014) *The Autism Spectrum and Depression.* London: Jessica Kingsley Publishers.

## Chapter 14

Agony Autie (2017) "Your Questions, Answered #1." Retrieved 27 March 2018, from www.youtube.com/watch?v=XmSL_GstC74&t=518s

Hallowell, E.M. and Ratey, J.J. (1995) *Driven to Distraction: Recognizing and Coping with Attention Deficit Disorder from Childhood through Adulthood.* New York, NY: Simon & Schuster.

Hallowell, E.M. (2015) *Driven to Distraction at Work: How to Focus and Be More Productive.* Boston, MA: Harvard Business Review Press.

Holtmann, M., Bolte, S. and Poustka, F. (2005) "Letters to the editor: ADHD, Asperger syndrome and high functioning autism." *Journal of the American Academy of Child and Adolescent Psychiatry 44*, 1101.

Moraine, P. (2015) *Autism and Everyday Executive Function: A Strengths-Based Approach for Improving Attention, Memory, Organization and Flexibility.* London: Jessica Kingsley Publishers.

Moyes, R. (2013) *Executive Function "Dysfunction": Strategies for Educators and Parents.* London: Jessica Kingsley Publishers.

Wikipedia (2017) "Gaslighting." Retrieved 5 August 2017, from https://en.wikipedia. org/wiki/Gaslighting

## Chapter 15

Cleveland Clinic (2017) "Mitochondrial Disease." Cleveland Clinic. Retrieved 13 April 2018, from https://my.clevelandclinic.org/health/diseases/17237-mitochondrial-disease

Lesko, A. (2017) *The Complete Guide to Autism and Healthcare*. Arlington, TX: Future Horizons.

Lum, M., Garnett. M.S. and O'Connor, E. (2014) "Health Communication: A pilot study comparing perceptions of women with and without high functioning autism spectrum disorder." *Research in Autism Spectrum Disorders 8*, 1713–1721.

Szakacs, G. and Davi, A. (2017) "Risk of Anesthesia Regression in Children with Autism Spectrum Disorder and Mitochondrial Dysfunction." Mitoaction.org. Retrieved 28 November 2017, from www.mitoaction.org/files/Risk%20of%20 Anesthesia%20Regression%20(2).pdf

## Chapter 16

American Psychological Association (2006) "Stress Weakens the Immune System." Retrieved 12 November 2017, from www.apa.org/research/action/immune. aspx

Arnold, C. (2016) "The invisible link between autism and anorexia." Spectrumnews. org. Retrieved 12 November 2017, from www.spectrumnews.org/features/ deep-dive/the-invisible-link-between-autism-and-anorexia

Attwood, T. (2008) *The Complete Guide to Asperger's Syndrome*. London: Jessica Kingsley Publishers.

Autism Key (2017) "Sensory Processing Disorder and Autism." Retrieved 12 November 2017, from www.autismkey.com/sensory-processing-disorder-and-autism

Autism Research Institute (2017) "Researchers investigate associations between autism and dyspraxia." Retrieved 12 November 2017, from www.autism.com/ autism_and_dyspraxia

Autism Spectrum Australia (2017) "Dyslexia." Retrieved 12 November 2017, from www.autismspectrum.org.au/content/dyslexia

Breaking the Vicious Cycle (2017) "Autism & GI Problems - Breaking the Vicious Cycle." Retrieved 12 November 2017, from www.breakingtheviciouscycle. info/p/autism-gi-problems/

Cage, E. (2017) "Autistic people aren't really accepted – and it's impacting their mental health." *The Conversation*. Retrieved 12 November 2017, from https://theconversation.com/autistic-people-arent-really-accepted-and-its-impacting-their-mental-health-86817

Centers for Disease Control and Prevention (2017) "Mitochondrial Disease – Frequently Asked Questions." Retrieved 12 November 2017, from www.cdc.gov/ ncbddd/autism/mitochondrial-faq.html

Conrad Stöppler, M. (2017) "Diabetes Symptoms (Type 1 and Type 2)." MedicineNet. Retrieved 12 November 2017, from www.medicinenet.com/diabetes_mellitus/article.htm

Dudova, I., Kocourkova, J. and Koutek, J. (2015) "Early-onset anorexia nervosa in girls with Asperger syndrome." *Neuropsychiatric Disease and Treatment 2015*, 11, 1639–1643.

Dyscalculia.org (2017) "Learning Disabilities." Retrieved 12 November 2017, from www.dyscalculia.org/learning-disabilities/autism

Dyspraxia Foundation (2017) "What is dyspraxia?" Retrieved 12 November 2017, from www.dyspraxiafoundation.org.uk/about-dyspraxia/

Ehlers-Danlos Society (2017) "What are the Ehlers-Danlos Syndromes?" Retrieved 12 November 2017, from www.ehlers-danlos.com/what-is-eds/

Lesko, A. (2017) *The Complete Guide to Autism and Healthcare.* Arlington, TX: Future Horizons.

Mayo Clinic (2017a) "COPD: Symptoms and causes." Retrieved 12 November 2017, from www.mayoclinic.org/diseases-conditions/copd/symptoms-causes/syc-20353679

Mayo Clinic (2017b) "High blood pressure (hypertension): Symptoms and causes." Retrieved 12 November 2017, from www.mayoclinic.org/diseases-conditions/high-blood-pressure/symptoms-causes/syc-20373410

National Autistic Society (2017) "Anxiety in autistic adults." Retrieved 12 November 2017, from www.autism.org.uk/about/behaviour/anxiety.aspx

WebMD (2017a) "Autism, ADHD Often Occur Together, Research Shows." Retrieved 12 November 2017, from www.webmd.com/brain/autism/news/20130606/autism-adhd-often-occur-together-research-shows#1

WebMD (2017b) "Sleep Apnea." Retrieved 12 November 2017, from www.webmd.com/sleep-disorders/sleep-apnea

Zaatreh, M. (2014) "The Connection Between Autism and Epilepsy." *HuffPost.* Retrieved 12 November 2017, from www.huffingtonpost.com/2014/05/30/connection-between-autism-and-epilepsy_n_5419003.html

## Chapter 17

Antony, P.J. and Shore, S.M. (2015) *College for Students with Disabilities: We Do Belong.* London: Jessica Kingsley Publishers.

Attwood, T. and Garnett, M.S. (2016) *Exploring Depression and Beating the Blues: A CBT Self-Help Guide to Understanding and Coping with Depression in Asperger's Syndrome.* London: Jessica Kingsley Publishers.

Baker, J. (2005) *Preparing for Life: The Complete Guide for Transitioning to Adulthood for Those with Autism and Asperger's Syndrome.* Arlington, TX: Future Horizons.

Berg, K.L., Shiu, C.-S., Acharya, K., Stolbach, B.C. and Msall, M.E. (2016) "Disparities in adversity among children with autism spectrum disorder: A population-based study." *Developmental Medicine and Child Neurology 58*, 11, 1124–1131.

Burke, L. and Stoddart, K.P. (2014) "Medical and Health Problems in Adults with High-Functioning Autism and Asperger Syndrome." In F.R. Volkmar, B. Reichow and J.C. McPartland (eds) *Adolescents and Adults with Autism Spectrum Disorders*. New York, NY: Springer.

Croen, L.A., Zerbo, O., Qian, Y., Massolo, M.L. *et al.* (2015) "The health status of adults on the autism spectrum." *Autism: The International Journal of Research and Practice 19*, 7, 814–823.

Fling, E.R. (2000) *Eating an Artichoke: A Mother's Perspective on Asperger Syndrome*. London: Jessica Kingsley Publishers.

Gassner, D.L. (2012) "You *are* Precious!" In L. Perner (ed.) *Scholars with Autism: Achieving Dreams*. Sedona, AZ: Auricle Books.

Gaus, V.L. (2007) *Behavioral Therapy for Adult Asperger Syndrome*. New York, NY: Guilford Press.

Gaus, V.L. (2011) *Living Well on the Spectrum: How to Use Your Strengths to Meet the Challenges of Asperger Syndrome/High-Functioning Autism*. New York, NY: Guilford Press.

Geurts, H.M. and Jansen, M.D. (2012) "A retrospective chart study: The pathway to a diagnosis for adults referred for ASD assessment." *Autism 16*, 3, 299–305.

Gillberg, C., Gillberg, C.I., Rastam, M. and Johansson, M. (1996) "The cognitive profile of anorexia nervosa: A comparative study including a community-based sample." *Comprehensive Psychiatry 37*, 1, 23–30.

Helbert, K. (2012) *Finding Your Own Way to Grieve: A Creative Activity Workbook for Kids and Teens on the Autism Spectrum*. London: Jessica Kingsley Publishers.

Hirvikoski, T. and Blomqvist, M. (2015) "High self-perceived stress and poor coping in intellectually able adults with autism spectrum disorder." *Autism 19*, 6, 752–757.

Hirvikoski, T., Mittendorfer-Rutz, E., Boman, M., Larsson, H., Lichtenstein, P. and Bölte, S. (2016) "Premature mortality in autism spectrum disorder." *The British Journal of Psychiatry 208*, 3, 232–238.

Holliday Willey, L. (1999) *Pretending to be Normal: Living with Asperger's Syndrome (Autism Spectrum Disorder)*. London: Jessica Kingsley Publishers.

Jones, L., Goddard, L., Hill, E.L., Henry, L.A. and Crane, L. (2014) "Experiences of receiving a diagnosis of autism spectrum disorder: A survey of adults in the United Kingdom." *Journal of Autism and Developmental Disorders 44*, 12, 3033–3044.

Kerns, C.M., Newschaffer, C.J. and Berkowitz, S.J. (2015) "Traumatic childhood events and autism spectrum disorder." *Journal of Autism and Developmental Disorders 45*, 11, 3475–3486.

Kristensen, Z.E. and Broome, M.R. (2015) "Autistic traits in an internet sample of gender variant UK adults." *International Journal of Transgenderism 16*, 4, 234–245.

Lai, M.-C., Baron-Cohen, S. and Buxbaum, J.D. (2015) "Understanding autism in the light of sex/gender." *Molecular Autism 6*, 1, 1–5.

Lai, M.-C., Lombardo, M.V., Auyeung, B., Chakrabarti, B. and Baron-Cohen, S. (2014) "Sex/gender differences and autism: Setting the scene for future research." *Journal of the American Academy of Child and Adolescent Psychiatry 54*, 1, 11–24.

Lawson, W. (1998) *Life behind Glass: A Personal Account of Autism Spectrum Disorder.* London: Jessica Kingsley Publishers.

Lawson, W.B. and Lawson, B.M. (2017) *Transitioning Together: One Couple's Journey of Gender and Identity Discovery.* London: Jessica Kingsley Publishers.

Maddox, B.B., Trubanova, A. and White, S.W. (2016) "Untended wounds: Non-suicidal self-injury in adults with autism spectrum disorder." *Autism: The International Journal of Research and Practice 21*, 4, 412–422.

McGraw, P.C. (2001) *Life Strategies: Doing What Works, Doing What Matters.* New York, NY: Random House.

Miller, J.K. (2003) *Women from Another Planet? Our Lives in the Universe of Autism.* Bloomington, IN: AuthorHouse.

Miller, R. (2015) *The iRest Program for Healing PTSD: A Proven-Effective Approach to Using Yoga Nidra Meditation and Deep Relaxation Techniques to Overcome Trauma.* Oakland, CA: New Harbinger.

Milovanov, A., Paquette-Smith, M., Lunsky, Y. and Weiss, J.A. (2013) "Prevalence and impact of significant life events for adults with asperger syndrome." *Journal on Developmental Disabilities 19*, 3, 50–54.

Nicolaidis, C., Raymaker, D., McDonald, K., Dern, S. *et al.* (2013) "Comparison of healthcare experiences in autistic and non-autistic adults: A cross-sectional online survey facilitated by an academic-community partnership." *Journal of General Internal Medicine 28*, 6, 761–769.

Overton, J., Lawson, W., Jackson, J., Debbaudt, D. *et al.* (2005) *Coming out Asperger: Diagnosis, Disclosure and Self-Confidence.* London: Jessica Kingsley Publishers.

Paradiz, V. (2002) *Elijah's Cup: A Family's Journey into the Community and Culture of High-Functioning Autism and Asperger's Syndrome.* London: Jessica Kingsley Publishers.

Paradiz, V. (2009) *The Integrated Self-Advocacy Curriculum: A Program Elijah's Cup: A Family's Journey into the Community and Culture of High-Functioning Autism and Asperger's Syndrome for emerging Self-Advocates with Autism Spectrum and Other Conditions (Student Workbook).* Shawnee Mission, KS: Autism Asperger Publishing Company.

Perner, L. (2012) *Scholars with Autism: Achieving Dreams.* Sedona, AZ: Auricle Books.

Prince-Hughes, D. (2004) *Songs of the Gorilla Nation: My Journey through Autism.* New York, NY: Harmony Books.

Rastam, M. (2008) "Eating disturbances in autism spectrum disorders with focus on adolescent and adult years." *Clinical Neuropsychiatry 5*, 1, 31–42.

Roux, A. and Kerns, C. (2016) "Awareness, Education, and Counseling: Supporting Mental Health for Adults with Autism." Drexel University Life Course Outcomes Research Program. Retrieved 13 April 2018, from http://drexel.edu/autismoutcomes/blog/overview/2016/March/Awareness-Education-and-Counseling-Supporting-mental-health-for-adults-with-autism

Shore, S. (ed.) (2004) *Ask and Tell: Self-Advocacy for and Disclosure for People on the Autism Spectrum.* Mission Falls, KS: Autism Asperger Publishing Company.

Wentz Nilsson, E., Gillberg, C., Gillberg, C.I. and Rastam, M. (1999) "Ten year follow-up of adolescent onset anorexia nervosa: Personality disorders." *Journal of the American Academy of Child and Adolescent Psychiatry 38*, 1389–1395.

White, S.W., Ollendick, T.H. and Bray, B.C. (2011) "College students on the autism spectrum: Prevalence and associated problems." *Autism: The International Journal of Research and Practice 15*, 683–701.

Whitlock, J., Muehlenkamp, J., Eckenrode, J., Purington, A. *et al.* (2013) "Nonsuicidal self-injury as a gateway to suicide in young adults." *Journal of Adolescent Health 52*, 4, 486–492.

Zaks, Z. (2006) *Life and Love: Positive Strategies for Autistic Adults.* Shawnee Mission, KS: Autism Asperger Publishing Company.

## Chapter 18

Goleman, D. (2004) *Destructive Emotions and How We Can Overcome Them.* London: Bloomsbury.

Maslow, A.H. (1943) "A theory of human motivation." *Psychological Review 50*, 4, 370–396.

## Chapter 19

Attwood, T. and Garnett, M.S. (2016) *Exploring Depression and Beating the Blues: A CBT Self-Help Guide to Understanding and Coping with Depression in Asperger's syndrome.* London: Jessica Kingsley Publishers.

Brown, B. (2016) *Daring Greatly: How the Courage to be Vulnerable Transforms the Way We Live, Love, Parent, and Lead.* London: Penguin Books.

Brown, B. (2017) *Braving the Wilderness: The quest for true belonging and the courage to stand alone.* New York: Penguin RandomHouse.

Davide-Rivera, J. (2013) "Love or Obsession: When a Person Becomes an #Aspie's Special Interest." Retrieved 20 September 2017, from http://aspiewriter.com/2013/05/love-or-obsession-when-a-person-becomes-an-aspies-special-interest.html

Harrop, C. and Kasari, C. (2015) "Learning when to treat repetitive behaviors in autism." *Spectrum Autism Research News.* Retrieved 20 September 2017, from https://spectrumnews.org/opinion/viewpoint/learning-when-to-treat-repetitive-behaviors-in-autism/

Malaquias, C. (2014) "'Too happy': France's censorship of award-winning World Down Syndrome Day video to be challenged in European Court of Human Rights." *Starting With Julius*. Retrieved 20 September 2017, from www.startingwithjulius.org.au/frances-censoring-award-winning-world-down-syndrome-day-video-to-be-challenged-in-european-court-of-human-rights/

Malaquias, C. (2017) "'Usefulness' is not a measure of human worth – it's a dangerous ideology." *Starting with Julius*. Retrieved 20 September 2017, from www.startingwithjulius.org.au/usefulness-is-a-dangerous-measure-of-human-worth

Schaber, A. (2014a) "Ask an Autistic #13 – What are Special Interests?" YouTube. Retrieved 20 September 2017, from www.youtube.com/watch?v=ytWwFr5_pbY

Schaber, A. (2014b) "Ask an Autistic #7 – What is Scripting?" YouTube. Retrieved 20 September 2017, from http://youtu.be/vtbbmeyh5rk

# Additional Bibliography

## Chapter 5

### Friendship

Bogdashina, O. (2005) *Communication Issues in Autism and Asperger Syndrome*. London: Jessica Kingsley Publishers.

Edmonds, G. and Beardon, L. (2008) *Asperger's Syndrome and Social Relationships: Adults Speak Out About Asperger's Syndrome*. London: Jessica Kingsley Publishers.

Edmonds, G. and Worton, D. (2008) *The Asperger Social Guide*. London: Paul Chapman Publishing.

Grandin, T. and Barron, S. (2005) *Unwritten Rules of Social Relationships*. Arlington, TX: Future Horizons.

### Marriage

Aston, M. (2003) *Aspergers in Love*. London: Jessica Kingsley Publishers.

Edmonds, G. and Worton, D. (2005) *The Asperger Love Guide: A Practical Guide for Adults with Asperger's Syndrome to Seeking and Maintaining Successful Relationships*. London: Paul Chapman Publishing.

Simone, R. (2016) *22 Things a Woman with Asperger's Syndrome Wants Her Partner to Know*. London: Jessica Kingsley Publishers.

Thompson, B. (2008) *Counselling for Asperger Couples*. London: Jessica Kingsley Publishers.

## Chapter 11

Bogdashina, O. (2016) *Sensory Perceptual Issues in Autism and Asperger Syndrome: Different Sensory Experiences, Different Perceptual Worlds*, 2nd edn. London: Jessica Kingsley Publishers.

## Chapter 12

Attwood, T. and Garnett M.S. (2016) *Exploring Depression and Beating the Blues: A CBT Self-Help Guide to Understanding and Coping with Depression in Asperger's Syndrome.* London: Jessica Kingsley Publishers.

Harris, R.L. (2017) *Contemplative Therapy for Clients on the Autism Spectrum: A Reflective Integration Therapy™ Manual for Psychotherapists and Counsellors.* London: Jessica Kingsley Publishers.

Miller, R. (2015) *The iRest Program for Healing PTSD: A Proven-Effective Approach to Using Yoga Nidra Meditation and Deep Relaxation Techniques to Overcome Trauma.* Oakland, CA: New Harbinger.

## Chapter 15

Lesko, A. and Grandin, T. (2018) *Temple Grandin: The Stories I Tell My Friends.* Arlington, TX: Future Horizons.

## Chapter 18

Aitken, K.J. (2012) *Sleep Difficulties and Autism Spectrum Disorders.* London: Jessica Kingsley Publishers.

Holliday Willey, L. (1999) *Pretending to be Normal.* London: Jessica Kingsley Publishers.

## Chapter 19

Association of Nature and Forest Therapy Guides and Programs (2017) "Nature and Forest Therapy." Retrieved 20 September 2017, from www.natureandforesttherapy.org

Brown, B. (2016) *Daring Greatly: How the Courage to be Vulnerable Transforms the Way We Live, Love, Parent, and Lead.* London: Penguin Books.

Brown, B. (2017) *Braving the Wilderness: The quest for true belonging and the courage to stand alone.* London: Ebury Publishing.

Chabot, S. (2017) "Trailer: The Gardener." YouTube. Retrieved 19 September 2017, from www.youtube.com/watch?v=daVoRtLAm3Y

Craft, S. (2016) "Females with Aspergers Syndrome Checklist by Samantha Craft." *Everyday Aspie.* Retrieved 19 September 2017, from https://everydayaspie.wordpress.com/2016/05/02/females-with-aspergers-syndrome-checklist-by-samantha-craft

Forleo, M. (2017) "Brené Brown Shows You How To 'Brave the Wilderness.'" YouTube. Retrieved 20 September 2017, from www.youtube.com/watch?v=A9FopgKyAfI at 32:52

Gregory, A. (2017) "Running Free in Germany's Outdoor Preschools." *New York Times.* Retrieved 20 September 2017, from www.nytimes.com/2017/05/18/t-magazine/germany-forest-kindergarten-outdoor-preschool-waldkitas.html

Hoopmann, K. (2007) *All Cats Have Asperger Syndrome.* London: Jessica Kingsley Publishers.

Levitin, D. (2006) *This Is Your Brain on Music: Understanding a Human Obsession*. New York, NY: Penguin Books.

MacGregor, R. (2015) *Canoe Country*. Toronto: RandomHouse Canada.

Malloy, A. (2017) "More Than a Walk in the Woods." *Sierra Club*. Retrieved 19 September 2017, from www.sierraclub.org/sierra/green-life/more-walk-woods

Mason, B. (2011) "Waterwalker." YouTube. Retrieved 20 September 2017, from www.youtube.com/watch?v=Dq7CqhbzPUs

National Autistic Society (2016) "Gardens and Health." YouTube. Retrieved 19 September 2017, from www.youtube.com/watch?v=bvMP-X-Hpqo

Ottawa Riverkeeper (2017) "Our Story." Retrieved 19 September 2017, from www.ottawariverkeeper.ca/home/who-we-are/our-story/

Prince-Hughes, D. (2004) *Songs of the Gorilla Nation*. New York, NY: Harmony Books.

Simone, R. (2010) *Aspergirls: Empowering Females with Asperger Syndrome*. London: Jessica Kingsley Publishers.

Wikipedia (2017) "Ernest Thompson Seton." Retrieved 19 September 2017, from https://en.wikipedia.org/wiki/Ernest_Thompson_Seton

Wikipedia (2017) "Laurent Mottron." Retrieved 19 September 2017, from https://en.wikipedia.org/wiki/Laurent_Mottron

# Recommended Resources

**Publications**

*22 Things a Woman Must Know If She Loves a Man with Asperger Syndrome*, Rudy Simone (Jessica Kingsley Publishers, 2009)

*22 Things a Woman with Aspergers Wants Her Partner to Know*, Rudy Simone (Jessica Kingsley Publishers, 2012)

*A Field Guide to Earthlings: An Autistic/Asperger View of Neurotypical Behaviour*, Ian Ford (Ian Ford Software Corporation, 2010)

*Am I Autistic? A Guide to Autism and Asperger's Self-Diagnosis for Adults*, Lydia Andal (New Idealist, 2015)

*An Adult with an Autism Diagnosis: A Guide for the Newly Diagnosed*, Gillan Drew (Jessica Kingsley Publishers, 2017)

*Asperger Syndrome in Adolescence: Living with the Ups, the Downs and Things in Between*, Liane Holliday Willey (Jessica Kingsley Publishers, 2003)

*Asperger Syndrome in the Family: Redefining Normal*, Liane Holliday Willey (Jessica Kingsley Publishers, 2001)

*Aspergirls: Empowering Females with Asperger Syndrome*, Rudy Simone (Jessica Kingsley Publishers, 2010)

*Aspergirls: Empowering Females with Asperger Syndrome*, Rudy Simone (Jessica Kingsley Publishers, 2010)

*Autism in Adulthood*, Quarterly Journal (Mary Ann Liebert Inc. Publishers, 2018)

*Autism in Heels: The Untold Story of a Female Life on the Spectrum*, Jennifer O'Toole (Skyhorse Publishing, 2018)

*Autism Spectrum Disorder in Mid and Later Life*, edited by Scott D. Wright, PhD (Jessica Kingsley Publishers, 2016)

*Been There. Done That. Try This! An Aspie's Guide to Life on Earth*, Tony Attwood, Craig Evans, and Anita Lesko (Jessica Kingsley Publishers, 2014)

*College for Students with Disabilities: We Do Belong*, Pavan John Antony and Stephen M. Shore (Jessica Kingsley Publishers, 2015)

*Contemplative Therapy for Clients on the Autism Spectrum: A Reflective Integration Therapy™ Manual for Contemplative Therapy for Clients on the Autism Spectrum*, Rachael Lee Harris (Jessica Kingsley Publishers, 2017)

*Everyday Aspergers*, Samantha Craft (BookLogix, 2016)

*Fifteen Things They Forgot to Tell You About Autism: The Stuff That Transformed My Life as an Autism Parent*, Debby Elley (Jessica Kingsley Publishers, 2018)

*Finding a Different Kind of Normal: Misadventures with Asperger Syndrome*, Jeanette Purkis (Jessica Kingsley Publishers, 2006)

*From Here to Maternity: Pregnancy and Motherhood on the Autism Spectrum*, Lana Grant (Jessica Kingsley Publishers, 2015)

*I Think I Might Be Autistic: A Guide to Autism Spectrum Disorder Diagnosis and Self-Discovery for Adults*, Cynthia Kim (Narrow Gauge Press, 2013)

*Life on the Autism Spectrum: A Guide for Girls and Women*, Karen McKibbin (Jessica Kingsley Publishers, 2015)

*M in the Middle*, The Students of Limpsfield Grange School (Jessica Kingsley Publishers, 2016)

*Mindful Living with Asperger's Syndrome: Everyday Mindfulness Practices to Help You Tune in to the Present Moment*, Chris Mitchell (Jessica Kingsley Publishers, 2013)

*National Autism Project: The Future I'd Like to See*, Dr. Catriona Stewart (www.nationalautismproject.org.uk/the-future-id-like-to-see-dr-catriona-stewart)

*Nerdy, Shy, and Socially Inappropriate: A User Guide to an Asperger Life*, Cynthia Kim (Jessica Kingsley Publishers, 2014)

*NeuroTribes: The Legacy of Autism and the Future of Neurodiversity*, Steve Silberman (Avery, 2015)

*Older Adults and Autism Spectrum Conditions: An Introduction and Guide*, Wenn Lawson (Jessica Kingsley Publishers, 2015)

*Pretending to Be Normal: Living with Asperger's Syndrome*, Expanded Edition, Liane Holliday Willey (Jessica Kingsley Publishers, 2014)

*Safety Skills for Asperger Women: How to Save a Perfectly Good Female Life*, Liane Holliday Willey (Jessica Kingsley Publishers, 2011)

*Scholars with Autism Achieving Dreams*, Temple Grandin and Valerie Paradiz (Auricle Ink Pub, 2012)

*Sensing the City: An Autistic Perspective*, Sandra Beale-Ellis (Jessica Kingsley Publishers, 2017)

*Sex and the Single Aspie*, ARtemisia (Jessica Kingsley Publishers, 2018)

*The Autism Spectrum Guide to Sexuality and Relationships: Understand Yourself and Make Choices That Are Right for You*, Dr Emma Goodall (Jessica Kingsley Publishers, 2016)

*The A–Z of ASDs: Aunt Aspie's Guide to Life*, Rudy Simone (Jessica Kingsley Publishers, 2016)

*The Complete Guide to Asperger's Syndrome*, Tony Attwood (Jessica Kingsley Publishers, 2006)

*The Complete Guide to Autism and Healthcare*, Anita Lesko (Future Horizons, 2017)

*The Guide to Good Mental Health on the Autism Spectrum*, Jeanette Purkis, Emma Goodall, and Jane Nugent (Jessica Kingsley Publishers, 2016)

*The Wonderful World of Work: A Workbook for Asperteens*, Jeanette Purkis, illustrated by Andrew Hore (Jessica Kingsley Publishers, 2014)

*Uniquely Human: A Different Way of Seeing Autism*, Barry M. Prizant, PhD (Simon & Schuster, 2016)

*Women and Girls with Autism Spectrum Disorder: Understanding Life Experiences from Early Childhood to Old Age*, Sarah Hendrickx (Jessica Kingsley Publishers, 2015)

## Websites

Asexual Visibility and Education Network (AVEN): www.asexuality.org

Asperger Services Australia (ASA): www.asperger.asn.au

Autism Queensland: www.autismqld.com.au

Autism Society (USA): www.autism-society.org

Autism Spectrum Australia (ASPECT): www.autismspectrum.org.au

Autism Spectrum Connection: www.aspergersyndrome.org

Autism Women's Network: www.autismwomensnetwork.org

Autistic Adults and other Stakeholders Engaged Together (AASET): www.autistichealth.org

Autistic Self Advocacy Network (ASAN): www.autisticadvocacy.org

Katherine Uher: Therapist, Speaker, Writer: www.thesensitivity
spectrum.com

Minds & Hearts: www.mindsandhearts.net

My Spectrum Suite, Everyday Aspergers: www.myspectrumsuite.
com

National Autistic Society (UK): www.nas.org.uk

Rachael Lee Harris: www.rlharrispsy.com/rit

Scottish Women's Autism Network (SWAN): www.swanscotland.com

Spectrum Women Magazine: www.spectrumwomen.com

The International Aspergirl® Society: www.aspergirlsociety.org

The Sisterhood Society: www.thesisterhoodsocietyaustralia.com

Tony Attwood: www.tonyattwood.com

World Autism Organisation (WAO): www.worldautismorganisation.
com

Yellow Ladybugs: www.yellowladybugs.com.au

Yes She Can Inc.: www.yesshecaninc.org

## Blogs

A Diary of a Mom: www.adiaryofamom.com

Agony Autic vlog: www.youtube.com/channel/UCN9fwImPnx16c8-
eThlKCWQ

Cherry Blossom Tree: www.iammyownexperience.com

Hello Michelle Swan: www.michellesuttonwrites.com

Jeanette Purkis: www.jeanettepurkis.wordpress.com

Judy Endow: www.judyendow.com/blog

Just Stimming: www.juststimming.wordpress.com

Live Positively Autistic: www.geekclubbooks.com/becca-positively-autistic

Ollibean: www.ollibean.com/blog

Musings of an Aspie: www.musingsofanaspie.com

Respectfully Connected: www.respectfullyconnected.com

The Silent Wave: www.thesilentwaveblog.wordpress.com

## Films

*Carrie Pilby* (2016; drama/comedy)

*Dina* (2017; a real-life romantic comedy)

*Mozart and the Whale* (2005; drama/comedy)

## Other

Integrative Restoration Institute: www.irest.us

National Autism Sleep Guidelines for Autism: www.autism.org.uk/about/health/sleep.aspx

Spectrumly Speaking (podcast): www.differentbrains.org/spectrumly-speaking

# Index